The Organized Teacher's Guide to

Substitute Teaching

The Organized Teacher's Guide to
Substitute Teaching

Steve Springer, MA
Kimberly Persiani, EdD

New York   Chicago   San Francisco   Athens   London
Madrid   Mexico City   Milan   New Delhi
Singapore   Sydney   Toronto

1 2 3 4 5 6 7 8 9   LHS   24 23 22 21 20 19

ISBN   978-1-260-45353-9
MHID   1-260-45353-7

e-ISBN 978-1-260-45354-6
e-MHID   1-260-45354-5

Interior illustrations by Steve Springer

Bonus Templates

In order to access the online templates, please go to http://www.mhprofessional.com/mediacenter. Enter the ISBN of this book: 978-1-260-45353-9

For further assistance, please see the instructions on the inside front cover ad to access the templates.

Contents

Preface xiii

chapter 1
Getting off to a good start
1

chapter 2
Behavior management
23

chapter 3

Kindergarten (5–6 years old)

49

chapter 4

First grade (6–7 years old)

65

chapter 7

Fourth grade (9–10 years old)
121

chapter 8

Fifth grade (10–11 years old)
141

chapter 9

Sixth grade (11–12 years old)

chapter 10

Secondary Grades (13–18 years old)

chapter 11

Professionalism

197

chapter 12

Extra activities and fillers

211

Preface

Who are the substitute teachers?

Substitute teaching has often been dismissed as a less-than-viable profession. Many regular classroom teachers have regarded substitute teachers as mere babysitters. Administrators have filled an absent teacher's position with little concern about the qualifications or competence of the substitute teacher. And substitute teachers have sometimes succumbed to this view, believing that they aren't legitimate teachers.

Fortunately, the attitude toward substitute teachers is changing, with more credentialed teachers choosing to substitute teach. In the past, substitute teachers tended to be retired teachers, people who were credentialed but hadn't gotten a full-time teaching position, and people who resorted to subbing because they weren't sure they wanted to be teachers. In recent years, however, substitute teaching has appealed to teacher candidates and retired administrators, as well as a younger group of credentialed teachers, many of whom hope that the substitute teaching experience and exposure will land them full-time teaching positions.

Most people choose substitute teaching to further their career in education, to gain classroom experience, or to continue their contribution to the teaching field after retirement. They ought to be held in high esteem and viewed as competent educators, not babysitters. Substitute teachers, in fact, can carry out the classroom teacher's responsibilities for a day, for a week, or for months.

Substitute teaching in the 21st century

In past decades, a substitute teacher may have shown videos, supervised extended physical education periods, and distributed busy work (worksheets and the like). Today, however, substitute teachers are qualified to implement the daily agenda in a classroom, with the result that no school day needs to be wasted by a teacher's absence. In fact, many substitute teachers now have training in a particular school district's curriculum and technology.

As a substitute teacher, you need to take the job very seriously. The regular classroom teacher is leaving his or her students in your care—a significant responsibility. You must be curriculum-savvy, up-to-date with teaching strategies and discipline techniques, and comfortable with technology and software.

You don't have to be fluent in every subject for every grade, but you should realistically assess your talents and abilities and be honest about what subjects and grades you are able to teach. In order to do this, you should have a general understanding of grade level standards, the curriculum for each grade, and the differences in students' attitudes and behavior at each grade level. This is complicated by the fact that many classrooms include multiple grade levels.

Beyond curriculum, you are expected to maintain control of the class and employ age-appropriate and relevant discipline techniques, in accordance with the regular classroom teacher's discipline plan.

Today's classrooms are not quiet. For students learning a second language, oral discussions are crucial. Some teachers make use of cooperative grouping, and students must talk out loud. Many classrooms include opportunities for students to do the teaching and call on others for assistance and responses. As a substitute teacher, you must know how to cultivate these experiences while managing the class, maintaining order, and completing the day's agenda.

It's important that you enter each substitute teaching experience with enthusiasm, confidence, flexibility, and open-mindedness. You may have had a bad day in a second grade classroom yesterday, but you have a clean slate as you enter a sixth grade classroom today. You should begin each day as a completely new experience.

The Organized Teacher's Guide to Substitute Teaching

This book is quick to read, and its ideas are practical and easy to implement. It is rich in ideas and activities that span the curriculum and support grade level standards. It includes dozens of templates that cover the gamut of classroom logistics, curriculum, discipline, activities, and substitute teacher evaluation and record keeping.

An entire chapter is devoted to each grade level, from kindergarten through secondary grades. Each of these chapters contains detailed information about behavior patterns; curriculum content in reading, writing, math, social studies, and science; and strategies and activities for each of these curricular areas. There's also a list of recommended books that you may want to put in your substitute teacher toolbox, as well as a list of websites that you can use in the computer lab, during computer center time, or when students finish work early. At the end of each of these chapters is a comprehensive demonstration of how to link a picture book or chapter book across the curriculum.

This book can serve as an indispensable reference tool for all your substitute teaching experiences. Today's substitute teachers meet up through e-mail, Facebook, conferences, college courses, and chats over coffee, and all of these played a role in developing the content of this book. We have brought the experiences, concerns, and voices of countless substitute teachers to its pages. We'd especially like to thank Warren Herr, Jennifer Santos, Ashley Desjardis, Nicole Rathje-Jones, and Michael Ulrich for their many ideas and contributions. This book is dedicated to them and to you—and to all the students you serve in classrooms across the country.

The Organized Teacher's Guide to

Substitute Teaching

chapter 1

Getting off to a good start

Substitute teachers must be prepared to meet a wide variety of classroom situations, including a diverse group of students, attitudes, school policies, and school cultures. These will differ from school to school and from district to district. It's critical that you be proactive: Your ability to assimilate to a variety of circumstances will help you succeed as a substitute teacher.

It's possible that you may teach in some classrooms or schools only once, never returning to them for a later assignment. You may even view each teaching assignment as completely separate, whether or not you return to the same classroom or school. This is most likely to be the case when things aren't going well and your day has become more about survival than anything else. Yet this can be shortsighted, and this view confines and limits the teaching experience, leaving little room for reflection and growth. A key to making each experience count is being prepared, and this first section of the book will help you do just that.

1

Survival kit

Every substitute teacher needs a survival kit. You have to be ready for the unexpected, such as any grade level, rainy days, no available lesson plans, or extra students in the classroom. You name it, and it can happen! Your own survival kit might be a heavy plastic box, a backpack with roller wheels, an accordion file, or any other container or organizer that works for you.

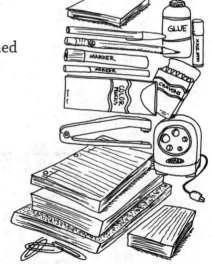

It's important to develop a list of essential items for your survival kit and to make sure that these items are easily accessible to you. We suggest several basic items that are helpful to have in your own personal survival kit.

Supplies

- **School supplies** that the regular classroom teacher might not have on hand
    - Colored markers (water-based)—both thick- and fine-tipped
    - Colored pencils
    - Crayons—large (lower grades) and standard (upper grades)
    - First-aid kit
    - Glue—white glue and glue sticks
    - Index cards
    - Paper—wide-lined (lower grades) and narrow-lined (upper grades); blank white paper; pack of multi-colored construction paper
    - Paper clips
    - Pencil sharpener
    - Pencils—large (lower grades) and standard No. 2 (upper grades)
    - Pens—black, blue, and red ink
    - Stapler and staples
    - Sticky notes in assorted sizes and colors
    - Tape—both masking and scotch

- ◆ **Teacher resource supplies** that can aid in instructional activities

  - ◆ Calendar pictures—Start a picture file of everything from animals to weather. Having these accessible to use in a lesson can be invaluable.
  - ◆ Measuring containers—cups, pints, etc., for measuring volume. You can pick them up at a garage sale for pennies.
  - ◆ Rulers—for measuring length in both inches and centimeters.

- ◆ **Incentives and rewards** are important to have. Students are easily motivated by something as simple as a sticker, a pencil, or a gel pen. On days where you have been assigned a particularly difficult class, these may be a necessity. Rewards can include

  - ◆ Certificates
  - ◆ Erasers
  - ◆ Pencils
  - ◆ Pens
  - ◆ Small spiral notebooks or scratch pads
  - ◆ Stamps (for use with an ink pad)
  - ◆ Stickers

  36
  Reward
  Certificates

  Rewards can be purchased on-line at www.orientaltrading.com and www.smilemakers.com.

Activities

Desk name tags

Have students create desk name tags as an opening activity. You'll be able to take a few minutes to get your bearings while the students are busy with the name tags. Students can show something about themselves (either written or illustrated) in each corner of a four-corner name tag made from a folded sheet of paper. They can share the information on their name tags with the rest of the class if time allows.

Because name tags are a great way to relate to students, especially the more difficult students, remember to create your own. Use the **Desk Name Tag** template.

Desk name tags for all grade levels will be helpful, especially if a seating chart isn't available. The quickest way to get students' attention is to call them by name, and it gives you a good way to both recognize them in a positive way and prevent behavior issues. Make sure the desk name tags are easy to see and read.

13
Desk Name
Tag

Be sure to make enough copies of desk name tags for a week, so you don't run out. If you are subbing in a class for multiple days, have students either save name tags in their desks or give them to you to hold for subsequent days.

13
Desk Name
Tag

If you don't use the **Desk Name Tag** template, you can bring a stack of large index cards and put one on each student's desk. Ask students to fold the card in half to create a name tag with first and last names on both sides, accompanied by pictures of their interests.

Another option is to arrive early, obtain the class roll, and write out name tags yourself. Create your own name tag with your name and pictures of your interests as an example for the students.

Information in the corners of desk name tags might include

- Favorite food
- Favorite hobby
- Favorite book
- Favorite movie
- Favorite entertainer
- Favorite singer
- Favorite dessert
- Favorite animal or pet
- Favorite sport

Picture books

Many children's books include extended lessons that are engaging and require few supplies. These are essential to a substitute teacher's survival kit for every grade level (K–1, 2–3, 4–6, 7–8). They may come in handy if you have extra time during the day or if you have no available lesson plans. Try to find the lighter and more compact versions of your favorite books so that they are more easily transportable. Having go-to lessons for all of the grade levels is key, and sample lesson ideas for books at each grade level can be found in Chapters 3 through 9. Note the list of suggested picture books in those chapters, which can be used to teach all curricular areas.

Picture books can calm a class or serve as a time filler, and they are great for reading aloud after recess, lunch, or before the end of the day. When reading a picture book to the class, keep the following things in mind.

- ◆ Introduce the book.
  - ◆ Title
  - ◆ Author
  - ◆ Illustrator
  - ◆ Copyright ("birthday of the book")
- ◆ Use an appropriately animated voice to read the story.
- ◆ Have fun.
- ◆ Hold the book in one hand so the class can see the pictures as you read it.
- ◆ Exercise "wait time" at the end of each page so students can take in the illustrations.
- ◆ During the story, ask students critical thinking questions.
  - ◆ "What do you think will happen next?"
  - ◆ "Has anything like this ever happened to you?"
  - ◆ "How would you handle the situation?"
- ◆ After the story, ask more questions!
  - ◆ What was the setting of the story?
  - ◆ Who were the main characters?
  - ◆ What was the main idea of the story?
  - ◆ What was the problem or conflict in the story?
  - ◆ How was the problem or conflict resolved?
- ◆ Have students sequence the story.

Reading strategies

When reading with students, several reading strategies can be used to increase reading comprehension, understanding, and interpretation. The **Bookmarks** template shows guides for these reading strategies in a fun format for the students. These bookmarks can be copied and laminated for use with every class you sub for. Make one set and keep it in your survival kit.

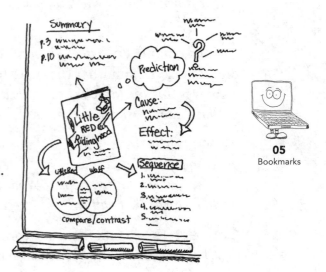

05
Bookmarks

You can use the language in the questions that follow when reading and discussing a story. Students should be able to go back to the text and find specific support (page numbers and quotes) for their answers.

Predict Have students predict what will happen in the story.
What do you think will happen next, or in the next chapter? Can anyone make a prediction about what might be coming?

Summarize Have students summarize what has happened in the story.
Who can summarize what happened on this page, in this chapter, so far?

Visualize Have students visualize the story, the setting, characters, and action; ask students to close their eyes and try to see the story.

Close your eyes. Can you visualize what it would be like to be in that situation? Can you describe the setting?

Interpret Have students derive meaning from the text and make an educated guess about an aspect of the story.

What does this mean in the story? How do you think the character feels? What is the message here? What is the author trying to convey?

Ask questions Have the students ask and/or discuss questions to understand the story.

What questions do you have? What do you think? What does it mean? How is . . . ? Would you . . . ?

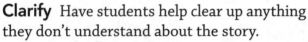

Reference Have students refer to a similar situation or research an aspect of the story.

How is this similar to what happened in . . . ? During this time in history, what happened . . . ? Have you experienced a similar situation in reference to . . . ?

Clarify Have students help clear up anything they don't understand about the story.

Can anyone clarify what happened . . . ? I would like to clarify . . . I am confused; What does . . . mean?

Compare and contrast Have students relate the story to another story or relate one character to another character (even from the same story).

How is this similar to . . . ? How is it different from . . . ? Can we compare . . . ? Can we contrast . . . ? What are the similarities? What are the differences?

Cause and effect Have students determine which event results in a specific outcome.

What caused this to happen? What was the effect? What were the actions of this character? What happened as a result?

Connect Have students make connections from the story to real life experiences.

What does this remind you of in your life? What connections can we make here? This is like . . .

Personally relate Have students relate personally to the story in some way.

This happened to me once . . . Has something like this ever happened to you? I don't like it when . . . Do you like it when . . . ? Do you enjoy . . . ?

Describe Have students use details from the story to describe what happened.

What is happening here? What details or examples support the story? Can you describe the setting, what is happening, how the character felt?

Author's point of view Have students interpret what the author is trying to say, what the author's opinion is. How does the author illustrate that point of view (with language, events)?

What is the author of this story trying to say? What does the author think about . . . ? How does the author get that point across? What does the author use in the story to support that opinion?

Author's purpose Have students determine what the author is trying to accomplish (for example, to entertain or inform).

Why do you think this story was written? Is this fact or opinion? What is the author trying to accomplish by telling this story?

Synthesize Have students bring it all together and summarize details, the author's purpose, connections, and inferences.

What can we say about this story? Can someone sum up the story? What was the main idea?

Sequence Have students put events of the story in time order sequence.

What is the sequence of events that happened in this story? What happened first? Next? Then? Last?

Story writing

It is essential to have creative writing assignments on hand that will engage students. These need to be well thought out, with a specific goal in mind for the assignment (such as persuasion, description, or narrative). They can also be used as time fillers, where students write silly stories using descriptive writing. See the list of suggested story starters in Chapter 11, Extra activities and fillers.

Students in the lower grades may write a few sentences and then illustrate them. For upper grades, story writing may take the form of a paragraph or a theme consisting of several paragraphs. The following is a general guide for leveled story writing.

- ◆ **Kindergarten** Simple words, inventive spelling, simple sentences with illustration
- ◆ **First grade** Three to five simple sentences with illustrations
- ◆ **Second grade** Simple sentences in a short paragraph
- ◆ **Third grade** One or two paragraphs related to a topic
- ◆ **Fourth grade** One to three paragraphs that relate to a topic and include supporting details
- ◆ **Fifth grade** Narratives of several paragraphs that relate to a topic and include supporting details
- ◆ **Sixth to twelfth grades** Well-developed narratives with paragraphs that relate to the topic of a story and include several supporting details

Students' paragraphs should have a basic structure, with a topic sentence and supporting sentences related to the topic sentence. Students should include details, and their stories should have enticing beginnings that grab the reader's attention. Encourage them to enhance their stories with vivid descriptions.

Try reading a picture book before the story writing activity, and encourage students to create a similar story of their own.

Ideas for writing stories based on a picture book can include the following.

- Write from the character's perspective. How would the character see the world? For example, write a story from the perspective of one of Santa's reindeer.
- Write about how to do something.
- Write a new ending to a story.
- Write a sequel to a story.
- Write an alternative solution to a story.
- Use a story starter for an idea.

If time permits, students can move through the writing process or a modified version of it. This includes the following steps.

1. Brainstorming/Prewriting (using graphic organizers)
2. Drafting
3. Editing/Revising
4. Proofreading
5. Publishing

Even if time does not permit students' moving through the full writing process, it is still important to have them brainstorm their ideas using a graphic organizer. You may use a template for one of the organizers found in this book: a **Sandwich Organizer**, two forms of a **Stair Organizer**, a **Story Organizer**, and a **Web Organizer**. Choose the graphic organizer that fits best with your writing project.

38
Sandwich Organizer
41
Stair Organizer 1
42
Stair Organizer 2
45
Story Organizer
62
Web Organizer

It may be necessary to model the story writing or have the class write a group story. Students can contribute their ideas with your guidance. This can be charted out and then copied by each student. Writing a group story can be especially helpful for students in the lower grades, English language learners, and classes that are struggling with their writing.

Stories can relate to holidays, events, or anything that grabs the students' attention. You want to help the students be motivated to write, engage the reader, and feel successful.

You can come up with your own ideas for a story writing activity or, if you aren't sure where to start, begin with one of the following three ideas.

"Monster Show-Not-Tell"

Have the students write in detail about a monster that they visualize. They might like to illustrate the monster they have written about.

Haiku poetry

Have students follow the three-line format for haiku poetry using five–seven–five syllables.

"The Grossest Dinner I Ever Ate"

Have students describe in great detail the grossest dinner they ever ate. Encourage them to use their imagination and to include details in their stories.

Students can be very creative, and they will enjoy this type of writing. You may also have them illustrate their story. Don't forget to write and illustrate your own story to share with the students.

Games and activities

Games and activities offer students a break during the school day. On rainy or snowy days, when students may not be allowed outside, being creative and thinking on your feet may be essential to your survival. Here are some ideas for easy games and activities that can be played indoors during inclement weather or at the end of the day.

Heads Up Seven Up

Select seven students to be "it." All other students put their heads down on their desks and cover their eyes. The seven students walk around the room, and each one touches a different person who has his or her head down. Once a person is touched, he or she should stick a thumb up. Once all seven people have touched someone, announce "Heads Up Seven Up!" Have the students with their thumbs up try to guess which of the seven students touched them. If a student guesses correctly, he gets to trade places with the person who touched him, but if he guesses incorrectly, he must remain in his seat. The person who touched that student gets to be "it" again.

Around the World

Use a set of flash cards for whichever mathematical concept you want the students to practice. Have a set of +, −, ×, and ÷ cards as backup. Have students sit in a circle. Choose a starting person, and have this student stand behind the next student in the circle. The teacher holds up a flash card. The first student to say the correct answer stands behind the next person in the circle. If a sitting student says the answer first, the standing student changes places with the sitting student. This process continues until at least one student makes it completely around the circle.

You may use weekly spelling words, vocabulary words, and even sight words, in addition to math flash cards. Make sure the flash cards are large enough for students to see from each seat. Advanced students or students that consecutively win can be asked to flash the cards.

Board games and travel games

Have a few small travel games like Scrabble, chess, checkers, or playing cards to offer as fillers if there is extra time before recess or lunch, or at the end of the day. There may also be full-size board games available in the classroom.

Flash cards

Have math flash cards on hand (+, −, ×, ÷). These help fill the 10 to 15 minutes before recess or lunch, when students have finished an assignment or are restless.

Tangrams

Tangram puzzles and a book such as *Grandfather Tang's Story* by Ann Tompert offer an opportunity for reading and math activities, along with a physical activity that students in many grades will enjoy. Photocopy the tangram puzzle pieces (using the **Tangrams 1** or **Tangrams 2** template) so students can cut them out and keep them. Then photocopy the **Tangram Picture Cards** on card stock, laminate them, and keep them in a file so they can be used over and over.

56
Tangram
Picture Cards
57
Tangrams 1
58
Tangrams 2

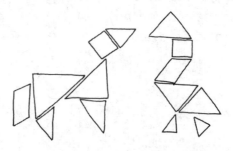

Sparkle

Sparkle provides good practice for the week's spelling words. Appoint a leader, and arrange the rest of the students in a line. The leader calls out a word. The first student in line calls out the first letter in that word; the second student calls out the second letter; the third student calls out the third letter; and so on. The student who provides the last letter in the word turns to the next student in line and says "sparkle." The person who is "sparkled" must return to his or her seat. If a word is misspelled, the student who has called out the wrong letter sits down, and the spelling of that word continues. After a student has been "sparkled," the leader calls out a new word. The game continues until only one student remains standing.

Learning relay

Learning relay can be used for several curricular areas. Divide the class into two or three groups to create teams with the same number of students. Choose a curricular area (spelling words, sentence correction, or computation, for example) as a focus for the activity. Have one student from each team come to the board. Give them a word or sentence to write or a math problem to solve. Whoever writes the correct answer first earns a point for their team. Repeat with the rest of the students until all students have had a turn. Keep track of team points, and offer a reward to the team that wins. The reward can be simple and easy, for example, first to be dismissed (for recess, for lunch, or at the end of the day), a sticker, or a pencil.

Word guess

Word guess provides good practice for the students' weekly spelling words or vocabulary words. On the board, write a line for each letter of a selected spelling word or vocabulary word. Call on students at random, asking them to call out a letter of the alphabet. If that letter is part of the word you have in mind, write the letter on the corresponding line or lines. If the called-out letter is not part of the word you have in mind, write it in a separate area of the board so students know that it has already been tried. Follow these steps until the word has been completed or until a student guesses what the word is. After five wrong guesses, fill in the missing letters to complete the word. To challenge students, when the word is complete, have them use the word in a sentence or give a definition for it.

Plans

Lesson plans

Most teachers prepare lesson plans for their class and have them available for substitute teachers. However, it is important for you to prepare emergency lesson plans for those times when you arrive at a substitute teaching assignment and find that no lesson plans are available. General lesson plans for math, reading, writing, history, and science classes can be prepared for each grade level ahead of time and saved in envelopes or folders. If you begin an assignment with no lesson plans provided by the regular classroom teacher and no assistance from other grade level teachers, you can pull out your own grade level folder and get the day going with your own emergency lesson plans. Use the template for a **Lesson Plan** using direct instruction to get started.

29
Lesson Plan:
Direct
Instruction
(with
instructions)

30
Lesson Plan:
Direct
Instruction
(without
instructions)

Fillers

Having extra activities for those students who fly through their work and then say, "I'm done. What's next?" is really helpful. Usually, classroom teachers have "Must Do" and "May Do" lists posted that show what students can do if they finish their work early. If this isn't in place, be sure to have some filler ideas or sponge activities of your own ready to go. Holiday activities are a good type of activity to have on hand for early finishers. A list of sponge activities can be found in Chapter 11, Extra activities and fillers.

Breaking up the day

"Chunk" the day—break the day up into a series of activities. This keeps the students engaged. For younger students, the blocks of time devoted to an activity will necessarily be smaller, because of their shorter attention span. Blocks of time for activities can be extended when working with students in the upper grade levels.

Morning routines

Arrive early! This is critical in getting off to a good start. There is nothing worse than rushing in, realizing the teacher didn't leave lesson plans for you, and then trying to find out from other grade level or subject area teachers what you should be teaching that day.

If you arrive early and are prepared with your personal survival kit, you can be calm in the knowledge that you will have plenty to get you and the students through the day. Your emergency lesson plans for each grade level plus appropriate grade level picture books will make sure of that. Following are a few other ideas to help both you and the students get started once they walk in the classroom door.

Morning message

Write a morning message to the students on the board or overhead. Tell them your name, that you will be their substitute teacher that day, and what you would like them to get started on. For example, *Good morning, second grade. My name is Mrs. Hillson. Your teacher will not be here*

today, but I am excited to be your substitute teacher. Please unpack quietly and create a name tag for yourself that has your first and last names. You may decorate the corners of your name tag with pictures of things that interest you. I have made mine as an example. Thank you!*

Attendance

After the bell rings, take attendance. If the teacher has not left information about the school's attendance procedure, ask about it in the office before the school day starts. Every school uses a different form of attendance (some are electronic); some schools ask you to call in attendance.

Use the seating chart if there is one. If you have no seating chart and no class list, ask the students in each row with an empty desk to tell you who sits there. This always works, and the students are more than happy to help. You can also hand out a blank seating chart and have students write in their names, which you can use for the rest of the day.

02
Attendance/
Task Log

Use the **Attendance/Task Log** template and have each student sign it. This log sheet can then be used throughout the day to track student behavior. At the end of the day, you can leave it with a note for the classroom teacher.

Morning chat

Talk with the students about being the substitute teacher for the class, how the day will unfold, and the expectations that you have for them. This might include a discussion about rules and consequences (see Chapter 2, Behavior management), bathroom breaks, and the day's agenda. Of course, you will want to share a bit about yourself with the students, too.

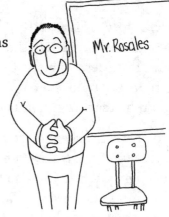

Restroom and water breaks The **Classroom Log** template can be used to track students who leave the classroom. Prepare a blank sign-out log and put it in a plastic sheet protector. Place this by the door with a transparency marker. The sign-out log ensures that you know who is out of the room at all times. If you think the students were abusing out-of-classroom privileges during the day, you can copy it for the teacher to see. You can use a fresh photocopy each time and leave it for the teacher to see if you prefer.

06
Classroom
Log

water
restroom
questions

If you notice students leaving the room one after the other, mention that you have a small surprise at the end of the day for any student who does not need to leave the room during instructional time that day (a sticker, pencil, or small eraser is a typical reward). Be sure to note that students are allowed to use the restroom or get water if needed by signing out. You don't want anyone to have an accident just because they want a reward.

Students are often out of their seats within the classroom—to get a drink of water, to sharpen pencils, or to access their backpacks when retrieving something or putting something away. Use the **Out-of-My-Seat Log** to track this behavior, and leave it for the regular classroom teacher. If students' time out of their seats is tracked, it makes it less likely that they will be out of their seats unnecessarily.

32
Out-of-My-
Seat Log

These morning routines help eliminate interruptions throughout the day from students telling you how things are done in their class. Presenting your expectations can cut down on "we don't do it like that" statements by 90 percent or more. The first few times you sub, the students will be eager to tell you how to do things. Be ready for this, or you could end up not getting anything done. It should take no more than a few minutes to hear what they have to say so that you know what they need from you.

Day-to-day substitute teaching

Substitute teaching assignments are generally for short periods of time, such as one to five days. Typically, if an assignment lasts longer than that, the experience is considered a long-term position. When you substitute teach in day-to-day situations, you should ask yourself, "How can I influence these students and their learning?" You have a very important role, because you are in a position to help reinforce skills that are standard for the grade level or that have been targeted by the regular classroom teacher. You give students an opportunity to meet new people in an authoritative role, possibly from a culture they are not familiar with. Be prepared, and arrive early enough to prepare yourself and the classroom for the day ahead in order to ensure a successful day with the class. Take the time to know what you are teaching, what materials you will need, and who will be there to help you.

Lesson plans

In most cases, the regular classroom teacher will leave you step-by-step lesson plans to follow. Some teachers will be more detailed than others. After a handful of experiences, you will get better at reading between the lines and understanding the curriculum. You can always ask the neighboring grade level teacher for help. Likely, that teacher will be doing similar work and can help you decipher the teacher's lesson plans. Here are some suggestions to help you prepare for the school day once you have arrived in the classroom.

- Locate the regular classroom teacher's lesson plans. Usually they can be found on the teacher's desk, on the desktop computer, a worktable, or near the whiteboard.
- Seek out the teacher's manual (referred to as the teacher's edition in some curriculums) if a plan calls for them.
- Preview the lessons for each curricular area in case you have a question about an element you will be teaching.
- Follow the plans set out by the teacher. It's helpful to make yourself a checklist if one is not provided for you.
- List the lessons in the order in which they should be delivered. Include the following information about each lesson.
  - Topics
  - Time periods
  - Teacher's manual page numbers
  - Workbook and textbook page numbers
  - Student work required

Check off each item as you and the students complete it.

Use the **Agenda Checklist** template to organize your day.

You should have emergency lesson plans prepared in case the teacher doesn't leave any for you; you can use the **Lesson Plan** templates for this purpose. Get to know the grade levels you teach most often, and be sure to have backup ideas for those grades. If you have been called in at the last minute because of an emergency, you might ask the neighboring grade level teachers what they're doing that day and then follow the same lesson plans with the class you're responsible for.

The classroom aide

A substitute teacher might not typically take into consideration the role of a classroom aide, especially for a day-to-day assignment. Not all schools have aides, so it's good to assume that you won't have an aide—but be prepared in case you do. Sometimes an aide can be a great help, especially when it comes to keeping students on track, letting you know who has special needs, and working in small groups or one-on-one. In any case, always remember that *you* are in charge. If you are prepared with a handful of ways in which an aide can assist you, it offers the aide a sense of productivity but also lets the aide know that you have a firm grasp on things. Let the aide know how you plan to carry

out the day, what rules and consequences you and the students will work with, and how you plan to manage behavior and discipline during your time in the classroom. If you let the aide know this up front, he or she will understand that you run a smooth and efficient classroom and will likely share this with the regular classroom teacher (thus ensuring a request for you in the future). Do look for instructions in the classroom teacher's lesson plans about how to utilize the aide, because the aide may have standard duties that the classroom teacher wants the aide to handle. Suggestions for using the classroom aide in productive ways include the following.

◆ **Assisting with the start of the day** Attendance, lunch tickets, unpacking, calendar, homework check, and other parts of the morning routine can all be more easily facilitated by an adult who is accustomed to the routine. If an aide is in the classroom at this time, take advantage of his or her help as you start your day with the class. It doesn't mean that you will sit back and do nothing. Remember that the aide will likely give informal feedback on your performance, so you should be actively involved in all aspects of the classroom.

- **Small groups** The classroom aide can work with a small group of students to target a specific skill, such as reviewing a math lesson, working on sentence structure, or using small whiteboards to solve logic problems.
- **One-on-one** The classroom aide can work with a student individually to target a specific skill, such as editing student writing, having a student read aloud, or helping a student practice sight words.
- **Circulating** The classroom aide can be a great asset by circulating through the classroom to students' desks or tables and checking on students who might need academic support, whether during a lesson or independent practice.
- **Behavior management** The classroom aide knows the students well, so he or she knows which students might get easily distracted, might be likely to daydream, or might have trouble sitting still and staying focused. The aide can watch for triggers that might set off negative behavior and tend to them before problems occur.
- **Administrative** The classroom aide can help with grading papers, putting up bulletin boards, making photocopies, and many other classroom needs.

Parent connections

Consider sending a note home to let parents know that you were the substitute teacher in their child's class that day. Decide whether sending a note home to parents is appropriate based on the school, the classroom, and the length of your substitute teaching assignment. In a note home to parents, introduce yourself and offer reassurance that you will be following the regular classroom curriculum. If you use one of the basic **Parent Letter** templates, you can fill it out and photocopy it at lunchtime or during an afternoon break so that it's ready to send home at the end of the day. You should also share this note home with the regular classroom teacher. The note could include the following basic information.

34
Parent Letter 1
35
Parent Letter 2

- Your name
- Regular classroom teacher's name
- Room number
- Grade or subject
- Dates of substitute teaching assignment
- Information about you
- Ways to contact you if necessary (for example, website, e-mail, school phone number)
- Short description of the day

Long-term substitute teaching

Lesson plans

You may be in charge of lesson planning during your extended stay, depending on how long the regular classroom teacher is out of the classroom. If the teacher is only going to be gone for a week, he or she will probably leave lesson plans for that time period. But after about a week, it will probably be up to you to create lesson plans for each day, using the required curriculum. It's important to contact your grade level and subject area team members and ask them to set a time for you to plan together.

♦ **Teacher's lesson plans** If the teacher knows that he or she will be absent for a long period of time (for example, for extended family care, a wedding, maternity or paternity leave, or a medical concern), the teacher may very well have you come in to observe the classroom, meet the students, and review the plans you will carry out during his or her absence. This is the ideal situation. Not only will the students already know who you are, but you'll have a better understanding of what the teacher expects in terms of routine, schedule, and curriculum. Although you'll be asked to follow the plans as they are spelled out for you, if you are able to meet with the teacher in advance, you'll be able to ask for clarification. If you have any questions after you've begun the assignment, you can check in with your grade level and subject area team members.

29
Lesson Plan:
Direct
Instruction
(with
instructions)
30
Lesson Plan:
Direct
Instruction
(without
instructions)

♦ **Creating your own lesson plans** If your time in the classroom is extended beyond a week, you'll need to be prepared to do lesson planning on your own. Of course, you may have the help of other teachers, but you will need to create daily and weekly lesson plans yourself. You might also have access to coaches or curriculum specialists for certain subject areas, and if you are going to be at the school for a month or more, you may be able to get training for some of the curriculum. Use the **Lesson Plan** templates to organize your daily and weekly plans in a simple and easy-to-follow format.

- **Emergency lesson plans** You might be called in for a long-term substitute teaching assignment in an emergency situation in which the classroom teacher has not been able to leave any lesson plans for you. In such a situation, use your already prepared emergency lesson plans to help you get through the first day or two. Then you'll be able to meet with the grade level and subject area teachers and plan with them.

- **Teacher's manuals** These materials will help you become familiar with the curriculum as a whole and can be an enormous help. Teacher's manuals often follow a pattern from lesson to lesson. Once you understand the pattern, planning will be much easier.

  - Look for consistencies in the introduction, guided practice, independent work, follow-up, extension, and assessment resources sections.
  - Read background knowledge overviews.
  - Review cross-curricular connections.
  - Watch for tie-ins to state and national standards.

Students can help in many ways, whether lesson plans have been prepared for you or not. Older students can be especially helpful in telling you which stories they have already read in their anthology, what spelling lesson they are on, what essay they have been writing, which chapter in social studies they are studying, what assignment they are completing in the computer lab, and which math concepts they have been addressing. If you don't have lesson plans at all, it is important to use your emergency lesson plans. But the first day of your assignment could simply be a day of discovery, where you randomly call on two girls and two boys to tell you what they are doing in the given subjects.

The classroom aide

If you are fortunate enough to have a classroom aide during your long-term substitute teaching assignment, you will want to meet with the aide during the first day or two to discuss how the aide is typically used on a day-to-day basis and how he or she might be used productively during the regular classroom teacher's absence. This is especially important if the classroom teacher didn't address this in the lesson plans. Since you will be in the classroom for some time, it's important that you and the aide work well together. Ask what the aide usually does and what he or she enjoys doing most to help ensure the best use of the aide's time in the classroom. Suggestions for areas where it might be good for the classroom aide to have responsibility follow.

- **Small groups** The classroom aide can work with a small group of students to target a specific skill. If you have students needing support for several different skills, the aide can work with several small groups for given amounts of time.

- **One-on-one** The classroom aide can work with a student individually to target a specific skill. You and the aide can put together a list of students and the skills each one needs help with. Students can rotate in and out during the day.

- **Circulating** The classroom aide can be a great asset by circulating through the classroom to students' desks or tables and checking on students who might need academic support, whether during a lesson or independent practice.

- **Special needs** Some classroom aides may be assigned to your classroom because a student with an Individual Education Plan (IEP) is required to have a one-on-one aide. However, the aide will also be able to help with other students when appropriate, which can be quite helpful if you have other students in the class with different instructional challenges. It will be up to you and the aide to decide which students he or she will work with.

- **Grading** Having help from the classroom aide with grading can alleviate the often overwhelming responsibilities of a long-term substitute teaching assignment. If you ask the aide to grade papers, make sure that you provide an answer key and that you review the work yourself. You still need to know where students are making mistakes so that you can target those skills in your teaching.

- **Assessments** The classroom aide can give make-up tests to students who were absent when a test was given. During downtime or recess, a classroom aide can proctor the test while the student completes it.

- **Bulletin boards** The classroom aide often knows how the teacher prefers handling bulletin boards, and he or she can be of assistance in planning and managing updates to the bulletin boards while you are in the classroom. Posting student work that was completed while you were in the classroom is one way you can leave your mark on the class. If you are only substituting in the classroom for a week or two, it may not be appropriate to make any changes to the bulletin boards, but for a more extended substitute teaching assignment, it is appropriate unless you have been instructed not to.

- **Tracking student grades** If the substitute teaching assignment is truly long-term, you may need to assign grades for the grading period, so it is critical that you keep detailed records and anecdotal notes. The classroom aide can be a valuable resource when you are assigning grades. Make sure that you can back up whatever formal grades you assign.

◆ **Organizing classroom materials and supplies** Because the classroom aide often knows the classroom teacher's organization system for the classroom, you can ask for the aide's assistance to make sure you know what materials and supplies are available and have easy access to them.

Parent connections

You will be with this same group of students for an extended period of time, so it is important to make sure that the students' parents are confident in your abilities to meet their child's needs and challenge their child. The first day you are in the classroom, send a note home letting the parents know that you will be the substitute teacher in their child's class. Introduce yourself and include the dates that you have been hired for. If you have the opportunity to meet with the regular classroom teacher before taking over his or her class, it might be possible to write a joint note home. You can use one of the **Parent Letter** templates or compose your own.

34
Parent Letter 1
35
Parent Letter 2

Parent conferences

If you are substitute teaching for a period of time that extends into parent and teacher conferences, you will have to conduct those meetings. Suggestions for successfully carrying out a parent and teacher conference include the following.

◆ Offer and schedule a variety of conference times. If school policy allows, consider including conference options such as before school begins, during lunch time, after school, in the evening, by phone, virtually, or by e-mail.

◆ Confirm the day, date, time, and option in advance. To the best of your ability and conforming with school policy, accommodate any changes that are necessary.

◆ If you can acquire home email addresses and phone numbers to make these confirmations, this will help ensure successful meetings with parents or guardians.

◆ Carry out your conference by beginning with a positive comment, then discuss areas needing improvement, and close the conference with another positive comment.

◆ Do not do all the talking. Allow parents to discuss their concerns with you.

◆ Take notes. This information can help you plan skill-based learning and will help you meet the needs of their child.

◆ Follow through on what is discussed. Be sure to note any modification that needs to be put in place.

- Never diagnose a child's learning or behavior issues. You are the teacher, but you are not qualified to diagnose. Leave that to a qualified professional. If a parent does ask you about a learning or behavior issue, just state what you have observed and recommend that they consult with school resource professionals or their family physician.

- Tell the parents tangible ways they can support their child at home in the areas of behavior, homework, sleep, and the like.

- Ask the office to provide a translator if you know that you and the parents will need one. Avoid putting students in charge of translating for their parents.

- Treat the parents with respect and courtesy. Remember that you are talking with them about their child.

Serving as a substitute teacher is no easy task, but being a long-term substitute teacher is even more demanding. In many cases, you take over most of the responsibilities of the regular classroom teacher and tend to all the needs of the students in the classroom. You are responsible to the parents, the administration, the classroom aide, the office staff, and, most important, to the students.

Never be afraid to ask for help. Utilize the expertise of your grade level team members, faculty, coaches, curriculum specialists, office staff, school staff, administrators, parent volunteers, and classroom aides. They are willing to assist you, but you need to let them know when you need their support. Be kind to all of them. Take the time to say hello, introduce yourself, and smile. You never know whose assistance you're going to need, and being friendly will benefit you when you do need help.

chapter 2
Behavior management

Handling classroom behavior as a substitute teacher can be a daunting task—reducing the best of intentions to frustrations and raising questions about one's abilities as a sub. You need to be able to manage inappropriate behavior quickly and efficiently.

The more prepared you are when you start the day, the fewer behavior concerns you will need to deal with. Keep students engaged and busy; if you make good use of student participation and use students as volunteers, there will be fewer disturbances in the classroom.

It is important that you find out right away how the regular classroom teacher runs his or her class and how you can utilize those strategies. Student behavior for every class is greatly influenced by the kind of system the teacher already has in place for behavior management, how the teacher manages the classroom on a day-to-day basis, and how well the classroom organization works. For every class you sub in, student behavior is also greatly influenced by your own organization, how well you transition into their established routine, and the tone you establish from the start.

Remember the following:

♦ You are a guest in the classroom, so respect its established system.

♦ Start off with a serious demeanor and an organized approach. In time, you will be able to determine what type of class you are dealing with and, if the situation allows, you can lighten up. It is hard to go the other way—from too friendly to serious.

♦ Establish your presence from the start. Tell them who you are and a bit about your past experience (if appropriate), and let them know that you expect to carry out the day as if the regular classroom teacher were in the room.

♦ Rewards in the classroom should be earned gradually. Don't rush to give too many, too soon; if you do, the effectiveness of the reward system will be diminished. And no regular classroom teacher would appreciate returning to find that all classroom rewards had been distributed or that a rewards jar was completely full, thus requiring an immediate reward for the class for filling it.

♦ Stay positive, and focus on the positives in the classroom.

♦ Be proactive, not reactive. Anticipate potential problems.

♦ Handle standard behavior management in the classroom to keep everything running smoothly, but, if possible, let the regular classroom teacher handle major offenses after returning. Unless a situation warrants immediate follow-through, because of personal danger, for example, leave a note about the offense for the teacher and let the regular classroom teacher handle it.

♦ Choose your battles. Because you are a sub, there will be students who test your boundaries. You have to decide what is truly important and what your limits are.

♦ Never let the students see you sweat. Stay calm. *You* are the adult.

♦ Manage the classroom's behavior on your own, without the need for outside assistance, as much as possible.

♦ Use a behavior management system in the classroom that the students can work with. Setting impossible goals—whether for the entire class or an individual student—can be counterproductive. Let the students experience success!

- Be consistent and follow through. Don't burn any bridges with students, because you may be called back. Be sure to have prizes readily accessible.

- Always get approval from the school office for any rewards that you bring in yourself. Avoid candy and other food items, because some of your students may have allergies, or the school may have a no junk food policy.

The classroom behavior management system

When you first arrive in the classroom, look for an already established behavior management system. It could take several different forms.

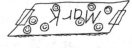

- **Individual sticker charts or cards** Charts or cards may be taped to the desk, and stickers are applied as students exhibit good behavior or participation. When a card is full (as determined by teacher), a reward is given.

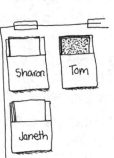

- **Behavior color cards** A chart with a pocket for each student may be displayed on a wall or bulletin board. Each student's pocket has a set of colored cards (such as green, yellow, red) in it. Students start the day with all cards in order. If inappropriate behavior is exhibited, students are asked to pull a card. The order of the cards indicates a student's behavior.

  - **First card**—may simply indicate a warning.
  - **Second card**—may indicate five minutes less recess time, and so on.
  - **Last card**—is usually reserved for major offenses.
  - **Additional card**—may be used to indicate appropriate behavior. Giving this special color card to those children who are behaving appropriately can motivate other students and set an example for them in a positive way.

  At the end of the day, those students whose card indicates good behavior can receive a sticker or some other reward.

- **Names on the board** Smiley and sad faces may be drawn on the board so that names can be added underneath as good or bad behavior is exhibited.

  - Checks can be added next to students' names during the day.
  - Names can be worked off the sad face list by erasing a few letters at a time for better behavior.
  - You may want to use only the positive smiley face as a way of focusing more on those who are caught doing something good, rather than on negative behavior.

- **Marble jar** Some teachers fill a jar or other container with marbles. As students exhibit good behavior, marbles are added until the jar or container is full, at which point the class earns a pre-established reward.

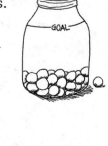

- **Table/Team point system** Working with an established point system, groups of students work together (by tables or in teams) to earn points. The points are tracked on the board or a chart, and winning groups can earn a prize.

- **Tickets** Tickets may be distributed as rewards for good behavior. Use the **Outstanding Student Tickets** template or the **Super Star Tickets** templates, and make sure you have a good supply of them on hand. Students can collect reward tickets and use them to "purchase" rewards and prizes on a designated day.

33
Outstanding Student Tickets
54
Super Star Tickets 1
55
Super Star Tickets 2

- **Traffic light clips** A traffic light with students' names (often written on clothespins) clipped onto it may be displayed in the classroom. All students' names start at green. They are moved to yellow as a warning and to red for a consequence. Students try to stay in the "green" with their behavior and can be rewarded for it.

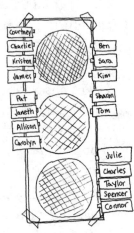

47
Student Behavior Tracker

- **Name chart** Create a name chart from the class roster that you can use throughout the day to make notations about how students are doing. The **Student Behavior Tracker** template includes columns for recording happy faces, checks, plus or minus symbols, or other notations, depending on students'

behavior. Leave this name chart with the regular classroom teacher along with your notes, and he or she can handle behavior issues upon returning. This system allows you to communicate privately with the classroom teacher about negative behavior in the classroom.

It is not your job to change the behavior management system in the classroom but to enforce it until the teacher returns. With younger students, it's very important to use the regular classroom teacher's behavior management system (assuming there is one). With older students, it's best to continue with the established behavior management system as much as possible, but in the absence of an established system, it's easier for older students to adhere to a system that you develop together as you begin your day in the classroom. What is most important is for you to track inappropriate behavior throughout the day, whatever system is used. Follow-through and consistency are key to any system.

Behavior interview

Conduct a behavior interview with the class to find out about the current behavior management system to determine if it's working. Keep things simple: If a system has already been established, you don't need to reinvent the wheel; if it's not broken, don't fix it. If there is an established system in place, it probably means that the students respond well to it.

The following questions will help you become familiar with the classroom's behavior management system, and they will remind students what you will hold them accountable for.

1. What are your classroom rules?
   As part of your behavior interview with the class, write the classroom rules on the board to help familiarize yourself with them and as a way to review them with the class.
2. What rewards are given when good behavior is exhibited?
   Write the rewards on the board. Explore the cause and effect relationship between the rules and the rewards with the class.
3. Where are points and rewards tracked?
   This may be on a chart, on the board, or in some other way.
4. When are rewards given?
   Rewards may be given out at the end of the week, at the end of the day, or even on the spot.
5. How is misbehavior handled?
   Find out about the hierarchy of consequences for misbehavior for this class. Some possibilities are a warning, a time-out, a note to the regular classroom teacher, and going to the office.

Students can be a great resource, and including their input as you get to know the classroom can be a tremendous help. Younger students are especially willing to help out. As you discuss classroom behavior policies with the students, jot down the names of those who were helpful and let them know that you will share their helpfulness with the classroom teacher. This will make students accountable for what they tell you, which is especially important with older students, who may try to get away with more.

Direct the conversation to help you understand the following about the behavior management system in the classroom.

1. **What?**
   What is the system? What are the classroom rules? What are the rewards and consequences?
2. **How?**
   How is it managed?
3. **When?**
   When are rewards distributed?

Conversations with students might go like these:

- ◆ **"My teacher gives us blue tickets."**

  - ◆ Ask the students, "How many tickets at a time are given out?" and "Where are the tickets kept?"
  - ◆ Reward tickets are usually a big hit with the students, and most teachers will tell you to give out as many as you want, as long as the rewards are earned. To keep the system operating effectively, don't make it too easy: Students should work for their tickets. Reward tickets are well received by most students in kindergarten through grade 12, as long as the reward is age appropriate (such as a Popsicle party for students in the lower grades, free homework passes for students in middle school or high school).

- ◆ **"Our teacher puts marbles in a jar."**

  - ◆ Ask the students, "What are you trying to earn with the marbles?"
  - ◆ Refer to the goal throughout the day, whenever you add marbles to the jar or take them out. The goal may be to earn a reward such as a field trip, a popcorn party, or a Friday movie.

- ◆ **"We earn team points."**

  - ◆ Ask the students, "Where are your points recorded?" and "What are you working toward?"
  - ◆ Team points are frequently used as a reward for students in all grades from kindergarten through grade 12. Teams may be composed of students who sit at the same table or in the same row, or who are grouped by another method.

List students' responses on the board, and assure them that you will refer to them throughout the day. Within the first hour of the school day, make a point to positively reinforce as much behavior as possible while employing this behavior management system.

Your own behavior management system

It's important for you to be prepared with several of your own behavior management strategies, even if the regular classroom teacher has given you some direction. If established classroom strategies are not available for you to use, it's even more critical to be prepared with some strategies of your own. Explain to the students how you will monitor their behavior during your time as the substitute teacher in the classroom.

For students at all grade levels, there are several subtle moves on your part that can often correct an inappropriate behavior.

1. A "teacher look" in the student's direction or eye contact with a quick shake of the head deters most unwanted behavior. These strategies don't even require that you know the student's name.
2. Your physical proximity to the student can be effective. As you are conducting a lesson, move closer to students who are talking or distracted; this can deter inappropriate behavior.
3. Jotting a few notes while the class is watching to let them know that you are tracking behavior gives students a powerful reminder that you mean business. It should in no way take away from your instruction; make it just a quick stop-and-jot.
4. Allowing students to observe (but not hear) a conference with a student can be a strong deterrent to further inappropriate behavior. Conference with the student in the hall, leaving the door open. Using a low voice that only the two of you can hear, explain why the student's behavior is an issue and what the consequences will be.

Rules and consequences

Rules and consequences provide structure and boundaries that offer students security, consistency, and a sense of organization in their environment. This in turn creates an atmosphere of low anxiety that allows students to perform well. No behavior management strategy will be effective if rules and consequences are not in place.

If classroom rules and consequences are not easily accessible to you when you arrive in the classroom, take the first 10 to 15 minutes of the school day to brainstorm appropriate behavior with the students. Have students help you develop a short list of rules (three rules for kindergarten through grade 3, five rules for grades 4 through 12) and a few consequences, using a hierarchy of increasing severity. More than five rules can be hard to track and may be counterproductive. Use the **Rule Planner** template so students can brainstorm and write their ideas down.

37
Rule Planner

State the rules in a positive manner. For example, "Do not hit" and "No fighting" can be stated as "Keep your hands and feet to yourself." Classroom rules will more likely be understood and followed during the day if the students have taken part in developing them. You'll want to give them a few examples to get them started.

Suggestions for classroom rules and consequences

Rules for kindergarten through grade 3

- Stay seated.
- Raise your hand.
- Use an inside voice.
- Take turns.
- Ask for help.
- Follow directions.
- Be prepared.
- Do your best.

Rules for grades 4 through 12

- Stay in your seat unless you have permission to leave it.
- Raise your hand to be heard.
- Use a quiet voice when working with a partner or in groups.
- Turn off all devices and stow them.
- Follow directions.
- Ask three friends for help before seeking help from the teacher.
- When asked to get started, begin working right away.
- Do your best.

Possible consequences for kindergarten through grade 12

- Warning
- Loss of recess time (anywhere from five minutes to the entire recess period)
- Conference (with you) plus a written assignment or behavior journal to be shared with the regular classroom teacher

- As a last resort, send the student to a designated buddy teacher or to the office, always with an assignment in hand. (Never send a student to another class with nothing to do.)

It may seem to you that it will take a lot of time to develop new rules and consequences with the students, but as you gain experience as a substitute teacher, you will find more ways to encourage the students to suggest rules and consequences. If you lead the discussion well, students won't be constantly telling you "we do this . . . , but we don't do that." This eliminates many of the disruptions that otherwise use up instructional time.

It is important to discuss the behavior in question without making it a personal issue or an attack on the student. It is acceptable to say

- "It is not you, but it's the behavior that I have an issue with."
- "We have rules, and we all need to follow them."
- "You have a choice. You decide what behavior you bring to the table. You know that there will be consequences for your behavior— good or bad."

It is *never* appropriate to

- Send a student to the hall or outside the classroom alone.
- Have a student stand or sit in a corner.
- Deface a student's person or work.
- Use inappropriate language with a student.
- Touch, grab, push, or pull a student in any way.
- Have a student miss lunch.
- Belittle or degrade a student in front of others.
- Threaten a student in any way.

Managing classroom behavior

Following is a listing by grade level of some of the typical behavior concerns that you may encounter in the classroom. Of course, many of these can occur at any grade level, since much of a student's behavior depends on maturity.

Tracking student behavior throughout the day can be tedious and a bit overwhelming, but you can minimize the problem situations if you are prepared with some behavior management strategies that are appropriate for the grade level you're teaching.

It is important to set clear expectations for rewards, so that students know what behavior you expect and what they can expect to earn for meeting your expectations. Tell students how you will track their behavior and when they will get their reward. Good follow-through is the key to a successful rewards system. Remember that not all students have the self-control to earn a reward. With more difficult students, it is important to find a behavior that you can reward them for in order to give them a chance at success too.

Suggestions for both behavior management strategies and rewards are included for each grade level.

Keep in mind that students often act out when other areas of their lives are not stable. Don't take anything personally. Remember that, as a sub, it is not your job to investigate or diagnose students for potential issues beyond the classroom. If there is an issue with a particular student, communicate that to the regular classroom teacher with a note; you can use a **Substitute Teacher Feedback Note** template. You should only include what you have observed. If you suspect abuse, advise an administrator, who will determine how it should be handled. If you are a long-term substitute for a class, make a point to know the school's policies and procedures for handling a referral or an abuse report.

50
Substitute
Teacher
Feedback
Note 1

51
Substitute
Teacher
Feedback
Note 2

Kindergarten

Typical behavior concerns

- Crying
- Hitting
- Inattention
- Kicking
- Laughing uncontrollably
- Making silly noises
- Pouting
- Pushing
- Responding to unanswered questions
- Rolling on the carpet
- Tantrums
- Teasing
- Throwing objects
- Wiggling

Appropriate behavior management strategies

For kindergartners, the following ideas will help you plan ahead and be prepared with an arsenal of strategies to keep your day running smoothly.

- Use a variety of attention-getters (catchy songs, clappers, small bell, and the like) to keep students engaged and keep behavior problems to a minimum. Ask students what they like to sing; they can teach you a favorite song.
- Keep the day moving. Think of your day as a series of activities, each one 20 to 30 minutes from start to finish, so that the students are constantly engaged. This gives students little time for misbehavior.
- Know your audience. Know when it is time to wrap something up, and don't try to drag an activity out just so you can say you have finished it.

- Turn an instructional activity into a game. Creating a fun way for students to collectively engage in a learning activity can be motivating and fun for younger students.
- A "teacher look" in a student's direction tunes him or her in quickly.
- A quick shake of the head is a fast attention-getter.
- A brief "talking to" is usually sufficient.
- Every once in a while, a time-out at the end of the day is necessary.
- At the end of the day, present awards for things like good citizenship, good helper, and active learner to students. Use the **Rewards Certificates** template, and customize it for your particular need.

36
Reward
Certificates

Rewards

Following are suggested rewards for kindergartners.

- Earning a job as classroom helper to pass out materials, straighten up bookshelves, and the like
- Extra active time (PE, recess, break) for finishing the day's agenda early
- Extra read-aloud story
- Free time
- Hand stamp
- Name on the board under "star students" or smiley face
- Pencil
- Praise for a job well done
- Sticker (such as a scented sticker)
- Thumbs-up, high five, class claps for a great student response
- Trip to the "author's chair" to share their work

First grade

Typical behavior concerns
- Acting silly
- Getting out of their seats without permission
- Inappropriate language
- Inattention
- Making noises
- Not completing assignments
- Not following directions
- Pushing
- Responding to unanswered questions
- Talking out of turn
- Teasing

Appropriate behavior management strategies

For first graders, the following ideas will help you plan ahead and be prepared with an arsenal of strategies to keep your day running smoothly.

- Use a variety of attention-getters (repetitive clap, complimenting students who are working hard, five-finger countdown, and the like). Ask students what strategies the regular classroom teacher uses to get their attention.
- Discuss briefly why a certain behavior was inappropriate; this is usually sufficient with this grade level.
- To track positive behavior, write students' names on the board under the heading "star students" and add stars next to the names as students are "caught" doing what is asked of them. (Try to catch every student doing something appropriate early in the day.)
- As a last resort, send students who are misbehaving to a designated classroom, with work in hand, for a time-out (roughly one minute per year of their age); make note of this for the teacher. Always try to handle the situation in class first. (Make sure this strategy is in line with school policy and procedure.)

Rewards

Following are suggested rewards for first graders.

- Stickers (scented stickers are a huge hit) to be given out when students are caught staying on task or following the rules
  - Timing is important for this type of reward: Don't give them out too frequently, but give them out frequently enough that they have significance.
- Super Star tickets, created from the **Super Star Ticket** templates
  - When you are in a classroom on a long-term assignment, students can collect tickets and turn them in for a reward at the end of the week, month, or unit.
  - Photocopy several sheets of Super Star Tickets in advance, so you always have them available. These are especially well received by younger students.
- Pencils
- Hand stamp
- Praise for a job well done
- Thumbs-up, high five, class claps for a great student response
- Extra active time (PE, recess, break) for finishing the day's agenda early
- Earning the right to be a "special helper"
- Free time or sponge activity
- Extra read-aloud story

54
Super Star
Tickets 1
55
Super Star
Tickets 2

Second grade

Typical behavior concerns

- Being silly
- Getting out of their seats without permission
- Inattention
- Not finishing class work or homework
- Not following classroom rules
- Talking back
- Talking out of turn

Appropriate behavior management strategies

For second graders, the following ideas will help you plan ahead and be prepared with an arsenal of strategies to keep your day running smoothly.

- Use a variety of attention-getters (repetitive clap, complimenting students who are working hard, five-finger countdown, and the like). Ask students what strategies the regular classroom teacher uses to get their attention.

- Have the student complete unfinished or extra work while the rest of the class is doing a fun activity, or during recess or play time after lunch.
- To track positive behavior, write students' names on the board under the heading "star students" and add stars next to the names as students are "caught" doing what is asked of them. (Try to catch every student doing something appropriate early in the day.)
- Have students work toward a whole-class reward. The class can earn tallies or marbles in a jar, which can earn them a collective reward, such as extra free time at the end of the day.
- As a last resort, send students who are misbehaving to a designated classroom, with work in hand, for a time-out (roughly one minute per year of their age); make note of this for the teacher. Always try to handle the situation in class first. (Make sure this strategy is in line with school policy and procedure.)

Rewards

- Playing games at the end of the day
- Stickers for those demonstrating positive behavior
- Super Star tickets, created from the **Super Star Ticket** templates
  - When you are in a classroom on a long-term assignment, students can collect tickets and turn them in for a reward at the end of the week, month, or unit.
  - Photocopy several sheets of Super Star tickets in advance, so you always have them available. These are especially well received by younger students.
- Pencils
- Erasers
- Notepads

54
Super Star
Tickets 1
55
Super Star
Tickets 2

- Hand stamp
- Praise for a job well done
- Thumbs-up, high five, class claps for a great student response
- Extra active time (PE, recess, break) for finishing the day's agenda early
- Free time or sponge activity (such as I Spy, Heads Up Seven Up) (See Chapters 1 and 11.)

Third grade

Typical behavior concerns

- Arguing
- Bullying
- Not being someone's friend
- Not completing class work or homework
- Not following class rules
- Passing notes
- Silly behavior
- Talking
- Tattling

Appropriate behavior management strategies

For third graders, the following ideas will help you plan ahead and be prepared with an arsenal of strategies to keep your day running smoothly.

- Tell students that you will track their behavior and will leave a note for their teacher.
- Give a time-out during a fun activity. Students may decide to complete their work quickly so they can participate.
- Pull students aside to have a conversation with them about the behavior. Try to connect with the student. It can also be helpful to talk with the student in a low voice, but in view of the class, to show the entire class that you mean business.
- Have students complete unfinished or extra work while the rest of the class is doing a fun activity, or during recess or free time after lunch.
- Have a whole-class incentive as one of your strategies.
  - Write a sentence on the board at the start of the day with part or all of it represented by lines or dashes.
  - Ask students to suggest letters to fill in the secret message at a point during the day when they have earned it.

- Erase a letter if the class gets too rowdy.
- Examples: "We had a _____ day!" (We had a SUPER day!) or "Your class did an _____ job!" (Your class did an INCREDIBLE job!) When the students are all on task, call on a student to suggest a letter. By the end of the day, they will have completed a positive message for the regular classroom teacher when he or she returns. The students will be proud of a message like "We had a SUPER day!"

- If you are asked to sub again in the class, you'll most certainly be asked if they'll be making a new secret message for their teacher. This strategy is easy and free—and it works.

- As a last resort, send students who are misbehaving to a designated classroom, with work in hand, for a 10- to 15-minute time-out; make note of this for the teacher. Always try to handle the situation in class first. (Make sure this strategy is in line with school policy and procedure.)

Rewards

Following are suggested rewards for third graders.

- Playing board games or travel games at the end of the day (if they are available in the classroom or if you have some in your survival kit)
- Super Star tickets, created from the **Super Star Ticket** templates
  - When you are in a classroom on a long-term assignment, students can collect tickets and turn them in for a reward at the end of the week, month, or unit.
  - Photocopy several sheets of Super Star tickets in advance, so you always have them available. These are especially well received by younger students.
- Pencils
- Erasers
- Notepads
- Praise for a job well done
- Thumbs-up, high five, class claps for a great student response
- Pulling a student aside to tell them how proud you are of their behavior or a turnaround in their behavior
- Extra active time (PE, recess, break) for finishing the day's agenda early
- Free time or sponge activity (such as I Spy, Heads Up Seven Up). (See Chapters 1 and 11.)

54
Super Star
Tickets 1
55
Super Star
Tickets 2

Fourth grade

Typical behavior concerns

- Bullying
- Daydreaming
- Excessive talking
- Incomplete work
- Not being someone's friend
- Rowdiness
- Rushing through assignments
- Sneaking out of class (such as asking to use the restroom when it's not necessary)
- Tricking the substitute (such as sitting in the wrong seat or giving the sub misinformation)

Appropriate behavior management strategies

For fourth graders, the following ideas will help you plan ahead and be prepared with an arsenal of strategies to keep your day running smoothly.

- Make it clear to students that you will be leaving a note for the teacher.
  - Throughout the day, recognize students who are doing a great job by name, so the class knows you are keeping track.
  - Write down the names of these students to add to your final note to the teacher.
  - Use the **Student Behavior Tracker** and/ or the **Substitute Teacher Feedback Note** templates, or write your own note to the regular classroom teacher.

47
Student Behavior Tracker
50
Substitute Teacher Feedback Note 1
51
Substitute Teacher Feedback Note 2

- Proximity. Circulate around the room. If a student is misbehaving, move closer to the student as a deterrent to unwanted behavior.
- Praise good behavior.
- Walk around the classroom with a clipboard, writing down names of students who are working hard and doing their best, as well as those students who are struggling. (It always settles students down when they see a teacher walking around with a clipboard.) Use the **Student Behavior Tracker** template. This information should be included in your note to the teacher at the end of the day.
- Pull students aside to have a conversation with them about the unwanted behavior. Try to connect with the student. It can also be helpful to talk with the student in a low voice, but in view of the class, to show the entire class that you mean business.

◆ As a last resort, send students who are misbehaving to a designated classroom to complete their unfinished work during recess or lunch (after they have eaten their snack or lunch and had a chance to use the restroom); make note of this for the teacher. Always try to handle the situation in class first. (Make sure this strategy is in line with school policy and procedure.)

Rewards

◆ Extra homework time
  ◆ Students appreciate being able to get started on their homework at school.
◆ Working in pairs
  ◆ Students may work in pairs or small groups as long as they are productive.
  ◆ If a group becomes unproductive, you need to tell the group that they must work individually, because they are not using their time effectively.
◆ Free time at the end of the day if the required work gets completed
◆ Extra computer time or time at other classroom centers
  ◆ Always be mindful of the set-up and organization of classroom centers. Make sure they are used appropriately and left the way they were found.

Fifth grade

Typical behavior concerns

◆ Being argumentative
◆ Bullying
◆ Cliques of friends, excluding friends
◆ Daydreaming
◆ Excessive talking
◆ Fighting
◆ Incomplete work
◆ Passing notes
◆ Rowdiness
◆ Rushing through assignments
◆ Sneaking out of class (such as asking to use the restroom when it's not necessary)

Appropriate behavior management strategies

For fifth graders, the following ideas will help you plan ahead and be prepared with an arsenal of strategies to keep your day running smoothly.

◆ Have all students evaluate their own performance that day. Use the **Student Self-Evaluation Form** template, or let students write their own evaluation. Leave students' evaluations for the classroom teacher.
◆ Circulate around the room. If a student is misbehaving, move closer to the student as a deterrent to unwanted behavior.

48
Student Self-Evaluation Form

- ◆ Praise good behavior.
- ◆ Have students who are struggling write a note to the teacher about the behavior issues they experienced that day. You can help these students address the concerns.
- ◆ Leave a positive note for the teacher. Let the students know that you are keeping a list of those students who were helpful and on task throughout the day, and that you will be leaving this list for the regular classroom teacher. Use the **Student Behavior Tracker** template or the **Attendance/Task Log** template to track student behavior, and the **Substitute Teacher Feedback Note** templates for your note to the teacher.
- ◆ Pull students aside to have a conversation with them about the unwanted behavior. Try to connect with the student. It can also be helpful to talk with the student in a low voice, but in view of the class, to show the entire class that you mean business.
- ◆ As a last resort, send students who are misbehaving to a designated classroom, with work in hand, for a 10- to 15-minute time-out; make note of this for the teacher. Always try to handle the situation in class first. (Make sure this strategy is in line with school policy and procedure.)

02
Attendance/
Task Log
47
Student
Behavior
Tracker
50
Substitute
Teacher
Feedback
Note 1
51
Substitute
Teacher
Feedback
Note 2

Rewards

Following are suggested rewards for fifth graders.

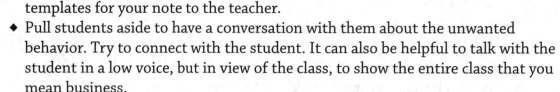

- ◆ Extra homework time
  - ◆ Students appreciate being able to get started on their homework at school.
- ◆ Working in pairs
  - ◆ Students may work in pairs or small groups as long as they are productive.
  - ◆ If a group becomes unproductive, you need to tell the group that they must work individually, because they are not using their time effectively.
- ◆ Free time at the end of the day if the required work gets completed
- ◆ An appropriate DVD shown at the end of the day if the required work gets completed

Sixth grade

Typical behavior concerns

- ◆ Abusing time during small group activities
- ◆ Boy/girl issues, crushes
- ◆ Bullying
- ◆ Chatting
- ◆ Daydreaming
- ◆ Falling asleep
- ◆ Fighting
- ◆ Cliques of friends, excluding friends
- ◆ Incomplete work
- ◆ Passing notes
- ◆ Rushing through assignments

Appropriate behavior management strategies

For sixth graders, the following ideas will help you plan ahead and be prepared with an arsenal of strategies to keep your day running smoothly.

- ◆ Have all students evaluate their own performance that day. Use the **Student Self-Evaluation Form** template, or let students write their own evaluation. Leave students' evaluations for the classroom teacher.

48
Student Self-Evaluation Form

- ◆ Circulate around the room. If a student is misbehaving, move closer to the student as a deterrent to unwanted behavior.
- ◆ Praise good behavior.
- ◆ Have students who are struggling write a note to the teacher about the behavior issues they experienced that day. You can help these students address the concerns.
- ◆ Leave a positive note for the teacher. Let the students know that you are keeping a list of those students who were helpful and on task throughout the day, and that you will be leaving this list for the regular classroom teacher. Use the **Student Behavior Tracker** template or the **Attendance/Task Log** template to track student behavior, and the **Substitute Teacher Feedback Note** templates for your note to the teacher.

02
Attendance/Task Log
47
Student Behavior Tracker
50
Substitute Teacher Feedback Note 1
51
Substitute Teacher Feedback Note 2

- ◆ Pull students aside to have a conversation with them about the unwanted behavior. Try to connect with the student. It can also be helpful to talk with the student in a low voice, but in view of the class, to show the entire class that you mean business.

◆ As a last resort, send students who are misbehaving to a designated classroom, with work in hand, for a 10- to 15-minute time-out; make note of this for the teacher. Always try to handle the situation in class first. (Make sure this strategy is in line with school policy and procedure.)

Rewards

Following are suggested rewards for sixth graders.

◆ Extra homework time
  ◆ Students appreciate being able to get started on their homework at school.
◆ Working in pairs
  ◆ Students may work in pairs or small groups as long as they are productive.
  ◆ If a group becomes unproductive, you need to tell the group that they must work individually, because they are not using their time effectively.
◆ Free time at the end of the day if the required work gets completed
◆ An appropriate DVD shown at the end of the day if the required work gets completed

Middle school

Typical behavior concerns

◆ Bullying
◆ Chatting
◆ Fighting
◆ Getting distracted by electronic devices
◆ Inattention
◆ Incomplete work
◆ Not following directions
◆ Talking back
◆ Talking out of turn
◆ Teasing
◆ Vandalism

Appropriate behavior management strategies

For middle school students, the following ideas will help you plan ahead and be prepared with an arsenal of strategies to keep your day running smoothly.

- Have all students evaluate their own performance that day. Use the **Student Self-Evaluation Form** template, or let students write their own evaluation. Leave students' evaluations for the classroom teacher.

48
Student Self-Evaluation Form

- Circulate around the room. If a student is misbehaving, move closer to the student as a deterrent to unwanted behavior.
- Praise good behavior.
- Leave a positive note for the teacher. Let the students know that you are keeping a list of those students who were helpful and on task throughout the day, and that you will be leaving this list for the regular classroom teacher. Use the **Student Behavior Tracker** template or the **Attendance/Task Log** template to track student behavior, and the **Substitute Teacher Feedback Note** templates for your note to the teacher.
- Find a way to relate to students by sharing something about yourself, possibly sharing a story about your own life or discussing your hobbies.

02
Attendance/ Task Log
47
Student Behavior Tracker
50
Substitute Teacher Feedback Note 1
51
Substitute Teacher Feedback Note 2

Rewards

Following are suggested rewards for middle school students.

- Extra homework time
  - Students appreciate being able to get started on their homework at school.
- Working in pairs
  - Students may work in pairs or small groups as long as they are productive.
  - If a group becomes unproductive, you need to tell the group that they must work individually, because they are not using their time effectively.
- Passes
  - Use the **Homework Pass** template if you are letting students skip a homework assignment.
  - Use the **Open Pass** template if you choose to modify an assignment, where you may allow students to do a smaller number of problems out of the assigned number (for example, if 20 problems were assigned, students who earn this reward can do fewer, such as 12 problems, instead.)

24
Homework Pass
31
Open Pass

- Less independent work, more work completed collectively
  - Complete some of the assigned work as a class: "If we can keep it together, I will work on this with you."

High school

Typical behavior concerns

- Bullying
- Chatting
- Fighting
- Getting distracted by electronic devices
- Inattention
- Incomplete class work and homework
- Not following directions
- Skipping class
- Talking back
- Talking out of turn
- Teasing

Appropriate behavior management strategies

For high school students, the following ideas will help you plan ahead and be prepared with an arsenal of strategies to keep your day running smoothly.

48
Student Self-Evaluation Form

- Have all students evaluate their own performance that day. Use the **Student Self-Evaluation Form** template, or let students write their own evaluation. Leave students' evaluations for the classroom teacher.
- Circulate around the room. If a student is misbehaving, move closer to the student as a deterrent to unwanted behavior.
- Praise good behavior.

02
Attendance/Task Log
47
Student Behavior Tracker
50
Substitute Teacher Feedback Note 1
51
Substitute Teacher Feedback Note 2

- Leave a positive note for the teacher. Let the students know that you are keeping a list of those students who were helpful and on task throughout the day, and that you will be leaving this list for the regular classroom teacher. Use the **Student Behavior Tracker** template or the **Attendance/Task Log** template to track student behavior, and the **Substitute Teacher Feedback Note** templates for your note to the teacher.
- Talk with students one-on-one.
- Find a way to connect with the students, perhaps by asking individual students to assist you.

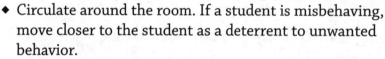

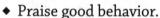
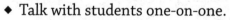

Rewards

Following are suggested rewards for high school students.

- ◆ Extra homework time
  - ◆ Students appreciate being able to get started on their homework at school.
- ◆ Working in pairs
  - ◆ Students may work in pairs or small groups as long as they are productive.
  - ◆ If a group becomes unproductive, you need to tell the group that they must work individually, because they are not using their time effectively.
- ◆ Free time for the last five minutes of the period

Showing you care

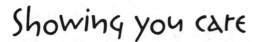

Kids need to know they are respected, heard, and cared for. This is true for every school in every location, for every grade level, and for every student—regardless of the make-up of the student body.

The following are suggestions for ways to show students that you care about them, whether you are subbing for one day, three days, weeks, or months at a time. Reflect on these ways to "show you care," and jot down ideas of your own. When you are having a hard day, review your list—and remember that showing you care about students can make a big difference in both their behavior and their work productivity.

Acquaint Get to know the students; learn students' names and use their names when addressing them.

Ask Ask students questions about their work; ask how would they do it differently.

Avoid Avoid negative comments.

Be consistent Establish your boundaries and rules, and be consistent in enforcing them.

Be present Keep an eye on what students are doing at all times.

Be real If you need help from the students, ask.

Compliment Find something to compliment each student on.

Encourage From class work to games, be a cheerleader for the students.

Follow-through Don't promise anything you can't follow through on.

Handle Deal with any conflict right away whenever possible.

Include Make sure that all students are included.

Inquire Spend a few minutes asking students about themselves.

Involve Include students in decisions for the day.

Laugh When appropriate, have fun with students.

Listen Listen to students' opinions, responses, and stories as time allows.

Model Model appropriate behavior for students, so that they know an alternate way of handling specific situations.

Motivate Be excited about what students are doing, and help them see the importance of what they do.

Move Circulate around the classroom.

Notice Pay attention to improvements or changes in performance.

Participate Join in games or classroom activities when appropriate.

Praise Build on good behavior by praising it.

Reach Set high—but realistic—expectations that encourage students to reach toward a goal.

Relate Share a little about yourself as a way to relate to students.

Show Applaud, high-five, or give a thumbs-up to show students you approve of their behavior and/or performance.

Support Ask questions that lead students to come up with good answers for their class work.

Substitute teachers need to be able to recognize patterns of student behavior, and they also must know how to respond in specific situations. Children are savvy, and they're quick to analyze responses to their behavior. They know very quickly which buttons to push and what they can get away with. In every classroom where you substitute teach, you must keep in mind that a substitute teacher's responses can actually trigger students' behavior—both appropriate and inappropriate.

The ideas and strategies presented in this chapter will prepare you to manage classroom behavior in many different types of situations. While suggestions for appropriate behavior management systems at different grade levels are included, you shouldn't be afraid to incorporate your own rules, consequences, strategies, and rewards, including advice you get from others. All this will help you—and your students—have a productive day in the classroom.

chapter 3

Kindergarten (5–6 years old)

This chapter provides a brief overview of kindergarten students and the learning that takes place at that grade level. Kindergarten is an important year socially. It is also a year of fundamental learning, when the printed word and number concepts are introduced. Students vary in personality and maturity at any grade level, so keep in mind that this is a general overview—a "sneak peek" at what you might expect. Be sure to address your own state standards when planning lessons.

Kindergartners—Who are they?

Kindergarten students are usually inquisitive and energetic. They tend to have a short attention span. They are developing their fine motor skills. These children need step-by-step guidance and require having procedures modeled for them and repeated many times. They enjoy singing, dancing, and pretending. Their world revolves around themselves. They are acquiring basic skills, as well as learning how to share and how to get along. This is an important year to help them build a foundation for appropriate social behavior.

What are they learning?

Reading

Kindergartners

... are learning their letters, sounds, and the basics of reading
... are learning that the printed word has meaning
... are acquiring knowledge from CVC (Consonant-Vowel-Consonant) words ("cat," "dog," etc.) to develop simple sentences
... are reading repetitive, simple text
... are reading rhyming patterns
... describe parts of a story
... enjoy having stories read to them

Writing

Kindergartners

... are starting to form letters of words (working with recognition of sounds)
... are building words from initial dictation to writing simple sentences
... are learning to write their first name and last name
... are using inventive spelling ("scl" can mean "school"; "dg" can mean "dog")
... are using simple spelling patterns
... are using pictures, letters (both upper- and lowercase), and some words to communicate in writing

Math

Kindergartners

... are writing, adding, and subtracting numbers from 1 to 10

$3 + 2 = 5$

... are counting to 30

... demonstrate patterning, comparing, ordering, and sorting by quantity and attributes

... show spatial relationships (top, bottom, in front of, behind)

... show physical differences (larger, smaller)

... identify shapes (square, rectangle, triangle, circle); identify plane vs. solid

... are learning time concepts (today, week, month) and telling time to the hour

... are using a calendar

... are learning about money (coins: penny, nickel, dime, quarter)

... are learning to graph objects and pictographs

... are learning to tally numbers

Social studies

Kindergartners

... are learning about their national history, patriotism, national symbols (such as the flag), and citizenship

... study simple maps and the globe

... study today vs. long ago

... learn about famous Americans and the holidays

... study their community and community helpers

... learn about cooperation, responsibility, and friendship

... are learning the concept that money buys goods

Science

Kindergartners

... make observations about the world around them

... learn about physical properties and attributes

... learn about water as a solid, liquid, or gas

... study the concepts of sink vs. float, plant vs. animal, the life cycle (for example, butterfly: egg, caterpillar, chrysalis, butterfly), weather (sunny, cloudy, rainy, snowy, foggy), shadows, and seasons (summer, fall, winter, spring)

... learn about land and water forms (mountains, valleys, rivers, oceans)

... learn about natural resources (for example, wood (natural) vs. plastic (man-made))

Activities for each curricular area

Whether you are substitute teaching in a class for one day, three days, a month, or longer, it's important to have a variety of grade level curriculum ideas and  activities in your personal survival kit. You may find that no lesson plans have been left for you; you may finish lessons more quickly than expected and have extra time at the end of a period; or you may have to do lesson planning on your own but need time to adjust to your current surroundings and the teacher's manuals you will be working with. The following lesson ideas and activities are suitable for kindergarten.

Reading activities

The following strategies and topics are ways to read to and with kindergartners.

Read aloud

- ◆ Read a book aloud to the class; it may include CVC words, rhyming patterns, and repetitive text.
- ◆ Do not stop to summarize or ask questions of the students unless prompted to do so by the curriculum guide.
- ◆ Students listen, but respond only if prompted to do so.
- ◆ A read-aloud is usually intended to be for the pure enjoyment of hearing a story.

Shared reading

- ◆ Read aloud a big book or text. Students view and follow as the substitute teacher points to the words being read.
- ◆ Model reading strategies, such as predicting, summarizing, visualizing, and the use of context clues.
- ◆ Students read aloud as the teacher tracks the words, if they are able to.
- ◆ Identify text with CVC words, rhyming patterns, or repetitive text.

Buddy reading

- A kindergarten student pairs with an upper grade student (from third, fourth, fifth, or sixth grade).
- Students read and discuss stories from age-appropriate books that may include CVC words, rhyming patterns, or repetitive text.
- The older student serves as a coach or reading mentor.

Guided reading

- Small groups at the same reading level.
- Students read same text.
- Teacher coaches students individually while other students read text silently or in a low voice.
- Teacher focuses on targeted 'aim' or 'skill'.

Reading Workshop

- Teacher introduces targeted 'aim' or 'skill' and models it in action.
- Students read books at their level/that they choose for a sustained period of time.
- Students have individual goals they work on as well as introduced skills.
- Teacher can informally conference with individual students, asking how they are applying a goal or the aim of the day.
- Whole group shares how skills were used.

Follow-up activities after reading stories

- Hold a class discussion or dialogue.
- Students respond to a story in their student journals (predicting, summarizing, sequencing), using simple sentences or illustrations.
- Students respond to a story by illustrating a favorite scene.
- Students retell the story on a storyboard, using simple sentences and/or illustrations. Use the **Storyboard Organizer** template.
- Students work in pairs, small groups, or as a whole class to describe parts of a story.

46
Storyboard
Organizer

Writing activities

The following strategies and topics are ways to teach writing to kindergartners.

Writing genres

- **Brief sentences** Students write words and brief sentences about topics they can relate to.
- **Narratives** Students write about things they know, especially themselves.
- **Autobiographies** Students write about themselves: their families, their friends, their pets, and so on.

Ways to write

- **Independent writing** There are a variety of forms (journals, labeling, student books, and so on) that work well with kindergartners. You may use sentence starters, where students complete a sentence, or you may also use "closed" sentences, where students fill in words that have been left out of a sentence.

Complete the sentence:

My favorite activity at school is

_____.

"Close" the sentences:

The dog is _____. The _____ is red.

- **Interactive writing** Students plan and write as a group by taking turns, working with the substitute teacher or classroom aide.

♦ **Shared writing** The substitute teacher writes simple sentences, and students copy them.

♦ **Guided writing** The substitute teacher and the students, who are grouped in pairs or small groups, write together as a community of writers.

♦ **Writer's workshop** Writers learn through their own experience, teacher models a skill, students write independently while teacher conferences with individuals on individual skills needs or the skill for that day and students share with class and get feedback.

Additional writing activities

◆ Students match pictures to words or letters (upper- and lowercase).

◆ Students create word lists, using words from current topics of study.

◆ Students use spelling words to write sentences.

◆ Students create word webs: They write a word in the center of a circle, and then draw lines from the word to points outside the circle where descriptors of the center word can be written. Depending on class level, this activity can be used for writing simple sentences.

◆ If school policy allows, use alphabet cereal to build words. This activity can be done at the end of the day so that it serves as a motivation throughout the day.

Math activities

The following strategies and topics are ways to teach math to kindergartners.

Number sense

25
Ice Cream
Sundae Math
Fact Families

◆ **Adding and subtracting from 1 to 10**
Lead students through a series of addition and subtraction fact families, using manipulatives or the **Ice Cream Sundae Math Fact Families** template. These fact families may be easy or difficult, depending on the class level.

◆ **Ordering and sorting** Using a bag of buttons, shells, rocks, and the like, students sort objects by attributes (color, texture, size, number of holes, shape). Students can use a sheet of paper folded into four quadrants or the **Sort-Order-Pattern Mat** template.

40
Sort-Order-
Pattern Mat

◆ **Patterning** Students create patterns with buttons, shells, rocks, and the like, and illustrate the patterns. Have students use the **Sort-Order-Pattern Mat** template to create patterns with Fruity Cheerios® (if school policy allows), or let students string cereal in patterns onto a piece of yarn for a necklace.

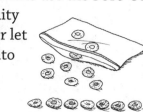

◆ **Money (coins)** Have a bag of real or plastic coins (pennies, nickels, dimes, quarters) on hand. Have students sort the coins by value. Model determining which coins equal given values, and then let students practice this. The values and number of coin combinations used will depend the level of knowledge of the students. However, values will primarily be small amounts, using only pennies, nickels, and dimes.

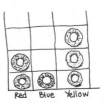

Graphing

◆ **Graphing objects** Using items such as Froot loops®, M&Ms®, and Fruity Cheerios® that have been placed in snack-sized plastic zipper bags, students sort by color, graph findings (line or bar graphs), and then tally the number for each color. This can serve as a motivation for students, who can take the treat home at the end of the day. Use the **Bar Graph** template.

04
Bar Graph
16
Geometric
Shape
Organizer

Geometry/Measurement

◆ **Identifying shapes** Using a bag of shapes (circles, squares, triangles, rectangles)

of various sizes and colors, students identify the shapes. Use the **Geometric Shape Organizer** template, or the class can collectively identify these shapes by finding them in common objects in the classroom. Students can go on a scavenger hunt to find each shape in the classroom, and then name and illustrate the objects in the classroom that have that shape. Students can then create patterns using the pieces (for example, circle, circle, square, circle, circle, square).

◆ **Calendar** Calendars can be used to teach about time in days, months, and years. They can be used to reinforce math skills such as counting, place value, and money. Use the calendar to teach weather (snowy, rainy, foggy, sunny), temperature (hot, cold, warm, cool), past, present, future, and tallies.

Social studies activities

The following strategies and topics are ways to teach social studies to kindergartners.

Being a good citizen

♦ Discuss character traits that are involved in being a good citizen: honesty, courage, determination, and individual responsibility. Include the importance of following rules (such as sharing and taking turns) and the consequences of breaking rules.

♦ Read aloud a book appropriate for discussing a character trait.

♦ When an appropriate book focusing on a character trait is not available, create role-playing activities that demonstrate the desired character trait.

♦ Read aloud a book such as *The Boy Who Wouldn't Share* by Mike Reiss, and discuss how important it is to share and take turns.

National symbols

♦ Share pictures of national symbols (found in nonfiction books or on the Internet), such as the national flag, the bald eagle, the Statue of Liberty, the White House, the Liberty Bell, and so on.

♦ Share a few simple facts about several national symbols, and let students choose a symbol to illustrate.

Jobs and community helpers

♦ Share descriptions of jobs that people do; discuss the names of related jobs at the school and in the local community.

♦ Write the names of several jobs on the board (principal, custodian, police officer, nurse, mayor, governor), and have students list the roles that people play in those jobs.

♦ Discuss jobs in the school and community, and ask students which job they would like to have.

♦ Students create their own community helper using the **Community Helper** template.

09
Community
Helper

People, places, and environments

◆ Help students become familiar with the school's layout. Take the class for a walk around the school campus, and either take pictures with a digital camera or have students illustrate places they've visited after the class has returned to the classroom. As a whole-class activity, draw a map of the school. Place photos or illustrations on the map to show where individual places such as the school office, bathrooms, nurse, library, auditorium, and cafeteria are located. (This activity is more suited for a long-term assignment.)

Events, people, and places of other times

◆ Plan activities around holidays like Thanksgiving, Independence Day, Washington's birthday, Lincoln's birthday, Martin Luther King Jr. Day, Memorial Day, Labor Day, Columbus Day, and Veterans Day. These provide a way to teach about historical and cultural perspectives.

◆ Create files for specific holidays that include simple activities that can be done in a reasonable amount of time. If you know you will be subbing during one of these holidays, visit the library to select relevant picture books to read aloud.

◆ Refer to resource books for ideas to use with lessons about holidays and/or important people.

Science activities

The following strategies and topics are ways to teach science to kindergartners.

Physical sciences

◆ Bring a variety of items (such as clay, cloth, paper, metal tabs from soda cans), and have students describe their characteristics and physical properties (for example, color, size, shape, weight, texture, flexibility). Create a chart listing each item, and write students' responses underneath each one.

Life sciences

◆ Identify major structures of common plants. Using a diagram of a plant, students identify each structure (such as stems, leaves, roots). Explain the importance of each one to the survival of plants.

◆ Identify major structures of common animals. Using a diagram or model of a bird, students identify each structure (such as wings, beak, feathers, legs). Explain the importance of each one to the survival of animals.

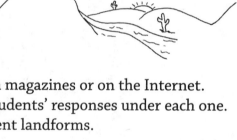

◆ Discuss with students: What makes a plant a plant? What makes an animal an animal? How do plants vary? How do animals vary? What do their structures help them do?

◆ Compare and contrast plants and animals through discussion or by using a **Venn Diagram**.

61
Venn Diagram

Earth sciences

◆ Students learn about the Earth and its composition (land, air, and water).

◆ Students learn the characteristics of mountains, rivers, oceans, valleys, deserts, and local landforms.

◆ Students identify the characteristics of landforms that can be seen in pictures found in magazines or on the Internet. Create a chart listing each landform, and list students' responses under each one.

◆ Students may illustrate and label several different landforms.

Environmental sciences

◆ Students learn to identify some of Earth's resources that are used in everyday life. They discuss ways of conserving many of the Earth's resources.

◆ Read aloud a picture book such as *The Giving Tree* by Shel Silverstein or *The Lorax* by Dr. Seuss. Students illustrate their favorite scene from the picture book or sequence the story, using some of the book's illustrations or creating their own sequenced storyboard. Assign parts of the story for specific students to illustrate and then assemble the illustrations into a class book.

◆ Students discuss the implications of using up the Earth's resources and what might happen if we do not conserve. Teach this from a positive perspective: With problems come opportunities for change; their generation has the exciting task of rethinking how things are done.

Investigation and experimentation

◆ Students learn how to ask meaningful questions and conduct investigations. Bring in a variety of common objects that can be used to demonstrate the five senses (a bell—sound, a lemon—taste, perfume—smell, neon green and pink paper—sight, fuzzy ball—touch). Let students explore these objects and describe them in relation to the five senses.

◆ Students describe the properties of objects, compare objects, and sort objects by physical attributes (such as color, shape, texture, size, weight). They communicate their observations orally and through drawings.

◆ Read aloud a picture book such as *My Five Senses* by Aliki.

Suggested books for kindergarten

Actual Size by Steve Jenkins (Houghton Mifflin, 2004)

Bee-Bim Bop! by Linda Sue Park, illustrated by Ho Baek Lee (Clarion Books, 2005)

The Boy Who Wouldn't Share by Mike Reiss, illustrated by David Catrow (HarperCollins, 2008)

Chicka Chicka Boom Boom by Bill Martin Jr. and John Archambault, illustrated by Lois Ehlert (Simon & Schuster, 1989)

Cleversticks by Bernard Ashley, illustrated by Derek Brazell (Crown Publishers, 1995)

David Goes to School by David Shannon (Blue Sky Press, 1999)

The Giving Tree by Shel Silverstein (HarperCollins, 1986)

I Can Read with My Eyes Shut by Dr. Seuss (Random House, 1978)

Knuffle Bunny Too: A Case of Mistaken Identity by Mo Willems (Hyperion Books for Children, 2007)

The Lorax by Dr. Seuss (Random House, 1971)

Mama Panya's Pancakes: A Village Tale from Kenya by Mary and Rich Chamberlin, illustrated by Julia Cairns (Barefoot Books, 2005)

My Five Senses by Aliki (HarperCollins, 1989)

One Potato, Two Potato by Cynthia DeFelice, illustrated by Andrea U'Ren (Farrar, Straus and Giroux, 2006)

The True Story of the 3 Little Pigs by Jon Scieszka, illustrated by Lane Smith (Viking Penguin, 1989)

Suggested websites for kindergarten

http://www.arcademicskillbuilders.com/games
http://www.bbc.co.uk/schools/wordsandpictures/index.shtml
http://www.brainpopjr.com
http://funschool.kaboose.com
http://www.internet4classrooms.com
http://kinderwebgames.com/index.html

http://www.learningplanet.com
http://www.primarygames.com
http://www.starfall.com
http://teacher.scholastic.com/clifford1/flash/confusable/index.htm
http://teacher.scholastic.com/clifford1/flash/phonics/index.htm
http://teacher.scholastic.com/clifford1/flash/story_4.htm

Link a picture book across the curriculum

A single picture book can be used to cover all curricular areas for kindergarten. These ideas can be tweaked and used at other grade levels as well.

One Fish, Two Fish, Red Fish, Blue Fish
by Dr. Seuss

PUBLISHER	Random House
PUBLICATION DATE	March 1960
AGE RANGE	2–6
SUMMARY	This is a book of rhyming adventures that take place in a fantasy world. It taps into simple rhyming patterns, using both real and nonsensical words. Children love the illustrations, and it is easy to learn the rhyming patterns.

Reading

◆ *One Fish, Two Fish, Red Fish, Blue Fish* is a perfect book to read aloud to younger children. The first time you read the story aloud to students, read it all the way through without stopping, but change the lilt in your voice as the rhyming patterns shift. Then read it aloud a second time, stopping along the way to point out the rhyming patterns. If you have access to a big book edition, be sure to point out the words as you read them aloud. If you have access to a document reader, you can project the book onto the whiteboard and read it aloud while students follow the words. Be sure to track the words with a ruler or pointer as you read them aloud.

Writing

- As a whole-class activity, have students help you create nonsensical poems. Write a few excerpts from the book on the board as a guide.
- Using words from the book, make word lists of numbers (one, two, three, four), colors (blue, red, yellow), and directions (here, there, everywhere, far, high, low). Have students use these words to help you write nonsensical poems.
- Teach students about antonyms by using examples from the book. Show corresponding pictures from the book so students can "see" the antonyms: longer/shorter, old/new, near/far, fast/slow, high/low.
- Teach adjectives, specifically those that describe physical attributes (fat, old, new, sad, glad, little, thin). Use examples from the book, and have students use these words as you work on nonsensical poems.
- Teach rhyming words, using combinations from the story (fear/ear/dear, mouse/house, old/gold/hold/cold, book/hook/nook/cook, swish/fish/dish, wink/drink/ink/pink, wet/pet). Then have students come up with as many rhyming words as they can. Write these on the board.

Math

- Use the numbers 1 to 11 to teach counting. Write these numbers on the board, and see if students can continue counting as far as 30. As they say the numbers out loud, write them on the board. Then have them help you count by twos. Place a circle around the twos as students call them out. Continue to do this for fives and tens.
- Teach students directions by using words from the book (here, there, far, near, high, low), and then have students stand up and respond to directions as you call them out. For example, "stand far away from your desk," "stand near your best friend," "get down low to the floor," "stand up high on your toes." Have only two to four students at a time to do this.

Social studies

- Several modes of transportation (air, land, sea) are mentioned in the book. Show pictures of a plane, a car, a bicycle, a boat, a train, and the like, and have students identify them. Ask students to share the types of transportation they have used. Then have students illustrate two modes of transportation they haven't experienced.
- The book introduces students to several different characters, some real and some made-up. An easy way to teach about diversity and individual differences is to have students help create a list of the ways we are all the same, and another list of the ways we are all different. Remind students not to use names of friends or family, but just to share likeness and difference in terms of attributes (hair color, wears glasses, height).

Science

- Students learn the differences between fish and land animals by comparing and contrasting body parts for each: Fish have gills, fins, a tail; land animals have four legs, a tail.

- Using types of weather mentioned in the book, have students draw what a day would be like if there was sunlight, rain, snow, or wind that day. Have them divide a sheet of paper into four boxes and draw one type of weather in each of the four boxes.

- Show an illustration from the book that demonstrates pulling and pushing, and describe what it means to push and to pull. Have volunteers come up to the front of the room and demonstrate the correct way to push objects, then the correct way to pull objects.

- Review the five senses (sight, smell, taste, hearing, touch) with the students. Bring a variety of items (horn, piece of fuzzy material, vanilla candle, M&Ms®, bright-colored paper) that involve a number of the senses. Have students focus on one sense at a time for several different items and explain what they are seeing, smelling, tasting, hearing, or feeling.

Art

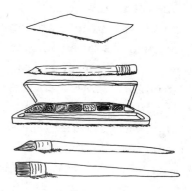

- Have students choose their favorite part of the book and illustrate it on their own. They can refer to a picture from the book, but encourage them to be creative.

- Draw large versions of the numbers from the book (1 through 11) and have students create a creature from a number they choose. Model this activity for the students. Use a lot of color and creativity.

chapter 4

First grade (6–7 years old)

This chapter gives a brief overview of first grade students and what learning takes place at that grade level. First grade is an important year in which many new skills are introduced. At this age, they have had some Preschool/TK schooling experiences and have some familiarity with school routines. Students vary in personality and maturity at any grade level, so keep in mind that this is a general overview—a "sneak peek" at what you might expect. Be sure to address your own state standards when doing any necessary lesson planning.

First graders—Who are they?

First graders are still learning how to multitask. They can focus on a task at hand and work in groups. First graders seek out validation for their work and can be sensitive to what others think. They enjoy learning through different experiences, such as hands-on activities, games, stories, and singing. First graders are still developing their basic social skills and need opportunities to practice skills such as sharing, getting along, and taking turns. A big transition takes place between kindergarten and first grade, where students have their own desk, take on more responsibility, do more homework, and so on. This year lays the foundation for developing good study skills and learning behaviors.

What are they learning?

Reading

First graders

... are working toward reading 60 words per minute by the end of the year in order to develop fluency and comprehension

... are learning letters and sounds with increasingly more complex spelling patterns (short and long vowel spellings)

... are learning about word families and rhyming

... are learning sight words, compound words, contractions, synonyms, and antonyms

... are reading simple sentences, repetitive text patterns, stories, and picture books

... are using word attack skills and decoding

... enjoy having stories read to them

... identify parts of a story and a book's setting, plot, conflict, and resolution

Writing

First graders

... move from simple sentences to paragraphs (stories of several sentences; narrative, expository, and friendly letters)

... develop their manuscript handwriting (printing)

... are working on punctuation and capitalization

... are learning the writing process for drafting and editing work

... are using simple parts of speech (noun, verb, adjective, adverb)

... are using possessives, both nouns and pronouns

... are adding details and description to their writing

Math

First graders

... count up to 100

... add and subtract to 20 and eventually to 100 with no regrouping

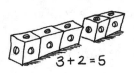

... learn place value (ones, tens, hundreds)

... are learning ordinal numbers to ten (tenth)

... are continuing patterning, sorting, and comparing ($>$, $<$, $=$)

... are counting by twos, fives, and tens

... engage in simple graphing

... identify shapes and solids

... measure simple lengths, volume, and weight

... are learning more about money (penny, nickel, dime, quarter, half-dollar, dollar), and add and compare values up to $1.00

... study the calendar

... carry out simple fractional parts (half, fourth)

... solve addition and subtraction facts up to 10

... compare shapes (number of sides or corners)

... tell time (hour, half hour)

... work with bar and picture graphs, and use tally charts

Social studies

First graders
... are learning about their place in time and space
... study family, the community, and community helpers
... study their role as a citizen, following rules, democracy, and contributing to a group
... learn about fair play and rules
... look at the past vs. the present
... study maps and their symbols
... study diverse communities (ethnic, religious, etc.) that are united by common principles
... learn about people in different locations as well as the weather, clothing, and diet of those people
... study American patriotic symbols and practices
... learn about famous Americans and legends
... learn that money can purchase goods and services

Science

First graders
... learn from observations of the world around them
... collect data, using simple sentences and drawing
... study states of matter
... study simple machines
... learn about weather and the effects of the sun
... learn about the characteristics, parts, and needs of plants and animals
... study life cycles
... learn about the sun and Earth (rotation, orbit)
... learn about the importance of reducing, reusing, and recycling to conserve resources

Activities for each curricular area

Whether you are substitute teaching for one day, three days, a month, or longer, it's important to have a variety of grade level curriculum ideas and activities in your personal survival kit. You may find that no plans have been left for you; you may finish plans more quickly than expected and have extra time at the end of a period; or you may have to do lesson planning on your own, but need time to adjust to your current surroundings and the teacher's manuals you will be working with. The following lesson ideas and activities are for first grade.

Reading activities

The following strategies and topics are ways to read to and with first graders.

Read aloud

- Read a book aloud to the class; it may include sight words, compound words, contractions, synonyms, and antonyms.
- Do not stop to summarize or ask questions.
- Students listen, and respond only if prompted to do so.
- A read-aloud is usually intended to be for the pure enjoyment of hearing a story.

Shared reading

- Read aloud a big book or text. Students view and follow as the substitute teacher points to the words and models tracking.
- Model reading strategies such as predicting, summarizing, visualizing, and the use of context clues.
- Students read aloud as the teacher tracks the words, if they are able to.
- Students identify text with CVC words, rhyming patterns, or repetitive text.

Buddy reading

- A first grade student pairs with an upper grade student (third, fourth, fifth, or sixth grade).
- Students read and discuss stories from age-appropriate books that might include simple repetitive sentences, CVC words, CVCC words, long vowel words, or rhyming patterns.
- The older student serves as coach or reading mentor.

Sustained Silent Reading (SSR)

- Students read independently and silently.
- Students read books at their instructional reading level.
- SSR provides reading practice and time for reading for pleasure.
- SSR is also known as Uninterrupted Sustained Silent Reading (USSR) or Drop Everything and Read (DEAR).

Choral reading

- ◆ Choral reading is also known as unison reading.
- ◆ It provides many opportunities for repeated readings of a selected piece.
- ◆ It provides an opportunity to practice oral reading.
- ◆ Choral reading is excellent for poetry, rhymes, and chants.

Partner reading

- ◆ Students pair up and share an agreed-upon book.
- ◆ Students take turns and assist one another.
- ◆ Designate a special place for partner reading in the classroom.
- ◆ You may want to pair students by reading ability: high/medium and medium/low.
- ◆ Students can sit knees-to-knees or shoulder-to-shoulder (sitting side by side but facing in opposite directions). Students should use their "six-inch" voices (low volume).

Timed reading

- ◆ Students work toward a designated number of words: 60 words per minute is the goal for first graders.
- ◆ Students read as much of a passage as they can in one minute in an attempt to reach the designated words per minute.
- ◆ Students read the passage twice, attempting to read further the second time; each reading is timed.
- ◆ Timed reading builds fluency.

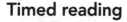

Guided reading

- ◆ Small groups at the same reading level.
- ◆ Students read same text.
- ◆ Teacher coaches students individually while other students read text silently or in a low voice.
- ◆ Teacher focuses on targeted 'aim' or 'skill'.

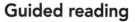

Reading Workshop

- Teacher introduces targeted 'aim' or 'skill' and models it in action.
- Students read books at their level/that they choose for a sustained period of time.
- Students have individual goals they work on as well as introduced skills.
- Teacher can informally conference with individual students, asking how they are applying a goal or the aim of the day.
- Whole group shares how skills were used.

Follow-up activities after reading stories

- Students think-pair-share about their favorite parts of a story. Ask students to think about the story for a limited period of time, and then have them turn to a partner to share and discuss it.
- Hold small group or class discussions about the author's purpose, the main idea, and so on, of a story.
- Students respond to a story by writing in their journals; they engage in predicting, summarizing, and sequencing, through simple sentences and/or illustrations.
- Students respond to a story by illustrating their favorite scene(s), which can then be sequenced on the board. Students may write captions under the pictures.
- Students retell a story on a storyboard through simple sentences and/or illustrations. Use the **Storyboard Organizer** template.
- Students describe parts of a story in pairs, in small groups, or as a whole class, using the pictures as a guide.

46
Storyboard
Organizer

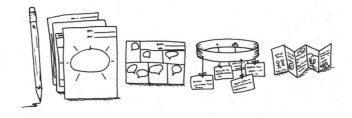

Writing activities

The following strategies and topics are ways to teach writing to first graders.

Writing genres

- **Brief narrative** Students write fictional or auto-biographical sentences that describe an experience.
- **Brief expository** Students write descriptions of real objects, people, places, or events, using sensory details.

Ways to write

- **Independent writing** There are a variety of forms (journals, mini-books, and so on) that work well for first graders. You may use sentence starters, where students complete simple sentences that have been started with a prompt and are related to a relevant topic.

- **Interactive writing** With the help of the substitute teacher or classroom aide, students work with a relevant topic, planning and writing as a group. They take turns, writing the story out on chart paper. This method works well for modeling corrections and edits. Use sticky notes or different colored markers to make changes.

- **Shared writing** The substitute teacher writes simple sentences, and students copy them from the teacher's model.

- **Guided writing** The substitute teacher and the students, who are grouped in pairs or small groups, write together as a community of writers.

- **Writer's workshop** Writers learn through their own experience, teacher models a skill, students write independently while teacher conferences with individuals on individual skills needs or the skill for that day and students share with class and get feedback.

Additional writing activities

- Students match pictures to words or letters (upper- and lowercase). Students then draw the picture on their own paper and write the matching word, once the combinations have been approved.
- Students create word lists, using words from current topics of study.
- Students use spelling words to write sentences.
- Students write to the author of a book that the class enjoys.
- Students write stories about the season or a holiday.
- Students write adventure stories about a teddy bear that you bring in.
  If you are subbing for a lengthy period, you may have students bring
  in a teddy bear or other toy for this activity.
- Students use a **graphic organizer** to organize data for a writing activity.
- Students sequence stories or ideas on a storyboard.
- Students write a friendly letter to a character from a story.
- Students journal about a learned activity in science or social studies. They may copy sentences or write their own.
- Students write out math word problems.
- Long-term substitute teachers may put together a backpack containing a journal book and teddy bear. The teddy bear visits a different student's home each evening, and the student journals about what the teddy bear saw and did.

38
Sandwich Organizer
41
Stair Organizer 1
42
Stair Organizer 2
45
Story Organizer
62
Web Organizer

Math activities

The following strategies and topics are ways to teach math to first graders.

Number sense

40
Sort-Order-Pattern Mat

15
Fraction Bars

- **Sorting, patterning, and comparing (>, <, =)** Prepare a small plastic zipper bag filled with M&Ms®, Froot loops®, Fruity Cheerios®, or a similar small treat for each student (if school policy allows). Students sort the contents of the bag by color. They then arrange the colored treats into a pattern (such as green, red, green, red: an ABAB pattern). Use the **Sort-Order-Pattern Mat** template. Introduce different patterns to the class, such as ABAB, ABCABC. Challenge students to create a specific pattern ("create an ABCABC pattern with your treats"). Students compare the number of treats of each color (for example, "9 red > 6 brown").

- **Fractional parts (one-half, one-fourth)** Show the students how to fold a paper in half, then in fourths; if students are advanced, you can show them other fractions. Using the **Fraction Bars** template, model for students how they can show one-half, one-fourth, three-fourths, and so on. Have students illustrate given fractions on a sheet of blank paper to turn in for assessment purposes. Then hand out the **Fraction Bars** template and have students cut out the fractional parts and place them in a plastic zipper bag to use over and over.

Graphing

04
Bar Graph

- **Simple graphing** Have a small plastic zipper bag filled with M&Ms®, Froot loops®, Fruity Cheerios®, or a similar small treat prepared for each student (if school policy allows). Show the students how to create a line graph or bar graph using the colored treats. (You can use the **Bar Graph** template.) You can also show them how to tally and chart the colored treats, using crayons to match the colors.

Geometry/Measurement

- **Measuring length** Be sure to have a ruler for every student. Before handing out the rulers, explain what an inch is and show them how to measure items that can be found in the classroom.

- **Measuring volume** Bring in containers of several capacities: cups, pints, quarts, half gallons, gallons, and a large tub. Show students how to measure and add volumes, using rice or beans. Allow students to take turns measuring volume. Students write volume equivalents and illustrate them (for example, 2 quarts = ½ gallon, 4 quarts = 1 gallon, etc.).

- **Telling time (hour, half hour)** Read aloud *The Grouchy Ladybug* by Eric Carle. Ask students to tell you what they know about time. After reading aloud the story and discussing the book, hand out the **Clock** template and have students make their own clock. Using the book as a guide, have students move the hands on their clock to show the times mentioned in the book.

07
Clock

Social studies activities

The following strategies and topics are ways to teach social studies to first graders.

Community helpers

- Share descriptions of people who help out in their community (such as police officers, nurses, librarians, and mail carriers).

- Write a chart on the board that lists jobs performed by community helpers, and have students list the roles that people play in those jobs.
- Students create their favorite community helper, using the **Community Helper** template. Then they write stories about their community helper on the back.

09
Community Helper

Role as a citizen

◆ Discuss with the students what it means to be a good citizen. Have them work in pairs or triads to consider their role as citizens at home, at their school, and within the community. Use the **Attributes Organizer**. Ask them to focus on the many volunteer opportunities available to them. Have each group share its ideas with the rest of the class. Transcribe students' responses onto the board or chart paper.

03
Attributes
Organizer

◆ Ask students to write down volunteering ideas they came up with. Suggest that they ask their parents to allow them to carry out one of the volunteer roles they listed (such as beautifying the community, volunteering to feed the homeless, collecting jackets for a local shelter).

◆ Arrange for students to volunteer at school. Possible volunteer opportunities might be helping in a kindergarten classroom, picking up trash in the yard, helping with clean-up in the lunch area, and so on. (This activity is more suited for a long-term assignment.)

Past vs. present

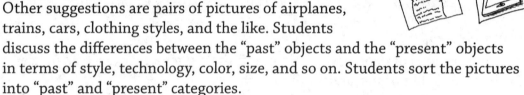

◆ Bring in pictures (perhaps printed from the Internet) that show objects from the past as well as pictures showing the same objects in the present. For example, bring in a picture of a one-room schoolhouse and a picture of their school (or a similar modern school). Other suggestions are pairs of pictures of airplanes, trains, cars, clothing styles, and the like. Students discuss the differences between the "past" objects and the "present" objects in terms of style, technology, color, size, and so on. Students sort the pictures into "past" and "present" categories.

◆ After a teacher-led discussion and presentation of vocabulary related to the topic, students write stories about a day at school in the past and a day at school now.

Maps

◆ Using the classroom's world map, show students north, south, east, and west. Ask volunteers to point to each of the directions on the world map. Have them stand up, and have students face each direction. Using landmarks that they would recognize, help them recognize north, south, east, and west in the classroom. Follow up by labeling the classroom walls with "North," "South," "East," and "West."

◆ Ask students to use directional words to tell you where a specific place is located on the school campus, for example, "The cafeteria is north of the classroom."

Money

◆ Make copies of play money, using the **Counting Coins** and **Incentive Money** templates. Have students cut out enough bills and coins to cover a shopping trip to a grocery store. Cut out pictures from the newspaper's grocery coupon section, and print pictures of food items from the Internet. Price each item appropriately, and set up a "store" where students can practice purchasing items. Select value amounts that are appropriate for their grade level. Give students an opportunity to count out money for each item you call out. Then call out two or more items, which will require students to add up their total purchase and show the correct total amount in bills and coins. This activity links social studies and math.

10
Counting Coins

26
Incentive Money

Science activities

The following strategies and topics are ways to teach science to first graders.

Physical sciences

◆ **States of matter** Use plastic zipper bags to explore the three states of matter. Base exploration on the following questions.

SPACE	Does it take up space?
WEIGHT	Does it have weight?
SHAPE	Does it hold its shape? Does it hold the shape of its container?
ATTRIBUTES	Can you hold it? Can you smell it? Can you see it?

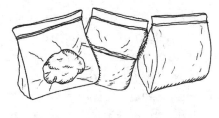

◆ **Solids** Place a solid (such as a rock or a ball) in a plastic zipper bag. Discuss the term "solid." Take out the item. Ask students to pass it around and feel it, look at it, and so on. Ask them, "Does it take up space?" "Does it have weight?" "Does it hold its shape?" Ask students for other examples of solids, and list them on the board or chart paper.

◆ **Liquids** Hold up a plastic zipper bag with water in it. Discuss the term "liquid." Hold up a second plastic zipper bag of water and allow students to observe and touch the bag. Ask them, "Does it take up space?" "Can you see it?" "Does it have weight?" "Does it hold its shape?" Pour the water into a cup so students can see that the liquid takes the shape of its container. Ask students for other examples of liquids, and list them on the board or chart paper.

◆ **Gases** Blow air into the third, empty plastic zipper bag. Discuss with the students what you just put into the bag. Ask them, "What's in the bag?"

"Does it take up space?" "Does it have weight?" (Accept the answer "no.") Ask them, "Does it hold its shape?" Let the air out of the bag and ask the students where it went. Ask them to inhale and see how lungs expand like a balloon. Ask students for other examples of gases, and list them on the board or chart paper.

Review from the board or chart paper all of the solids, liquids, and gases that you listed. Talk about the properties of each.

- **Sink or float** Set up a tub or small bucket filled with water, and have five to ten small items available for demonstrating sinking and floating. (Some items should sink and some should float.) Have students stand in a circle around the water. Ask them to say what floating and sinking mean. Hold up one item at a time, and ask students if they think that item will sink or float. After they make their prediction, put the item in the water to see what happens. Discuss their prediction and what actually happened. Do this with each item, and have students record the findings on a chart.

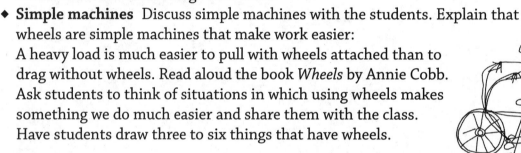

- **Simple machines** Discuss simple machines with the students. Explain that wheels are simple machines that make work easier: A heavy load is much easier to pull with wheels attached than to drag without wheels. Read aloud the book *Wheels* by Annie Cobb. Ask students to think of situations in which using wheels makes something we do much easier and share them with the class. Have students draw three to six things that have wheels.

Earth sciences

- **Weather** Play a recording of weather-related sounds, such as "spring rain" or "strong winds." (Nature CDs may be found at the library.) Students may hear sounds such as rain falling on a rooftop or the sidewalk, wind, hail, water running through gutters, thunder, snow being crunched under car tires, construction work on a sunny day, or waves crashing against the rocks. Have students draw the "sounds" of weather that they have heard. As a whole-class activity, list other weather-related sounds.

- Have students listen to a recording of weather-related sounds and identify the weather that's being represented. Let students illustrate each of the scenes; more advanced students may write a few sentences about it. If a recording is not available, have students discuss weather-related sounds and illustrate them from memory.
- Bring in pictures that show different types of weather, and use them to teach weather-related vocabulary (sunny, foggy, hot, cold, snowy, windy).

Life sciences

◆ **Life cycle of a butterfly** Read aloud *The Very Hungry Caterpillar* by Eric Carle. Discuss each stage of a caterpillar's life cycle and record each stage on the board, listing a few descriptive facts under each one. Have students divide a paper plate into quarters to use as a chart, labeling each section with the name of a stage in the life cycle of a butterfly. Students may glue different types of uncooked pasta to the plate to represent each stage (such as an elbow for the egg, a fusilli (spiral shape) for the caterpillar, a shell for the chrysalis, and a bowtie for the butterfly). They may decorate the background and write facts in each section. Other materials may be used if no pasta is available: dried seeds for eggs, cotton ball for cocoons, pipe cleaners for caterpillars, and a pipe cleaner with tissue paper wings for the butterfly, for example. Students may draw a picture of each stage, cut it out, and glue it to the plate.

Environmental sciences

◆ Read aloud a book about recycling, such as *Reduce and Reuse* by Sally Hewitt or *Stuff!* by Steven Kroll. Engage students in a discussion about the 3 R's—reduce, reuse, and recycle.

◆ Ask students to think of ways that they can reduce, reuse, and recycle. Chart students' responses on a three-column class chart.

◆ Have students complete the following sentences:
  ◆ Ways I can reduce waste are . . .
  ◆ Things I can reuse include . . .
  ◆ Things I can recycle are . . .

  ◆ As a whole-class activity, create a KWL chart (what they Know, what they Want to know, and what they Learned) with a focus on reduce, reuse, and recycle. Use the **KWL Organizer** template.
  ◆ Have students make posters to take home that encourage their families to reduce, reuse, and recycle.

28
KWL
Organizer

Suggested books for first grade

Alexander and the Terrible, Horrible, No Good, Very Bad Day by Judith Viorst, illustrated by Ray Cruz (Atheneum Books for Young Readers, 1972)

The Apple Pie That Papa Baked by Lauren Thompson, illustrated by Jonathan Bean (Simon & Schuster Books for Young Readers, 2007)

Clementine by Sara Pennypacker, illustrated by Marla Frazee (Hyperion Books for Children, 2006)

Dad, Jackie and Me by Myron Uhlberg, illustrated by Colin Bootman (Peachtree Publishers, 2005)

The Empty Pot by Demi (Henry Holt and Co., 1990)

How I Became a Pirate by Melinda Long, illustrated by David Shannon (Harcourt, 2003)

M is for Music by Kathleen Krull, illustrated by Stacy Innerst (Harcourt, 2003)

Miss Smith's Incredible Storybook by Michael Garland (Dutton Children's Books, 2003)

The New Girl . . . and Me by Jacqui Robbins, illustrated by Matt Phelan (Atheneum Books for Young Readers, 2006)

Reduce and Reuse by Sally Hewitt (Crabtree Publishing, 2009)

Stuff!: Reduce, Reuse, Recycle by Steven Kroll, illustrated by Steve Cox (Marshall Cavendish, 2009)

The Very Hungry Caterpillar by Eric Carle (Philomel Books, 1969)

Wheels! by Annie Cobb, illustrated by Davy Jones (Random House Books for Young Readers, 1996)

Widget by Lyn Rossiter McFarland, illustrated by Jim McFarland (Farrar, Straus and Giroux, 2001)

Suggested websites for first grade

http://www.arcademicskillbuilders.com/games
http://www.bbc.co.uk/schools/wordsandpictures/index.shtml
http://www.brainpopjr.com
http://funschool.kaboose.com
http://www.internet4classrooms.com
http://www.learningplanet.com
http://www.primarygames.com
http://www.starfall.com
http://teacher.scholastic.com/clifford1/flash/confusable/index.htm
http://teacher.scholastic.com/clifford1/flash/phonics/index.htm
http://teacher.scholastic.com/clifford1/flash/story_4.htm

Link a picture book across the curriculum

A single picture book can be used to cover all curricular areas for first grade. These ideas can be tweaked and used at other grade levels as well.

The Very Hungry Caterpillar
by Eric Carle

PUBLISHER	Penguin Group
PUBLICATION DATE	1994
AGE RANGE	2–6
SUMMARY	This is one of the most well-known Eric Carle stories. It is funny and full of colorful illustrations. The story, written in narrative form, is about a hungry caterpillar that grows up to be a beautiful butterfly.

Reading

◆ *The Very Hungry Caterpillar* is a wonderful book to read aloud. Interrupting the reading at strategic places in the story allows you to summarize and predict. Ask students to tell what is going on and what is going to happen next. If you have access to a big book edition, be sure to point out the words as you read them aloud. If you have access to a document reader, you can project the book onto the whiteboard and read it aloud while students follow the words. Be sure to track the words with a ruler or pointer as you read them aloud.

Writing

◆ Have students create a flip book to show the sequence of the story. (See Chapter 11, Extra activities and fillers.) Model this with large construction paper so the students can see what you expect. Choose at least five events from the story, illustrate each of the events, and label them for the students to use as a guide when they make their own. The front will be the title page. Prepare the students' blank flip books in advance, using regular white paper. Hand out the prepared flip books and ask the students to illustrate their own, using yours as a guide.

- Have students write a sequel for the butterfly. After reading the book aloud, ask students to brainstorm ideas about what happens to the butterfly. Where does it go? Where does it live? What does it eat? Who are its friends?
- Have students write a letter to the hungry caterpillar (with your help). Have students contribute ideas as you demonstrate how to write a friendly letter to the caterpillar. Talk about the adventures he has had, all the food he ate, and what it must be like to form a cocoon. Ask the caterpillar if he is excited or scared to turn into a butterfly.
- After reading the story, review the story again, page by page, and create a list of all the foods that the caterpillar ate. Have students include additional food items they might have wanted to eat if they were caterpillars.
- Sequence the story using circles cut from construction paper. On each circle, students draw and/or label a part of the story. Then they paste the circles together in order. They may add a face and legs as well.

Math

- Review counting: Have students count the number of holes punched out for the specific food that the caterpillar eats each day. Then have students count the different types of foods the caterpillar eats on Saturday.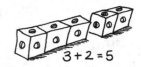
- Using the text from the book, teach students to compare greater than and less than. Ask students questions such as "Did the caterpillar eat more on Tuesday than on Friday, or did he eat less on Tuesday than on Friday?"
- Have students sequence the story by using ordinal numbers (first, second, third, etc.).

Social studies

- As part of a whole-class discussion, make a list of the workers in the community who help people meet their nutritional needs. Some possible responses are farmer, baker, chef, grocery store employee, doctor, and nutritionist.
- Discuss the ways in which these workers help people in the community be more healthy.

Science

- Review the life cycle of the butterfly, using pictures from the story. You may photocopy the pictures that show the stages of the life cycle.
- Introduce the food pyramid, since this story includes healthy foods and foods that are not healthy. Using the foods mentioned in the story, have students name the part of the food pyramid where each of the food items would fit. Have each student share a favorite food and decide where it would fit on the food pyramid.

Art

- Teach children how to make new colors from primary colors. Have them layer tissue paper, placing a sheet of one color on top of another (for example, blue layered on top of yellow makes green; red layered on top of blue makes purple; yellow layered on top of red makes orange).

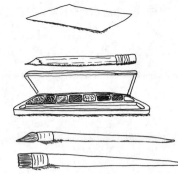

- Have students make caterpillars, using torn construction paper and glue, in imitation of Eric Carle's style of art (collage made from torn paper). You may have to tear some of the paper for them in advance. Students may do this on their own, but you should model it for them first.

chapter 5
Second grade (7–8 years old)

This chapter gives a brief overview of second grade students and what learning takes place at that grade level. Second grade reviews first grade skills and extends the concepts. The children in this age range are looking forward to becoming "big kids" next year when they head into the transitional third grade year. Students vary in personality and maturity at any grade level, so keep in mind that this is a general overview—a "sneak peek" at what you might expect. Be sure to address your own state standards when doing any necessary lesson planning.

Second graders—Who are they?

Second grade largely reviews first grade curriculum and expands upon it. Students are able to solidify primary skills in both learning and socialization. Students are growing up. They are more independent and self-confident, but they still seek out validation. At this point, they work well in groups and are conscious of others around them. They are more aware of their surroundings and environment, including material things. They take more academic and personal risks, as they are more self-assured. Second graders are more curious about how and why things work. They are becoming young students and defining more who they are. When they leave second grade, they have a good grasp of fundamental skills in math, reading, and writing.

What are they learning?

Reading

Second graders
... are working toward reading fluency of 80 words per minute
... read with increased fluency and comprehension
... understand complex text for meaning, purpose, and enjoyment
... have an easier time with comparing and contrasting
... learn how to read and write poetry
... learn how to analyze, compare, and predict text
... identify parts of a story (setting, plot, etc.)
... engage in more complex spelling patterns (diphthongs, special vowels, etc.)
... are learning word attack skills, decoding, and sight words
... learn about abbreviations, plurals, synonyms, antonyms, and cause and effect

Writing

Second graders

... develop more detailed stories with a beginning, middle, and end

... use the writing process

... are writing narratives (personal experience) and friendly letters (parts of a letter)

... create sentences that are complete and use correct punctuation (commas, quotation marks), subject-verb agreement, spelling, and grammar

Math

Second graders

... understand numbers up to 1000

... are adding and subtracting to 100 with regrouping

... are learning place value to 1000

... count to 100 by twos, fives, and tens

... review ordinal numbers to 20 (twentieth)

... compare numbers (>, <, =)

... learn fractions (½, ⅓, ¼, ⅛, ⅒)

... learn about similar (equivalent) fractions

... learn about plane vs. solid shapes

... find simple perimeters

... add, subtract, and count money

... solve transactions up to three-digit numbers

... understand more complex concepts about money, such as coins and bills (penny, nickel, dime, quarter, half-dollar, dollar), adding and comparing values up to $2.00

... study simple multiplication

... study data graphs, tally charts, range, and mode

... review measurement (inches, centimeters)

... learn about time to the quarter-hour

... learn about temperature (Fahrenheit, Celsius) to the nearest ten degrees

Social studies

Second graders

... study time lines

... learn about family trees, including their own

... study urban vs. rural

... study the North American map, community, government, laws, patriotic symbols, and economics (with regard to producers and consumers)

... learn about citizenship and voting

... study contributions from the past that influence the present (China, Egypt, Native Americans)
... study historical figures
... continue to learn about maps (title, legend, compass rose)
... study world maps and geography (seven continents, four oceans)
... study local and state maps and geography
... learn about natural vs. capital resources
... learn about multiculturalism

Science

Second graders
... observe and learn about life cycles and changes from one stage to another
... learn about gravity
... study motion (pushing, pulling)
... study magnets
... examine sound (vibrations)
... study rocks (physical properties, weathering), soil, and fossils
... learn about solids, liquids, and gases
... study plants, including fruits and flowers, and the roles these play in our lives
... study basic weather patterns

Activities for each curricular area

Whether you are substitute teaching for one day, three days, a month, or longer, it's important to have a variety of grade level curriculum ideas and activities in your personal survival kit. You may find that no plans have been left for you; you may finish plans more quickly than expected and have extra time at the end of a period; or you may have to do lesson planning on your own, but need time to adjust to your current surroundings and the teacher's manuals you will be working with. The following lesson ideas and activities are for second grade.

Reading activities

The following strategies and topics are ways to read to and with second graders.

Read aloud

- Read a book aloud to the class; it may include complex text, abbreviations, plurals, synonyms, antonyms, cause-and-effect relationships, and sight words.
- Do not stop to summarize or ask questions.
- Students listen, and respond only if prompted to do so.
- Select stories that are more mature in theme, (setting, plot, climax, solution, etc.).
- Consider poetry as a text to read aloud.
- A read-aloud is usually for the pure enjoyment of hearing a story. Second graders still enjoy being read aloud to.

Shared reading

- Read aloud a big book or from a textbook or other printed material.
- Model reading strategies such as predicting, summarizing, visualizing, and the use of context clues.
- Students read aloud as the teacher tracks the words, if they are able to.

Buddy reading

- A second grade student pairs with an upper grade student (fourth, fifth, or sixth grade).
- Students read and discuss stories from age-appropriate books that might include text or situations that involve comparisons.
- The older student serves as coach or reading mentor.

Sustained Silent Reading (SSR)

- Students read independently and silently.
- Students read books at their instructional reading level.
- SSR provides reading practice and time for reading for pleasure.
- SSR is also known as Uninterrupted Sustained Silent Reading (USSR) or Drop Everything and Read (DEAR).
- Make available a variety of books that students are interested in.

Partner reading

- Students pair up and share an agreed-upon book.
- Students take turns and assist one another.
- Designate a special place for partner reading in the room.
- You may want to pair students by reading ability: high/medium and medium/low.

Choral reading

- Choral reading is also known as unison reading.
- It provides many opportunities for repeated readings of a selected piece.
- It provides an opportunity to practice oral reading.
- Choral reading is excellent for poetry, rhymes, and chants.
- Choral reading is useful with repetitive text.

Timed reading

- Students work toward a designated number of words: 80 words per minute is the goal for second graders. However, student proficiency will vary.
- Students read as much of a passage as they can in one minute in an attempt to reach the designated words per minute.
- Students read the passage twice, attempting to read further the second time; each reading is timed.
- Timed reading builds fluency.

Guided reading

- Small groups at the same reading level.
- Students read the same text.
- Teacher coaches students individually while other students read text silently or in a low voice.
- Teacher focuses on targeted "aim" or "skill".

Reading workshop

- Teach introduces targeted "aim" or "skill" and models it in action.
- Students read books at their level/that they choose for a sustained period of time.
- Students have individual goals they work on as well as introduced skills.
- Teacher can informally conference with individual students, asking how they are applying a goal or the aim of the day.
- Whole group shares how skills were used.

Follow-up activities after reading stories

- Students think-pair-share about their favorite part of the story. Have students think about their favorite part of the story and then turn to a partner and discuss their thoughts. They then share their thoughts with the class.
- Hold small group and class discussions about the author's purpose, the main idea, and so on, of a story.
- Students respond to a story by writing in their journals; they engage in predicting, summarizing, and sequencing, through simple sentences and/or illustrations.
- Students respond to a story by illustrating their favorite scene(s).
- Students retell a story on a storyboard through simple sentences and/or illustrations. Use the **Storyboard Organizer** template, or students can create their own by folding a sheet of paper into the appropriate number of sections.
- Students describe designated parts of a story in pairs, in small groups, or as a whole class, using the pictures as a guide.

46
Storyboard
Organizer

Writing activities

The following strategies and topics are ways to teach writing to second graders.

Writing genres

- **Narratives** Students write narratives that tell a story, use imagination, and give a personal account. The narratives are written in first or third person.
- **Friendly letter** Students write letters that convey information and that include the date, a greeting, the body of the letter, a closing, and a signature.

Ways to write

- **Independent writing** There are a variety of forms (journals, mini-books, and so on) that work well for second graders. You may use sentence starters, where students complete simple sentences that have been started with a prompt and are related to a relevant topic. If it's in the middle of the school year or later, you might have students use a graphic organizer to write short paragraphs or essays. Use the **graphic organizer** template that is most appropriate for the assignment.

38
Sandwich
Organizer
41
Stair
Organizer 1
42
Stair
Organizer 2
45
Story
Organizer
62
Web
Organizer

- **Interactive writing** With the help of the substitute teacher or classroom aide, students will plan and write as a group, taking turns.

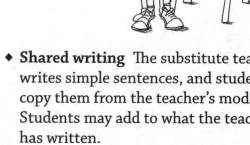

- **Shared writing** The substitute teacher writes simple sentences, and students copy them from the teacher's model. Students may add to what the teacher has written.

- **Guided writing** The substitute teacher and the students, who are grouped in pairs or small groups, write together as a community of writers.

- **Writer's workshop** Writers learn through their own experience, teacher models a skill, students write independently while teacher conferences with individuals on individual skills needs or the skill for that day and students share with class and get feedback.

Additional writing activities

- Students create word lists, using words from current topics of study.
- Students use spelling words to write sentences.
- Students write a friendly letter to the author of a book that the class enjoys.
- Students write a friendly letter to a character in the book.
- Students use graphic organizers to organize ideas for a writing activity.
- Students sequence stories or ideas on a storyboard, using simple sentences and illustrations.
- Students use index cards to write out and illustrate the sequence of a story.
- Students create a book cover for a book that the class has read. It should include a book summary, cover illustration, and author information.
- Students create a comic strip based on a book or a scene from a book.
- Students use picture prompts to write narratives.
- Students create a collage from magazine pictures. They then use the collage as the basis for writing a story.

Math activities

The following strategies and topics are ways to teach math to second graders.

Number sense

- **Compare numbers (>, <, =)** Draw >, <, and = on a standard sheet of construction paper. Teach the students basic math vocabulary: ">" means **greater than (more than)**, "<" means **less than (fewer than)**, and "=" means **equal to (the same as)**.

The greater-than symbol can be likened to an alligator's open mouth: The alligator always eats the larger number. Then, using the students to demonstrate the concepts, have three students stand to your left and two students stand to your right. Use the symbols that you drew on construction paper, and ask other student volunteers to hand you the correct symbol to indicate whether there are more than, fewer than, or an equal number of students to your left or right.
  - At the board, students work with problems using the concepts of greater than, less than, and equal to.
  - Students write sentences about an alligator that ate a larger quantity, for example, "There are 10 sandwiches on one plate and 5 sandwiches on another. The alligator ate the 10 sandwiches." The pages with their sentences can be collected and placed in a class book.

- **Fractions (½, ¼, ⅛, ¹⁄₁₆)** Hand out sheets of 8½" × 11" white drawing paper to students. Model for the students to fold the paper in half, then open it to show them the two halves. Fold it in half again to show fourths; fold it in half again to show eighths; and again to show sixteenths. Have students use crayons to color in one fourth of the sheet, then have them use a different crayon to color in three eighths of it, and so on. You may also use the **Fraction Bars** template.

15
Fraction Bars

16
Geometric
Shape
Organizer

Geometry/Measurement

- **Describe shapes** Draw shapes on the board, such as square, triangle, rhombus, rectangle, trapezoid, and hexagon. Write the name for each shape on short sentence cards or index cards. Have volunteers come to the board and label each shape. Describe a shape by its attributes, and have students guess the shape: "I have four vertices and four sides. What am I?"
  - Students determine the number of sides and corners for each shape. Use the **Geometric Shape Organizer** and have the students draw and label each shape.

- **Perimeter** Teach the students that the perimeter is the sum of the lengths of the sides of an object. To demonstrate this, trace the outline of a book on the whiteboard, and then use a ruler to measure each side and write the measurement of each side on the board. Next, add the lengths of all four sides to show the perimeter. Let students measure plane objects they find in the classroom. Students can use string or yarn to measure around solid objects such as their desktop, pencil box, books, and so on.

- **Time to the quarter-hour** Ask students to tell you what they know about time. After some discussion, hand out the **Clock** template and have students make their own clock, using paper plates, with brads to fasten the clock hands to the face of the clock. Write specific times on the whiteboard and have students move the hands on their clock to show these times. Have students note the pattern of "quarter hour."

07
Clock

Social studies activities

The following strategies and topics are ways to teach social studies to second graders.

Historical persons and events

- **Historical persons** Choose a biography of a famous historical person that is appropriate for the time of the year, and read it aloud to the class. Historical persons are recognized during several months of the year, often during the month of their birth. If a biography is not available, research and print a biography from the Internet to share with the students, or read biographical information from an available text. Have students list five to 10 facts about the historical figure you have read about. Students can then draw a picture of this person. Use the **KWL Historical Person/Event Organizer**.

27
KWL Historical Person/Event Organizer

- **Time lines** Using the biography of the historical person you have read about as a guide, help students create a time line of the life of that person. Use both illustrations and text. Students may create their own time line, or you may choose to assign an event to each student in order to create a class time line. Students' pictures can be used to sequence events. Use the **Historical Person/Event Time Line** template.

23
Historical
Person/Event
Time Line

Maps

◆ **Explore maps (continents, oceans)** Write the name of each continent and ocean on a small sheet of paper, and place the papers in a jar. Show students the classroom's world map, and using a pointer, locate each of the seven continents, focusing specifically on North America. Point out each of the oceans. Ask a volunteer to point out a continent or an ocean on the world map as its name is drawn from the jar. Have each student label and color the continents and oceans on a blank map of the world. Use the **World Map** template.

63
World Map

Role as a citizen

◆ **Voting** Voting is an important part of living in a democratic society, and it can also be an important part of classroom life. Ask students to brainstorm issues that are sometimes controversial in their class or school (for example, games at recess, a dress code, what to do during free time, and the like). Discuss the importance of voting and the impact of a vote on those who do not vote with the majority. Using an issue the students have suggested, hold a mock vote in the classroom. Tally the votes, and then discuss its impact on the class. Discuss how important it is to hold true to your values and opinions even if they are not in the majority.

Diversity

◆ **Multiculturalism** Read aloud *Children Just Like Me* by Anabel Kindersley. In a whole-class discussion, talk about several of the children in the book. If a document reader is available, project pages from the book onto the whiteboard, and use the images to launch a discussion about similarities and differences. Compare and contrast the lives of the students in the class with those of the children in the book. Always be aware that you need to be culturally sensitive and respectful when teaching multiculturalism lessons. Make sure that nothing you teach can be misconstrued or taken the wrong way. If this book is not available, bring in pictures and biographies of children from the Internet, or have students in the class share personal experiences: What are some of your family traditions? How do you celebrate birthdays or holidays? What foods do you eat in your home?

Science activities

The following strategies and topics are ways to teach science to second graders.

Physical sciences

- **Motion (push/pull)** Demonstrate the motion of pushing to the students by leaning into a heavy object such as a bookcase or the teacher's desk (be careful not to hurt yourself). Then demonstrate the motion of pulling by pulling a chair toward you. After demonstrating both motions, give students a series of scenarios and let them decide whether it would be better to push or pull in that scenario. For example, when opening your front door using the handle, would you push or pull? Would you push or pull to open the door of the refrigerator? Would you push or pull a boulder through the dirt?

  - Think of eight to 10 scenarios that involve pushing or pulling, plus additional scenarios that you can demonstrate (at least a couple of each type). Have volunteers show what they would do in each scenario. What simple machines assist us with pulling? with pushing? Responses include wheels, ramps, pulleys, and levers. Have students illustrate and label a simple machine in the action of pushing or pulling an object.

- **Magnets** Locate magnets in the classroom, or see if magnets can be borrowed from another teacher. Show the magnets to the students and ask students to tell you what they are and how they work. (Common refrigerator magnets will work too.) Show the students that a magnet attracts certain items, such as a paper clip, but does not attract other items, such as a plastic lid.

  - Have students work in small groups to explore whether items they find in the classroom will stick to magnets or not. Students can make a prediction and then test their "hypothesis." Some possibilities include (but are not limited to) magnets, a glass jar, wood, paper, a pencil, paper clips, tacks, a spoon, keys, a comb, marbles, blocks, place value cubes, foil, cork, cardboard, coins, a plastic bag, a battery, tissue, a balloon, buttons, a ruler, scissors, a filing cabinet, and table legs. Students will make a chart showing their findings.

◆ **Sound (vibrations)** Have students make a sound cone to amplify sounds that are coming from a particular direction. Students can roll a piece of tag board or poster board (about 18″ × 24″) into a cone shape, leaving a small hole (about ½″ to 1″ across) at the pointed end, and leaving the big end as large as possible. They then tape the edges so that the cone will hold its shape. Have students take the cones outside, and instruct them to listen carefully by putting the small end of the sound cone close to their ear and pointing the cone in different directions. Have them try to listen to the same sounds without the sound cone. Ask students to take notes about the sounds they hear, both with and without the sound cone. Encourage students to listen for at least three to five sounds (such as birds, the wind, leaves blowing, dogs barking, cars driving by, a teacher's voice, students' voices, and the like).

◆ Have students take turns speaking through a sound cone. Ask students whether voices sound louder or softer when the speaker uses a sound cone to speak through.

◆ Have students string two cups together with about 10 feet of string, and then speak to one another through the cups. This demonstrates sound vibration and travel.

Earth sciences

03
Attributes
Organizer

◆ **Fossils** Find pictures of fossils on the Internet and print them out to show to students. If a document reader is available, project the pictures onto the whiteboard. Otherwise, show the pictures so that all the students can easily see the fossils. Discuss the characteristics of fossils, and have students list the characteristics that they have observed. Use the **Attributes Organizer**. If any fossils are available in the classroom or from another teacher, pass them around and let the students examine them. Students can then make a rubbing of an object found in the classroom, using the side of a crayon and a sheet of construction paper. They will observe how images are imprinted on the paper in much the same way that fossils are created.

- ◆ **Basic weather patterns** Read aloud *Cloudy With a Chance of Meatballs* by Judi Barrett. After reading the book, discuss with the class what weather needs the people in Chewandswallow had, and how those needs were met. List the needs on the board. Using a graphic organizer such as a **Venn Diagram**, have students work in pairs to compare and contrast their own needs with those of the people in the book. After completing the Venn diagram, students may share their ideas with the whole class.

61
Venn Diagram

- ◆ If the book is not available, discuss different weather patterns with the students. What are their characteristics? How do they affect a community's needs? After discussion, have students fold a sheet of paper into quarters and illustrate a weather pattern that was discussed in each section of their paper.

Suggested books for second grade

Baseball Saved Us by Ken Mochizuki, illustrated by Dom Lee (Lee & Low Books, 1993)

Chig and the Second Spread by Gwenyth Swain (Dell Yearling, 2003)

Children Just Like Me: A Unique Celebration of Children Around the World by Barnabas and Anabel Kindersley (Dorling Kindersley Publishing, 1995)

Cloudy with a Chance of Meatballs by Judi Barrett, illustrated by Ron Barrett (Atheneum Books for Young Readers, 1978)

Dear Max by Sally Grindley, illustrated by Tony Ross (Simon & Schuster, 2006)

Diary of a Worm by Doreen Cronin (HarperCollins, 2003)

A Fine, Fine School by Sharon Creech, illustrated by Harry Bliss (HarperCollins, 2001)

Gator Gumbo: A Spicy-Hot Tale by Candace Fleming, illustrated by Sally Anne Lambert (Farrar, Straus and Giroux, 2004)

Mr. George Baker by Amy Hest, illustrated by Jon J. Muth (Candlewick Press, 2004)

Sam and the Lucky Money by Karen Chinn, illustrated by Cornelius Van Wright and Ying-Hwa Hu (Lee & Low Books, 1995)

Sneakers, the Seaside Cat by Margaret Wise Brown, illustrated by Anne Mortimer (HarperCollins, 2003)

Why The Sky Is Far Away: A Nigerian Folktale by Mary-Joan Gerson, illustrated by Carla Golembe (Little, Brown, 1992)

Suggested websites for second grade

http://www.starfall.com
http://www.primarygames.com
http://www.brainpopjr.com
http://funschool.kaboose.com
http://www.learningplanet.com
http://www.bbc.co.uk/schools/wordsandpictures/index.shtml
http://www.arcademicskillbuilders.com/games
http://www.internet4classrooms.com

Link a picture book across the curriculum

A single picture book can be used to cover all curricular areas for second grade. These ideas can be tweaked and used at other grade levels as well.

Alexander and the Terrible, Horrible, No Good, Very Bad Day
by Judith Viorst

PUBLISHER	Simon & Schuster
PUBLICATION DATE	July 1987
AGE RANGE	5–9
SUMMARY	This story is about a boy named Alexander, who starts his day off in a terrible way—and it only gets worse. Readers are taken through a series of humorous events that create a terrible, horrible, no good, very bad day for Alexander. Children will relate to the comical events of this story.

Reading

◆ Read aloud *Alexander and the Terrible, Horrible, No Good, Very Bad Day* with a focus on repetition. The book repeats "It was a terrible, horrible, no good, very bad day" several times. Allow the students to chime in when this line occurs. If you have access to a big book edition, point to each of the words in this repeated line and, instead of saying it out loud with the students, let them say it as you point to each word in that sentence.

Writing

- ◆ Discuss the events of the story, and have students choose the four events that they think are the most important. Have students sequence the story by putting these four events in the proper order.
- ◆ Students create a paper plate viewer for four events from the story. Hand out two paper plates and a brad to each student. Students mark one paper plate to divide it into four equal pie-piece shapes. They illustrate one event from the story in each section and add a sentence to explain it. Then they cut a one-fourth pie piece section out of the second plate, which they place on top of the illustrated plate, fastening them together with the brad. The top plate is rotated to reveal each illustrated event with the accompanying text explaining what is being seen.
- ◆ Students write about how they can relate to this very bad day by writing about a very bad day of their own.
- ◆ Students write a letter to Alexander, sympathizing with him.
- ◆ Students rewrite the ending to the story.
- ◆ Students write a story about Alexander's wonderful, perfect, super, good day.

Math

- ◆ Have students review the text of the story and count how many times Alexander runs into trouble. Students base their own stories (about their own very bad day or Alexander's good day) on the same number of events that they have identified in the story about Alexander's day.

- ◆ Have students use the story line and items presented in this book to create math word problems (for example, a word problem using lima beans).

Social studies

- ◆ After reading *Alexander and the Terrible, Horrible, No Good, Very Bad Day,* teach a lesson that focuses on character traits such as perseverance, sportsmanship, and getting along with others. (Teacher resource books like *The Organized Teacher's Guide to Building Character* provide lesson ideas for this type of lesson.)

Science

- ◆ If you are subbing in a long-term assignment, incorporate a unit in which the students grow lima beans. Use lesson plans from the Internet or a teacher resource book such as *The Creative Teacher* by Steve Springer, Kimberly Persiani, and Brandy Alexander.

Art

- ◆ Have students create a new book cover that shows an event from the story.

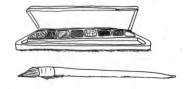

chapter 6
Third grade (8–9 years old)

This chapter gives a brief overview of third grade students and what learning takes place at that grade level. Third grade, like first grade, is a year when many new concepts—from cursive writing to multiplication—are introduced. Students vary in personality and maturity at any grade level, so keep in mind that this is a general overview—a "sneak peek" at what you might expect. Be sure to address your own state standards when planning lessons.

Third graders—Who are they?

Third graders are in a transitional stage—they are no longer in early childhood, nor are they the big kids on campus. They tend to be enthusiastic about their learning. They still love school and their teachers. Third graders are more socially aware of others, their moods, and their differences. They want acceptance from others. They understand popularity, music, current trends, and the like. Third graders are more apt to test limits and boundaries, and they take more risks. They know more about who they are, what they like and dislike. They are mature enough to take responsibility for their actions and are more reflective.

What are they learning?

Reading

Third graders

... are working toward reading fluency of 110 words per minute

... are using phonics, word parts (prefixes and suffixes), and context clues to read and derive meaning

... are reading for understanding and information in both fiction and nonfiction, including biographies and autobiographies

... are predicting and interpreting text

... are reading more chapter books and stories from around the world

... are reading independently for longer periods of time

... use the dictionary, thesaurus, encyclopedia, Internet, and other reference materials

Writing

Third graders

... are learning cursive handwriting

... are using the writing process to write paragraphs with topic sentences, details, correct spelling, punctuation, subject-verb agreement, verb tense, person, and capitalization

... use and understand the dictionary and thesaurus

... are writing narratives, descriptive writing, and both friendly and formal letters, with a length of up to several paragraphs

Math

Third graders

... are counting and learning place value to 10,000

... are rounding to the nearest ten, hundred, and thousand

... are adding and subtracting to 10,000 with regrouping

... are learning basic multiplication and division facts to 12

... are learning to determine unit cost

... are using higher-level thinking and problem-solving skills (word problems)

... are learning about basic probability of outcomes

... are adding and subtracting fractions with like denominators

... understand equivalent fractions and decimals (tenths, hundredths)

... solve problems using money (dollars and cents) up to $5.00

... study metric and US customary units of measure for length, volume, and weight

... identify attributes of polygons, quadrilaterals, triangles, and solid forms

... find area and perimeter

... tell time within the nearest 5-minute interval

... are learning more about temperature (Fahrenheit, Celsius)

Social studies

Third graders

... study immigration in America and abroad

... learn about cultural diversity and its role in the United States

... learn about early exploration of America

... study local government, laws, and rules

... study national and local symbols

... study the map as a research resource

... study geologic features of local regions

... study American Indian nations and their interactions with settlers, along with the impact on settlers in terms of religion, economics, traditions, and contributions

... learn about the production of goods and services

... learn about famous American heroes and their role in American history and freedom

Science

Third graders

... learn to use scientific tools in order to engage in scientific investigation

... review forms of energy (stored, heat, motion) and matter (solid, liquid, gas)

... learn about atoms and elements

... study the properties of light

... study the physical characteristics of rocks and minerals

... explore simple machines and their uses

... learn about ecosystems, animal adaptations, and the relationships of animals to one another (herbivore, predator, etc.), as well as how they survive in their environments

... discover patterns and cycles of nature

... learn about the water cycle (precipitation, percolation, evaporation, condensation)

... study types of soil and the role they play in plant growth

... review the sun, moon, planets, and stars, and their positions in the sky

... explore human and natural events as they influence the species and its survival

... understand energy resources (renewable and nonrenewable)

Activities for each curricular area

Whether you are substitute teaching for one day, three days, a month, or longer, it's important to have a variety of grade level curriculum ideas and activities in your personal survival kit. You may find that no plans have been left for you; you may finish plans more quickly than expected and have extra time at the end of a period; or you may have to do lesson planning on your own, but need time to adjust to your current surroundings and the teacher's manuals you will be working with. The following lesson ideas and activities are suitable for third grade.

Reading activities

The following strategies and topics are ways to read to and with third graders.

Read aloud

◆ Read a book aloud to the class; it may be either fiction or nonfiction, a biography, an autobiography, or multicultural stories. Fiction will include setting, plot, climax, and resolution.

◆ Do not stop to summarize or ask questions.

◆ Students listen, and respond only when prompted to do so.

◆ Reading selections may include poetry and chapter books.

◆ Reading selections may include stories that allow for prediction and interpretation.

- A read-aloud is usually intended to be for the pure enjoyment of hearing a story. Third graders still enjoy being read aloud to.

Shared reading

- Read aloud a big book or from a textbook or other printed material.
- Model reading strategies such as predicting, summarizing, visualizing, and the use of context clues.
- Students view and follow as the substitute teacher points to the words being read.
- Students read aloud as the teacher tracks the words, if they are able to.

Buddy reading

- A third grade student pairs with an upper grade or lower grade student: Upper grade students will support the third graders; if third graders are paired with lower grade students, the third graders serve as the coach or reading mentor.
- Students read and discuss stories from age-appropriate books that might include text or situations involving comparisons.

Sustained Silent Reading (SSR)

- Students read independently and silently.
- Students read books at their instructional reading level.
- SSR provides reading practice and time for reading for pleasure.
- Students read chapter books or picture books that are organized by the students' interests.
- SSR is also known as Uninterrupted Sustained Silent Reading (USSR) or Drop Everything and Read (DEAR).

Partner reading

- Students pair up and share an agreed-upon book.
- Students take turns and assist one another.
- Designate a special place for partner reading in the room.
- You may want to pair students by reading ability: high/medium and medium/low.

Timed reading

- Students work toward a designated number of words: 110 words per minute is the goal for third graders. However, student proficiency will vary.
- Students read as much of a passage as they can in one minute in an attempt to reach the designated words per minute.
- Students read the passage twice, attempting to read further the second time; each reading is timed.
- Timed reading builds fluency.

Guided reading

◆ Small groups at the same reading level.
◆ Students read same text.
◆ Teacher coaches students individually while other students read text silently or in a low voice.
◆ Teacher focuses on targeted "aim" or "skill".

Reading workshop

◆ Teach introduces targeted "aim" or "skill" and models it in action.
◆ Students read books at their level/that they choose for a sustained period of time.
◆ Students have individual goals they work on as well as introduced skills.
◆ Teacher can informally conference with individual students, asking how they are applying a goal or the aim of the day.
◆ Whole group shares how skills were used.

Follow-up activities after reading stories

◆ Students think-pair-share about their favorite parts of a story.
◆ Hold small group and class discussions about the author's purpose, the main idea, and so on, of a story.
◆ Students respond to a story by writing in their journals; they engage in predicting, summarizing, and sequencing, through simple sentences and/or illustrations.
◆ Students respond to a story by illustrating their favorite scene(s).
◆ Students retell a story on a storyboard through meaningful sentences and illustrations. Use the **Storyboard Organizer** template.
◆ Students describe designated parts of a story in pairs, in small groups, or as a whole class, using the pictures as a guide.

46
Storyboard
Organizer

- Students identify word parts (prefixes and suffixes) while reading.
- Students read in teams of four. Assign each team member a job (vocabulary finder, summarizer, illustrator, and discussion leader). Have students discuss the story, with each team member performing that particular job throughout the discussion. Teams then present to the entire class.
- Have students read a story out loud, and assign character parts or specific sections to different students.
- Students present the news, reading parts of a selection as if they were anchoring a news show.

Writing activities

The following strategies and topics are ways to teach writing to third graders.

Writing genres

- **Narratives** Students write narratives that tell a story, use imagination, and give a personal account. The narratives are written in first or third person.
- **Friendly letter** Students write letters that convey information and that include the date, a greeting, the body of the letter, a closing, and a signature.
- **Descriptive writing** Students write pieces that describe setting, characters, and plot. Descriptive writing is good practice in using adjectives and is often referred to as writing that shows rather than tells. It is usually written in first or third person.

Ways to write

- **Independent writing** There are a variety of forms (journals, mini-books, and so on) that work well for third graders. You might use sentence starters for paragraphs, where students complete essays that have been started with a prompt related to a relevant topic. You might have students use a graphic organizer to write short essays. Use the **graphic organizer** template that is most appropriate for the assignment.

38
Sandwich
Organizer

41
Stair
Organizer 1

42
Stair
Organizer 2

45
Story
Organizer

62
Web
Organizer

- **Interactive writing** With the help of the substitute teacher or classroom aide, students plan and write on a relevant topic as a group, taking turns.

- **Shared writing** The substitute teacher writes a short paragraph or sentences, and students transcribe them and add their own writing to them.

- **Guided writing** The substitute teacher and the students, who are grouped in pairs or small groups, write together as a community of writers.

- **Writer's Workshop** Writers learn through their own experience, teacher models a skill, students write independently while teacher conferences with individuals on individual skills needs or the skill for that day and students share with class and get feedback.

Additional writing activities

- Students create relevant word lists, using words from current topics of study.
- Students use spelling words to write sentences.
- Students write a friendly letter to another student; that student responds with a friendly letter.
- Students write a friendly letter to the author of a book that the class enjoys.
- Students use graphic organizers to organize ideas for a writing activity.
- Students sequence a story or ideas on a storyboard.
- Students create a tri-panel brochure for a book that the class is studying. They may include a cover, book summary, character bios, about the author section, opinion, and illustrations, for example.
- Students create and write a dialogue scene from a story.
- Students write a description based on something that the class is studying (for example, a detailed description of a volcano).

Math activities

The following strategies and topics are ways to teach math to third graders.

Number sense

- **Multiplication and division to 12** Students make flash cards out of 3″ × 5″ index cards, or you may use the **Flash Cards** template. Have students begin with the levels they have recently mastered. This will likely be posted in the classroom; if not, give the class a mixed multiplication/division timed test to determine their level of mastery of multiplication and division facts. Once their flash cards have been made, students pair up and practice their multiplication and division facts. Playing "Around the World" with the flash cards is a fun way to practice.

14
Flash Cards

- **Money (dollars and cents), up to $5.00** Select four to eight unique objects to use as items for "purchase." You might use items found in the classroom, such as a stapler, scissors, a book, markers, and the like,

or items that you bring in. Put a price on each item, using sticky notes. Have some items priced at less than a dollar and others that are priced in dollars and cents up to, but not including, $5.00. Show these items to the students. List the name and price of each item on the board. Then have students choose items that have a total cost as close to $5.00 as possible. Do this several times as a whole class, then let students continue to make selections in pairs or small groups.

 - Variation: Use take-out menus from local restaurants. Collect several sets of menus and have students select a restaurant; give them a budget. Advanced students may calculate tax and a tip.

Geometry/Measurement

 - **Polygons: triangles, quadrilaterals, pentagons**
Write the following definition on the board: *A polygon is a closed figure made by joining line segments, where each line segment intersects exactly two others.* Then draw several shapes on the board that represent polygons, including triangles, quadrilaterals, and pentagons. Ask student volunteers to describe which of the polygons each drawing represents.

   - Have students list and/or illustrate common polygons found around them in everyday life (stop sign, flat screen TV, sheet of paper, etc.). Use the **Geometric Shape Organizer**.
   - Have students draw a specified item (such as a space ship, a robot, or a cityscape) by using a designated number of polygons (for example, use four rectangles, two pentagons, five triangles).

16
Geometric
Shape
Organizer

 - **Perimeter** Review what it means to find the perimeter of an object by measuring each side of an object and adding the measurements. You might demonstrate this by using a yardstick to measure each side of a desk and then add the lengths of the sides to find the perimeter. Group the students into teams and ask them to find the perimeter of at least five objects in the classroom. Teams will list each object with its perimeter; they should show their math.

   - Variation: Have students use string to help them understand the concept of perimeter as an outer edge. Lengths of string can then be compared to one another to show differences in perimeters.

Probability/Statistics

 - **Probability** Bring a few decks of cards to school if you know you'll be teaching probability, so you can teach students to play this card game. Model it before having students play in teams: Place three cards face up on the table. Select one of those cards to be the target card, then turn the cards face down and quickly mix them up. A student volunteer tries to find the target card by turning over one card. If the student finds it, the student earns a point. If the student doesn't select the target card, the substitute teacher earns a point. The probability in this case is one out of three. Play for five rounds.

What is the probability of each round? Does playing more rounds change the probability? Keep track of who is winning. Discuss the probability of winning for both the teacher and the student. Let the students play the game in teams.

- ◆ Variation: Select 10 cards and discuss the change in probability. Does the probability of correctly choosing the target card increase or decrease with more cards? What about the probability of correctly selecting one card *or* another card (independent events)? Does the probability change for the second draw? What if you have a dependent event—the probability of correctly selecting one card *and* a second card? How does this affect the probability? Working with a set of 10 makes it easier to figure probabilities using decimals and percentages. (Probability can also be calculated using M&Ms® in brown paper bags, but make sure that school policy allows using food items in classroom activities.)

Social studies activities

The following strategies and topics are ways to teach social studies to third graders.

Civil rights

- ◆ **Civil Rights in America** Read aloud *The Story of Ruby Bridges* by Robert Coles to the class. After the read-aloud, post the following five questions:

  1. Who was Ruby Bridges?
  2. What made Ruby so different from everyone else?
  3. How would you feel if you were Ruby?
  4. What would you do in that situation if you were Ruby?
  5. In what ways has Ruby's strength and courage made you question your own privileges?

Have students number themselves from one to five. Divide the class into small groups. Have each student respond to the question that matches his or her assigned number. Each student shares his or her response within the small group, and then the whole class discusses the students' responses to the five questions.

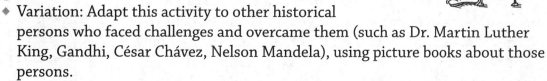

- ◆ Variation: Adapt this activity to other historical persons who faced challenges and overcame them (such as Dr. Martin Luther King, Gandhi, César Chávez, Nelson Mandela), using picture books about those persons.

◆ Variation: If no picture books are available on these persons, share research and pictures gathered from the Internet. Consider creating a PowerPoint presentation about a historical person, and carry it on a flash drive for future use.

Diversity

◆ **Cultural diversity in the United States** Have students draw and color an apple, then cut it out. Tell students to pay attention to their apple's unique characteristics. Apples have similarities and differences, just like people do. Have them make up a story about their apple and tell it to a partner, focusing on the apple's various characteristics. Have students place their apples together on a table. Mix the apples up and ask the students to try to find their own apple. After they return to their seats with an apple, ask how they knew which apple was theirs. Ask, "What does this have to do with people?" Have students make a list of the ways in which people are different, and discuss why this is important. Then have them make a list of the ways in which people are the same, and discuss why that is important. You may have students create the lists in small groups and then share them with the whole class. Have students write their names on their apples, and then glue all of them to a poster or a cut-out of a bushel basket. Engage students in a whole-class discussion about how everyone is part of the bunch; include discussion by asking, "Does one bad apple spoil the whole bunch?" Allow for critical discussion.

Exploration

◆ **Exploration of America** Working with the whole class, examine a time line of early American explorers from England, Spain, and France. (This will require research ahead of time; if computers are available, you may have students do the research.) Show students pictures of explorers; you may have notes about them and their exploration written on the back. Use the pictures to sequence events. Discuss what was brought to the New World and what was taken back to the explorers' countries of origin (for example, through the Columbian Exchange). Using the classroom's map of the world, trace the exploration routes on the map with a pointer. Give students a blank world map, and ask them to color it and add the explorer's route on their own map. Use the **World Map** template.

◆ **Geologic features of local regions** Have students draw a rough outline of their state to use for this activity. Use the **United States Map** template as the basis for their state map. Help students identify the agricultural and natural resource regions of the state, then color and label each of those regions on the outline map that they have drawn. Ask students to describe why these regions are suitable to farming or specific industries, how they affect the economy, and what part they play in the local communities. Have students list the state's major crops and resources.

60
United States Map
63
World Map

114

Historical persons and events

◆ **Famous American heroes** In a whole-class discussion, identify several characteristics of a hero. Share newspaper or online articles you have collected that focus on local heroes, as well as heroes from other parts of the state, the country, and the world. Using the articles, have students identify characteristics of some of the featured people that qualify them as heroes. Then have students think of a person in their own life that they view as a hero, and have them write a short essay about him or her.

Science activities

The following strategies and topics are ways to teach science to third graders.

Physical sciences

◆ **Travel of light** Discuss the visible light spectrum and the fact that light scatters when it hits particles in its path. The sky appears blue because sunlight is scattered by dust particles in the atmosphere. If this scattering did not occur, the sky would appear dark, like it does at night or from outer space. Demonstrate this with a flashlight, water, and a small amount of milk. Fill a large glass jar with water. Shine a bright flashlight through the water from one side. Students will be able to see some dust particles; these appear white, but they are few in number, which makes the beam of light appear bright but colorless. Add milk, a few drops at a time, and have students look at the beam of light from the side of the jar. The milk contains particles of protein and fat, which scatter the light. The light is separated into shorter blue and green light rays, giving a blue appearance to the light when it is observed from the side. Students are observing a simulation of the path of sunlight from directly overhead. When students look straight into the beam, the longer orange and red rays become more visible, and this gives the light a more reddish color. This simulates the reddish color of the sky at sunrise and sunset. With the addition of more milk, this becomes even more apparent. Have students observe the beam of light from all sides in order to see the differences. Discuss with the class the change in light and how this relates to the sun. Have students draw a picture of what they have observed.

Life sciences

◆ **Ecosystems** Discuss with students the following terms in reference to ecosystems.

  ◆ Ecosystem: community of living and nonliving things that work together in a balanced system (lake, pond, forest, desert, jungle)
  ◆ Producers (autotrophs): produce food (green plants)
  ◆ Consumers (heterotroph): obtain food from other living organisms (antelope)
  ◆ Decomposers (saprobes): feed on decay (bacteria and fungi)
  ◆ Carnivores: feed on other animals (lions, hyenas)
  ◆ Predators: hunt and kill for food (lions)
  ◆ Scavenger: feed on dead bodies of other animals (hyenas)
  ◆ Herbivores: feed on plants
  ◆ Omnivores: feed on both animals and plants

Have students write in their journals about what life would be like without insects. Ask the whole class to share their responses, and transcribe their responses on the board. Then break the class into small groups and assign each group one of the following elements of an ecosystem (producers, consumers, decomposers, and predators). Each small group is responsible for designing and constructing a mobile that illustrates the element of an ecosystem that they have been assigned. Have the groups share their mobiles with the class.

Earth sciences

◆ **Rocks and minerals** If a set of rocks and minerals is available in the classroom or from another teacher, students will be able to hold them, make observations, and classify them. A set of 10 to 20 small rocks is sufficient to rotate through pairs of student teams. In the absence of samples of rocks and minerals, gather pictures of rocks and minerals for students to use. Have students examine the rocks and minerals, considering texture, composition, color, hardness, and weight. Show students how to do a streak test in order to classify rocks as igneous (origin from magma and lava), sedimentary (origin from accumulations), or metamorphic (origins from pressure and heat). Research rocks and minerals on the Internet for accurate descriptions. Have students make mini-books in which they sketch and write about the rocks they have observed.

◆ **Types of soil** Explain to students that soil is a natural resource and that there are many types of soil (such as clay, silt, and sand). Let students know that soil only makes up 10 percent of the Earth's surface. Discuss several aspects of soil with the students: how farmers have to be careful about the type of soil they plant certain crops in, that soil can be a home for animals and insects, that soil can be used to filter waste and water, that soil can store and heat water, and that soil produces and stores gases

116

like carbon dioxide. Read aloud a book such as *Soil* by Sally Walker to help students learn what soil is all about. Then have students help you complete a short question-and-answer exercise, using sentences directly from the book. Prepare five to eight sentences from the book. Leave out one word from each sentence, and ask students to recall the information to help you complete the sentences.

◆ **Water cycle** Ask the students, "What happens when water is heated?" "What happens when water cools down?" Have students perform an experiment so they can see for themselves what the water cycle involves. Hand out materials (small jar lids, plastic zipper bags, masking tape, water, eyedropper), and have each student place five to eight drops of water in the lid and carefully place it into a bag, sealing the bag tightly. Have students tape the bags to the inside of a window that gets a lot of sun, and leave the bags in the sun for most of the day. Near the end of the day, have the students observe the bags. What do they see? (Most of the water should be gone from the lid, and the top of the bag should look cloudy, showing water vapor. Students may also see droplets of water on the sides of the bag.) As a class, discuss the following: "What happened to the water?" (Response: It evaporated from the lid.) "What might have happened if the bags were left open?" (Response: Water would evaporate into the air in the room.) Have students draw a picture illustrating the water cycle and label it. Discuss with the class that this process happens on a larger scale on the Earth, and include the terms *precipitation, condensation, evaporation, run-off, percolation,* and *transpiration* in your discussion.

Suggested books for third grade

I Love Saturdays y Domingos by Alma Flor Ada (Atheneum Books for Younger Readers, 2002)

La Mariposa by Francisco Jiménez, illustrated by Simón Silva (Houghton Mifflin, 1998)

My Name is Maria Isabel by Alma Flor Ada, illustrated by K. Dyble Thompson, translated from Spanish by Ana M. Cerro (Atheneum Books for Young Readers, 1993)

The Quiltmaker's Journey by Jeff Brumbeau, illustrated by Gail de Marcken (Orchard Books, 2005)

The Rag Coat by Lauren Mills (Little, Brown, 1991)

Stellaluna by Janell Cannon (Harcourt, 1993)

The Story of Ruby Bridges by Robert Coles, illustrated by George Ford (Scholastic, 1995)

Thank You, Mr. Falker by Patricia Polacco (Philomel Books, 1998)

Suggested websites for third grade

http://www.arcademicskillbuilders.com/games
http://www.internet4classrooms.com

Link a picture book across the curriculum

A single picture book can be used to cover all curricular areas for third grade. These ideas can be tweaked and used at other grade levels as well.

The Giving Tree by Shel Silverstein

PUBLISHER	HarperCollins
PUBLICATION DATE	1986
AGE RANGE	6–10
SUMMARY	In this book, students are exposed to the gift of giving and the notion of love. Readers are taken on a journey through the life of a boy who grows to be a man, and a tree that selflessly and generously gives him her bounty throughout his lifetime.

Reading

◆ *The Giving Tree* is considered a chapter book, but it can easily be read within a 20-minute time period. Read it aloud one time without interruption, and then revisit the parts of the book that show the boy taking and the tree giving. Have students think about the parts of the book where this occurs. You may want to designate a couple of students as recorders who take notes as the book is read aloud; attach sticky notes to pages that you will revisit so that it is easier to find them quickly.

Writing

◆ Sequence the story by discussing each of the events and listing them on the board. Have the students tell you the proper order for the events, and number them on the board. Then have students fold a sheet of paper into six or eight sections, which they use to illustrate and label the events of the story in the proper order.
◆ An important aspect of this story is the fact that the boy has taken so much from the tree. Have the students write a letter of apology from the boy to the tree.

Math

- Teach students to measure the diameter of something by measuring the diameter of round items that can be found in the classroom, such as cups or storage containers.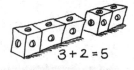
- Have students collect leaves from trees on the school property (or ask them to bring in leaves from their neighborhood). In the classroom, have students sort their leaves by color, texture, or size. Then have students combine their groups of leaves into class groupings. Count the leaves in each group and graph the results.

Social studies

- Discuss with students the economic aspects of trees. Ask them to help create a list of things that they know are made from trees. Discuss the process of trees being cut down, made into a product, and sold to a consumer. Discuss what can happen if too many trees are cut down and not enough are planted.
- Discuss with students a character trait such as empathy, kindness, being selfish vs. being selfless, or friendship. Refer to resource books such as *The Organized Teacher's Guide to Building Character* by Steve Springer and Kimberly Persiani.

Science

- If Internet access is available, have students research topics that are related to trees (for example, classifications: deciduous and coniferous) online.
- Discuss the life cycle of a seed, then have students illustrate each stage and label their drawing.
- Discuss with students the kinds of natural resources that are available to them and then discuss how to conserve natural resources.
- Students research the forest as a habitat for animals and trees.

Art

- Have students use watercolors and white construction paper to paint trees, using several different watercolors. You may show them a variety of pictures of flowers as a guide as they begin their own paintings.
- Take pencils and clipboards with paper outside and have students sketch trees.
- Go for a walking field trip on school property, and have students collect a variety of natural resources for creating an art piece made from found objects (such as leaves, twigs, and grass).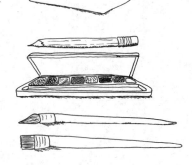

chapter 7
Fourth Grade (9–10 years old)

This chapter gives a brief overview of fourth grade students and what learning takes place at that grade level. The fourth grade curriculum reviews and solidifies many of the skills taught in third grade while creating new challenges. Students vary in personality and maturity at any grade level, so keep in mind that this is a general overview—a "sneak peek" at what you might expect. Be sure to address your own state standards when doing any necessary lesson planning.

Fourth graders—Who are they?

Fourth graders are becoming much more mature than their primary counterparts in kindergarten through third grade. They are more aware of ability levels and the similarities and differences between themselves and other students. They understand humor better. They compare their work to that of fellow students. Fourth graders have a better sense of self-worth and their place in the world than they did a year earlier. They are more introspective and can carry on deeper conversations about the consequences of actions. Fourth graders are independent and enjoy opportunities to solve problems and to investigate why and how things work.

What are they learning?

Reading

Fourth graders

... are working toward reading fluency of 130 words per minute

... read fiction and nonfiction text for a purpose and for pleasure

... engage in research by using the Internet and additional resources for informational text

... understand elements of text (figures, tables, pictures, etc.) and apply them to meaning

... derive meaning for new words from previous word knowledge, prefixes and suffixes, root words, and context clues

... use a thesaurus and dictionary

... use prior knowledge and text elements to connect ideas and comprehend new information

... are able to compare and contrast different forms of writing

... collect information in order to distinguish fact vs. opinion

Writing

Fourth graders

... use the writing process to develop multiparagraph essays and compositions, including supporting sentences about the topic or central idea with facts, details, and descriptions

... use correct spelling, grammar, punctuation, and capitalization

... include quotations and citations to support their writing

... use and understand the elements of resources such as the dictionary, thesaurus, encyclopedia, and Internet for writing

... write narratives, responses to literature, expository essays (informational reports), poems (rhymed and unrhymed) and summaries with a clear focus and purpose

... write in cursive

Math

Fourth graders

... understand and compare (>, <, =) whole numbers to the millions

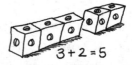

... add, subtract, multiply, and divide whole numbers and decimals to two places

... order fractions (like and unlike denominators), decimals, and mixed numbers

... round to the nearest ten, hundred, thousand, ten thousand, and hundred thousand

... compare equivalent fractions and decimals

... add and subtract fractions with like and unlike denominators

... explore concepts such as factoring prime numbers

... use a number line with positive and negative integers, fractions, mixed numbers, and decimals

... use variables in an expression or formula

... explain mean, median, and mode for data

... continue to solve basic probability problems

... find perimeter and area, and describe geometric solids, triangles, and quadrilaterals by attributes

... compare lines (perpendicular, parallel, intersecting), study metric units of measurement, and examine conversions between metric and US customary units of measure

Social studies

Fourth graders

... learn about the history of their home state

... study the state constitution, state and federal government, and roles of elected officials

... continue learning about geography and maps (longitude and latitude), state and regional history, prominent locations, regional divisions, and their state flag

Science

Fourth graders

... learn about electricity (simple circuits) and magnetism
   (repel and attract, Earth's poles, compass)
... study energy as heat, light, and motion
... discover more about habitats, the food chain, food webs,
   and the producers, consumers, and decomposers of an ecosystem
... learn how plants and animals adapt to ecosystems
... work toward an understanding of the basic anatomy of a plant, including
   reproduction and photosynthesis
... learn more about rocks and minerals, including their formation, types, and
   properties (identification)
... study erosion, change in land formations, and other factors (wind, ice, water,
   earthquakes, etc.) that affect these changes

Activities for each curricular area

Whether you are substitute
teaching for one day, three
days, a month, or longer,
it's important to have
a variety of grade level
curriculum ideas and

activities in your personal survival kit. You may find that no plans have been left for
you; you may finish plans more quickly than expected and have extra time at the end
of a period; or you may have to do lesson planning on your own, but need time to
adjust to your current surroundings and the teacher's manuals you will be working
with. The following lesson ideas and activities are suitable for fourth grade.

Reading activities

The following strategies and topics are ways to read to and with fourth graders.

Read aloud

◆ Read a book aloud to the class; it may be either fiction or nonfiction, a biography,
   an autobiography, multicultural stories, or informational text. Fiction will include
   setting, plot, climax, and solution.
◆ Do not stop to summarize or ask questions.

- Students listen, and respond only when prompted to do so.
- Reading selections may include poetry and chapter books.
- Reading selections may include stories that allow for comparing and contrasting, or for determining fact vs. opinion.
- A read-aloud is usually intended to be for the pure enjoyment of hearing a story. Fourth graders still enjoy being read to.

Shared reading

- Read aloud from a textbook or other printed material.
- Model reading strategies such as predicting, summarizing, visualizing, and the use of context clues.
- Students view and follow as the substitute teacher reads aloud.
- Students read aloud as the teacher tracks the words.

Buddy reading

- A fourth grade student pairs with an upper (fifth or sixth) grade student or lower (kindergarten, first, second, third) grade student. The older student of the pair serves as coach or reading mentor.
- Students read and discuss stories from age-appropriate books that might include text or situations involving comparisons.

Sustained Silent Reading (SSR)

- Students read independently and silently.
- Students read books at their instructional reading level.
- SSR provides reading practice and time for reading for pleasure.
- Students read chapter books or mature picture books.
- SSR is also known as Uninterrupted Sustained Silent Reading (USSR) or Drop Everything and Read (DEAR).

Partner reading

- Students pair up and share an agreed-upon book.
- Students take turns and assist one another.
- Designate a special place for partner reading in the room.
- You may want to pair students by reading ability: high/medium and medium/low.

Guided reading

♦ Teacher coaches students individually while other students read text silently or in a low voice.
♦ Teacher focuses on targeted "aim" or "skill."
♦ The teacher and students work together as they read, think about, and talk through the text.
♦ The teacher and student "echo read."
♦ Small groups at the same reading level.
♦ Students read the same text.

Popcorn reading

♦ The teacher asks a student to begin reading aloud; any willing student can start. When the student stops, he or she selects the next student, and that student continues reading (without direction from the teacher). This process continues until all students have taken a turn reading.
♦ A variation is to alternate boys and girls.
♦ Popcorn reading builds student responsibility for participation.

Timed reading

♦ Students work toward a designated number of words: 130 words per minute is the goal for fourth graders. However, student proficiency will vary.
♦ Students read as much of a passage as they can in one minute in an attempt to reach the designated words per minute.
♦ Students read the passage twice, attempting to read further the second time; each reading is timed.
♦ Timed reading builds fluency.

Reading workshop

♦ Teach introduces targeted "aim" or "skill" and models it in action.
♦ Students read books at their level/that they choose for a sustained period of time.
♦ Students have individual goals they work on as well as introduced skills.
♦ Teacher can informally conference with individual students, asking how they are applying a goal or the aim of the day.
♦ Whole group shares how skills were used.

Aim: Author's Purpose

Follow-up activities after reading stories

- Students think-pair-share about their favorite parts of a story.
- Hold small group and class discussions about the author's purpose, the main idea, and so on, of a story.
- Students respond to a story by writing in their journals; they engage in predicting, summarizing, and sequencing, through simple sentences and/or illustrations.
- Students respond to a story by illustrating their favorite scene(s).
- Students retell a story on a storyboard through meaningful sentences and illustrations. Use the **Storyboard Organizer** template.
- Students describe designated parts of a story in pairs, in small groups, or as a whole class, using the pictures as a guide.
- Students identify word parts (prefixes and suffixes) while reading.

46
Storyboard
Organizer

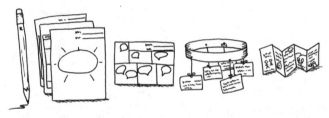

Writing activities

The following strategies and topics are ways to teach writing to fourth graders.

Writing genres

- **Narratives** Students write narratives that tell a story, use imagination, and give a personal account. The narratives are written in first or third person.
- **Responses to literature** Students respond to literature, using strategies such as inference, prediction, personal connection, and opinion.
- **Summaries** Students summarize a document, maintaining the integrity of the original document and using its main ideas to make a point.
- **Expository essays (informational reports)** Students explain, define, and give information, while presenting facts and statistical information, cause-and-effect relationships, and examples. Expository essays are usually written in third person.
- **Poems (rhymed and unrhymed)** Students write an arranged composition using sound and rhythm. The composition may use any one of many forms, including haiku, cinquain, limerick, closed verse, lyric, nonsense verse, narrative, jump rope, and concrete (shape) poetry.

Ways to write

♦ **Independent writing** There are a variety of forms (journals, mini-books, and so on) that work well for fourth graders. You might use sentence starters for paragraphs, where students complete essays that have been started with a prompt related to a relevant topic. You might have students use a graphic organizer to write short essays. Use the **graphic organizer** template that is most appropriate for the assignment.

38
Sandwich Organizer
41
Stair Organizer 1
42
Stair Organizer 2
45
Story Organizer
62
Web Organizer

♦ **Interactive writing** With the help of the substitute teacher or classroom aide, students plan and write on a relevant topic as a group, taking turns.

♦ **Shared writing** The substitute teacher writes a short paragraph or sentences, and students transcribe them and add their own writing to them.

♦ **Guided writing** The substitute teacher and the students, who are grouped in pairs or small groups, write together as a community of writers.

- **Writer's workshop** Writers learn through their own experience, teacher models a skill, students write independently while teacher conferences with individuals on individual skills needs or the skill for that day and students share with class and get feedback.

Additional writing activities

- Students create relevant word lists, using words from current topics of study.
- Students use spelling words to write sentences and paragraphs.
- Students write a friendly letter to the author of a book that the class enjoys.
- Students use graphic organizers to organize ideas for a writing activity.
- Students sequence a story or ideas on a storyboard.
- Students create silly poems about real-life situations.
- Students write paragraph responses to questions across the curriculum.
- Students write multiparagraph summaries of a book.
- Students draw a monster and write a description of their monster. They then exchange papers with a partner, and each student tries to draw a monster based on the partner's descriptive writing.
- Students change the ending of a story or write a sequel to a story.
- Students write a role-play scenario with dialogue based on a class discussion or lesson.
- Students create a comic strip with dialogue.
- Assign each student a page from a shared book, and have students summarize and illustrate their page. Students then sequence their pages, and the pages can be assembled into a class book.
- Produce a class newspaper: Assign small groups of students to different sections of the newspaper: sports, entertainment, business, technology, and so on. Students will write stories and draw pictures for their section.
- Review paragraph structure with the class: an opening sentence, an example of that sentence, two or three extension sentences that support the example, and a closing sentence.

Math activities

The following strategies and topics are ways to teach math to fourth graders.

Number sense

◆ **Number line** Demonstrate on the board how to set up a positive and negative number line, with zero in the center. Hand out blank sentence strips to the students and have them create their own number line on the sentence strips. After the students have created their number line, write addition and subtraction problems on the board, and have students practice using their number line by solving these problems.

◆ Variation: Turn this into a class activity by drawing an empty number line on the board. Write fractions, decimals, mixed numbers, and positive and negative numbers on squares of paper and tape them to a separate section of the board, using doubled-over masking tape. Call on students to place numbers on the board in the correct order.

◆ **Order fractions** Working at the board, review converting fractions to decimals with the students. Encourage student participation by having them name the steps as the computation is carried out. Then have students help decide the order of the decimal numbers. Transcribe students' responses in sequential order and have the entire class agree on the placement of each one.

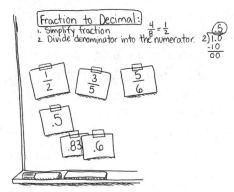

Geometry/Measurement

◆ **Geometric solids** As a whole class, discuss the characteristics of geometric solids. If the classroom has a set of geometric solids (possibly stored with the rest of the math manipulatives), show them to the students

as you discuss their properties: Each solid has flat sides called faces; each solid has edges to connect the faces; and each solid has corners (vertices) that connect the edges. Break the class into groups of six students each. Use the **Geometric Solids** templates, and assign one of the geometric solids (cone, cube, cylinder, rectangular prism, triangular prism, triangular pyramid) to a student in each group. Students assemble their geometric solid and then note the number of edges, flat sides, and corners it has. Each group reports its collective findings to the entire class.

- **Compare lines (parallel, intersecting)**
Discuss the properties of lines and line segments
with students: Two lines or line segments can
either *intersect* (cross) each other or be *parallel*
(side by side) to one another. Remind students
that parallel lines never meet one another, no matter how far they
extend in either direction. Demonstrate this with your arms to
show students the difference, then draw examples on the board.
Discuss real-life examples, such as an intersection, the framework
of a house, or a windowpane for intersecting lines; and railroad
tracks, steps, or yellow lines on a highway for parallel lines. Have
students work in groups to brainstorm additional real-life examples for both,
and then share them with the entire class. Ask students to draw pictures showing
at least three examples of parallel lines and three examples of intersecting lines.

Probability/Statistics

- **Mean, median, and mode** If school policy allows, use M&Ms® to teach students
about finding the mean, median, and mode. Graphing and sorting activities can
also be easily incorporated. Give each student a small bag of
M&Ms, but tell them not to open the bags. First, ask students
to predict the total number of M&Ms in the bag and how
many of each color there are. Have students graph their
predictions by color. Next, have students open the bag, sort
the candy by color, and count the M&Ms of each color. In small groups, have the
students compare their results. Then have them find the mean, median, and mode
for the number of different colored M&Ms in their bag.

> EXAMPLE 15 M&Ms (4 red, 3 yellow, 2 blue, 3 red, 3 brown)
>
> Mean (average): 4 (red) + 3 (yellow) + 2 (blue) + 3 (red) + 3 (brown)
>   = 15 M&Ms ÷ 5 (different colors) = **3**
>
> Mode (most frequently occurring number of each color): **3**
>
> Median (middle number after they have been placed in order): 2, 3, **3**, 3, 4

Social studies activities

The following strategies and topics are ways to teach social studies to fourth graders.

State history

43
State Facts
44
State Profile

- ◆ **History of home state** Have students research information about their home state. Use the **State Facts** or **State Profile** template, and model the activity for the students, using a different state. Information that the students might research includes the state flower, bird, tree, fish, flag, seal, geography, location, climate, resources, agriculture, parks, population, and capital. You may want to group students into pairs or triads for this assignment. Gather resource materials from the class and school libraries to have available for students to use. Have students complete the information required on the chosen template.
  - ◆ Have students create a postcard about the state. Their postcard could include a "Welcome to _____" tagline, a famous attraction, state flower, state bird, and the like. Students may illustrate the front, and then use the back to write a message about what they are doing on a trip in the state.
- ◆ **The Constitution** In the United States, each state has its own constitution. Typically, state constitutions are longer than the 7,500-word federal constitution and they are more detailed with regard to the day-to-day relationships between the state government and the people. For this activity, hand out copies of the Tenth Amendment to the United States Constitution, which is part of the Bill of Rights. It provides that "The powers not delegated to the United States by the Constitution, nor prohibited by it to the States, are reserved to the States respectively, or to the people." The Guarantee Clause of Article 4 of the United States Constitution states that "The United States shall guarantee to every State in this Union a Republican Form of Government." These two provisions give states the authority to adopt a constitution, which is the fundamental document of state law. Read these two provisions aloud as the students follow along. Then hold a whole-class discussion about what it means. Have students work in small groups to analyze specific sections of their state's constitution and put it in their own words. Have each group share their new understanding of what their section of the state's constitution means.

132

◆ **Roles of city and state elected officials**

Discuss with students what it means to be an elected official. Begin a whole-class discussion with this statement: *An elected official is someone who holds an office in an organization of government and participates in the exercise of authority, either his own or that of his superior and/or employer, public or legally private*. Divide the class into six groups. Have each group of students work together to research the role of one of the following elected officials: City Mayor, Governor, Lieutenant Governor, Secretary of State, State Treasurer, or Attorney General. Make information about each position available for the students to use, either from a classroom text or printed from the Internet. Have each group write a summary of what they learned about the role they researched and then share it with the entire class. Draw a triangle on the board, and have students determine how to represent the hierarchy of these elected officials on the triangle. The Governor should be placed at the peak of the triangle, and other elected officials should be placed appropriately in one or more rows below.

◆ **State flag** Show students a picture of their state's flag. If a document reader is available, project a picture of the state flag onto the whiteboard so it's easy for all the students to see. Ask students to list as many elements as they can find on the flag, or list at least five things that make their state's flag unique. Students then share their ideas with the entire class. Have students draw the state flag on their own.

Geography and maps

◆ **Maps (longitude, latitude)** Introduce key vocabulary words: *latitude, longitude, equator, and prime meridian*. Point them out on the classroom map of the world. Hand out tongue depressors to each student and have the students tape them together, creating a plus sign. Tell students to hold up their sticks so that one is parallel to the classroom walls and the other is parallel to the floor. Have them write "top" in small letters on the part of the stick closest to the ceiling. Then ask students which of the two sticks measures latitude and which measures longitude. Explain that the vertical stick represents longitude and the horizontal stick represents latitude. Draw a representation of this on the board. Have students write "longitude" going up and down on one stick (the one with "top" written on it); have them write "latitude" going across on the other stick. Students may use their sticks as a reminder of the meanings of latitude and longitude.

◆ **Globe (equator, prime meridian)** Show students a world globe, and point out that it is bisected north to south between the poles by an imaginary line called the prime meridian, and east to west through its center by the equator. Put a thin piece of colored tape around the globe at both the prime meridian and the equator, and pass the globe around for students to see. Explain that the globe shows the entire planet marked with a series of vertical and horizontal lines that form a grid by which any point on the Earth's surface can be specified. Longitude lines run north to south, yet measure distance east to west. Latitude lines run east to west, yet measure distance north to south.

Science activities

The following strategies and topics are ways to teach science to fourth graders.

Physical sciences

◆ **Electricity** Have students explore how an object receives an electrical charge and the effect of bringing objects with like or unlike charges near one another. Ask students to help demonstrate electrical charges: Have the students inflate three balloons to the same size and tie a string to each balloon. Then have them give two of the balloons a negative charge by rubbing them with a wool cloth or against their hair. Both balloons become negatively charged.

  ◆ If the two negatively charged balloons are held close to each other, electrons on the surface of the two balloons push away from one another, because like charges repel. Therefore, the balloons do not "cling" to one another.

  ◆ If a "charged" balloon is held next a neutral balloon, electrons on the surface of the neutral balloon move away from its surface because like charges repel. This in turn creates a positively charged surface. The opposite charges attract, and this results in "clinging" between the negatively charged balloon and the now positively charged balloon. (Balloons can be neutralized by misting them with water.)

  ◆ Have students inflate several more balloons and attach a string to each. Then have students rub the balloons on their hair or with a wool cloth to create a negatively charged surface, and let students hold the balloons up toward the ceiling and observe what happens. Do the balloons cling to the ceiling? Why? (Remember to get the balloons down before the end of the day.)

Life sciences

- **Plant reproduction and photosynthesis**
  Introduce the following terms to the
  students and discuss their meanings: *roots,
  stems, leaves, photosynthesis, flowers, pistil,
  stamen, fertilization, stigma, style, fruit,
  seeds*. Draw a picture of a plant or flower
  on the whiteboard (or, if a document reader

  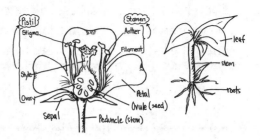

  is available, project the outline of a plant onto the whiteboard). Using the
  vocabulary presented, have students identify each part of the plant or flower.
  Discuss how each part of a plant contributes to photosynthesis. Students
  may create a detailed poster of the parts of a plant or flower, complete with
  explanations. If you have a long-term assignment in the classroom, you may
  want to let students grow some plants, so that you can continue discussion
  about how plants grow.

- **Adaptation of animals to ecosystems** Have students work
  in small groups to brainstorm ways that animals adapt
  (both physically and behaviorally) to the conditions of their
  environment in order to survive. Divide the class into six
  groups of students and designate two groups to research
  each of the following three ecosystems: rain forest, desert, and ocean. Have
  groups identify the primary adaptations made by both animals and plants in each
  of the three ecosystems. Then have groups share their responses with the entire
  class. Students' responses can be charted and posted in the classroom. If you have
  a long-term assignment in the classroom, one day can be devoted to a discussion
  about what ecosystems are and how plants and animals survive in them; the
  second day can be devoted to data collection; and the third day can be used for
  sharing their results. During the sharing by groups, you may have students record
  the results for each ecosystem on paper that has been folded into three sections,
  creating a column for each ecosystem. Students list adaptations for each
  ecosystem and draw a picture to illustrate it.

Earth sciences

- **Erosion (water, wind, ice)** Help students find the
  Grand Canyon on the classroom map of the United
  States. Find the Colorado River, and trace its route
  from east to west through the canyon. Show
  students a photo of the Grand Canyon. Write the
  word *erosion* on the board, and ask students if they
  know what it means. Guide the discussion toward

  this definition: "the way material like sand and rock is worn away from the Earth's
  surface by water, wind, or ice." Share pictures that show how the ocean's waves,
  over time, change the way rocks on the coastline look by washing away little
  pieces of the rocks. Discuss with students that erosion can be caused by water,
  wind, ice in glaciers, and even chemicals. Show students pictures of examples

135

of erosion caused by water, wind, and ice (possibly from the Internet, especially if you have Internet access in the classroom and are able to project images onto the whiteboard). Explain that the climate and landscape of northern Arizona when the canyon's layers were forming were very different from what they are now. During much of that earlier time, the Arizona landscape was covered with water. After the discussion, have students demonstrate what they have learned about erosion: Have students fold a sheet of white paper three times to create eight boxes; they then label their paper with the word *Erosion* in one box and write the definition of *erosion* in the second box. In the remaining three pairs of boxes, have students show examples of erosion resulting from three different causes. Each pair of boxes should have an illustration in one box, and its label with a description in the companion box. Students then share their work with the class.

◆ **Identification of rocks and minerals**

For this activity, you will need access to rocks and minerals (or detailed pictures of rocks and minerals), a magnifying glass for each student, and sheets for recording student observations. Use the **Attributes**

03
Attributes
Organizer

Organizer template. Display several rocks and minerals on a large table; label each one. Ask students to look at them and think of words or phrases that could be used to describe them. Record their responses on the board in chart form (for example, if "Slate" were the heading, descriptive words below it would be "sharp edges, gray in color, rough"). As a whole-class activity, chart descriptions of up to three rocks and minerals on the board. Then have students illustrate the items, label them, and record the characteristics of each one on their **Attributes Organizer**. Students should consider texture, composition, color, hardness, and weight. They can do a streak test to classify rocks as igneous (origin from magma and lava), sedimentary (origin from accumulations), and metamorphic (origin from pressure and heat). Have students continue working on their own, taking turns examining the rocks and minerals, and recording their observations. Discuss with students the importance of observation and creating an organized system of categorizing items. How does this help us? Does it make discussion easier? If you were designing a system of categorizing, what would be important to include and why?

Suggested books for fourth grade

Centerfield Ballhawk by Matt Christopher, illustrated by Ellen Beier (Little, Brown, 1994)

A Chair for My Mother by Vera B. Williams (Greenwillow Books, 1982)

Crickwing by Janell Cannon (Voyager Books, 2005)

Grandfather Counts by Andrea Cheng, illustrated by Ange Zhang (Lee & Low Books, 2000)

How Much Is a Million? by David M. Schwartz, illustrated by Steven Kellogg (HarperCollins, 1985)

Math Curse by Jon Scieszka, illustrated by Lane Smith (Viking, 1995)

The Misadventures of Maude March by Audrey Couloumbis (Yearling, 2007)

The Patchwork Quilt by Valerie Flournoy, illustrated by Jerry Pinkney (Dial Books for Young Readers, 1985)

Radio Man: A Story in English and Spanish by Arthur Dorros, translated by Sandra Marulanda Dorros (HarperCollins, 1993)

Sadako and the Thousand Paper Cranes by Eleanor Coerr, illustrated by Ronald Himler (G. P. Putnam's Sons, 1977)

Suggested websites for fourth grade

http://www.arcademicskillbuilders.com/games
http://www.internet4classrooms.com

Link a picture book across the curriculum

A single picture book can be used to cover all curricular areas for fourth grade. These ideas can be tweaked and used at other grade levels as well.

Stone Soup by Marcia Brown

PUBLISHER	Scholastic Press
PUBLICATION DATE	1997
AGE RANGE	4–10

OR

Stone Soup by Jon J. Muth

PUBLISHER	Simon & Schuster
PUBLICATION DATE	2003
AGE RANGE	4–10
SUMMARY	In most versions of this classic folktale, soldiers march down the road toward a village, but the peasants see them coming, and suddenly they become very busy. They know that soldiers are usually hungry, so the villagers hide their food. When the soldiers begin to make "stone soup," the curious villagers begin to share one ingredient at a time, as one villager adds a carrot, another adds some meat, and yet another adds an onion. Eventually, a pot of real soup is made. This community of people comes together as a result of working together.

Reading

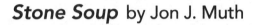

This text provides several opportunities for you to stop and summarize, clarify, or predict as you read the book aloud. If several copies of the book are available, you might do this as a shared reading activity, where you read the text aloud as the students follow in their books. Be sure to have a discussion about teamwork and coming together as a community after the story has been read.

Writing

- *Stone Soup* lends itself to being retold in a dramatic presentation. List the roles of the different characters on the board. Have student volunteers (or randomly called-on students) choose roles, and then have these students act out the story for the rest of the class.
- Have students rewrite the ending of the story so that the villagers remain selfish and don't share their food.

- Have students create a comic strip, using the characters from the story and events from the storyline.
- Have students sequence the story. Ask students to fold a sheet of paper into six or eight boxes, depending on how many events you want them to show. The first box should include the title and author of the book as well as the student's name and date. Students can be creative with illustrations and short sentences to sequence the events of the story in the remaining boxes.

Math

- Pretend to cook stone soup. Have students work in small groups to come up with fractional measurements and instructions for making their version of stone soup.
- As a challenge, have students determine how to double or triple the "recipe."

Social studies

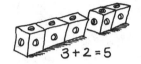

- *Stone Soup* is a good example of cooperation and teamwork within a community that comes together for a common goal. Use teacher resource books such as *The Organized Teacher's Guide to Building Character* by Steve Springer and Kimberly Persiani for lesson ideas on teaching character traits such as sportsmanship and teamwork.

Science

- Reading *Stone Soup* suggests working with stones— or rocks and minerals. If you have access to a set of rocks and minerals, have students use them to test their observational skills. Have students fold a sheet of paper in half two times so they have four boxes in which to illustrate and describe the rocks and minerals they have examined.
- Have students sort rocks and minerals by color, texture, size, and shape.

Art

- Have students draw their favorite scene from *Stone Soup*.
- Have students create a label for a can of Stone Soup.
- Have students create an advertisement for Stone Soup in a can.
- Have students redesign the cover of the book.

chapter 8

Fifth grade (10–11 years old)

This chapter gives a brief overview of fifth grade students and what learning takes place at that grade level. Students vary in personality and maturity at any grade level, so keep in mind that this is a general overview—a "sneak peek" at what you might expect. Be sure to address your own state standards when doing any necessary lesson planning.

141

Fifth graders—Who are they?

In many places, elementary school ends at fifth grade. These students are on the verge of leaving their elementary school, yet they are still children. They can handle more independent work, and they are able to work for longer periods of time. They are sensitive to how they are perceived in the world. Conflict may arise over friendships and loyalties. They understand the differences between boys and girls much better at this age. In addition, they are beginning to become interested in members of the opposite sex and/or same sex as they continue to develop their identities. Fifth graders thrive on projects that allow them to be original with their ideas and thinking. They are more responsible and can be given more opportunities for leadership roles. Fifth graders can be challenged more with problem solving.

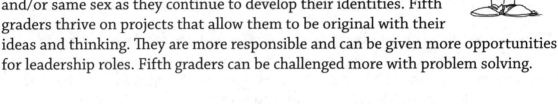

What are they learning?

Reading

Fifth graders

... are working toward reading fluency of 140 words per minute

... read fiction and nonfiction text

... can more easily analyze and interpret poetry

... use prior knowledge, comprehension strategies, and inference to understand text

... understand prefixes and suffixes, and use context clues to derive meaning

... use additional aspects of text (including diagrams, tables, and charts) to assist in understanding what they are reading

... understand the main idea, key concepts, symbolism, literary devices, cause-and-effect relationships, comparisons, and intention of the author of a selected reading

Writing

Fifth graders

... use the writing process to write narratives, research reports, persuasive letters and compositions, and responses to literature that are several paragraphs in length and have a clear focus and intention

... use purposeful writing to describe, inform, entertain, and explain

... use correct grammar, spelling, sentence structure, punctuation, and voice in writing

... focus on word-attack skills, understanding, and context to derive meaning

... write in cursive and use a keyboard more fluently

... use a dictionary, thesaurus, encyclopedia, and the Internet to research, gather, and clarify information

Math

Fifth graders

... add, subtract, multiply, and divide whole numbers (multidigit, long division)

... understand the use of decimals through the thousandths

... study fractions (like and unlike denominators), mixed numbers, and positive and negative integers

... round from millions down to thousandths

... plot positive and negative integers, fractions, decimals, and mixed numbers on a number line

... graph, plot with four quadrants, and work with ordered pairs of integers (x, y) on a grid

... select and plot appropriate graphs for data sets

... interchange, add, subtract, multiply, divide, order, and compare fractions (like and unlike denominators), mixed numbers, decimals, and percents

... understand probability (fractions or decimals 0 to 1)

... solve range, mode, outliers, median, and mean for a set of data

... review and measure area, perimeter, and volume, as well as angles (classify)

... understand circumference of a circle (diameter, radius)

... work with prime factorization (as factors and exponents), measure length, weight, volume, and temperature

... convert between metric and US customary measurements

Social studies

Fifth graders

... study US history to the late 1800s: Native Americans, settlers, early explorers, and historical persons

... learn about life during the colonial era and its influence on future generations

... study the Revolutionary War, the Declaration of Independence, and the US Constitution

... study slavery and the Civil War

... learn about the US government and the 50 states and their capitals

... spend significant time learning about their personal heritage

Science

Fifth graders

... study sound (transmission, applications) and light (characteristics, behavior)

... learn more about the solar system (planets, Earth, sun, moon)

... understand matter (atoms, elements, molecules) and its chemical and physical properties

... gain more in-depth knowledge about plants vs. animals (respiration and photosynthesis vs. digestion), carbon dioxide and oxygen, and the roles and cycles of plants and animals

... learn about the basic functions of cells

... study the water cycle (evaporation, condensation, precipitation)

... learn more about the ocean environment (physical, biological)

... study more about the classification of rocks and minerals

Activities for each curricular area

Whether you are substitute teaching for one day, three days, a month, or longer, it's important to have a variety of grade level curriculum ideas and
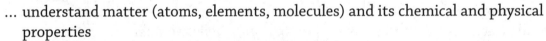
activities in your personal survival kit. You may find that no plans have been left for you; you may finish plans more quickly than expected and have extra time at the end of a period; or you may have to do lesson planning on your own, but need time to adjust to your current surroundings and the teacher's manuals you will be working with. The following lesson ideas and activities are suitable for fifth grade.

Reading activities

The following strategies and topics are ways to read to and with fifth graders.

Read aloud

- Read a book aloud to the class; it may be either fiction or nonfiction, a biography, an autobiography, multicultural stories, or informational text. Fiction will include setting, plot, climax, and resolution.
- Do not stop to summarize or ask questions.
- Students listen, and respond only when prompted to do so.
- Reading selections may include poetry and chapter books.
- Reading selections may include a focus on the main idea, key concepts, symbolism, literary devices, cause and effect relationships, comparing and contrasting, and intention of the author.
- A read-aloud is usually intended to be for the pure enjoyment of hearing a story. Fifth graders still enjoy being read to.

Shared reading

- Read aloud from a textbook or other printed material.
- Model reading strategies such as predicting, summarizing, visualizing, and the use of context clues.
- Students view and follow as the teacher reads aloud.
- Students read aloud as the teacher tracks the words.

Buddy reading

- A fifth grade student pairs with an upper (sixth) grade student or lower (kindergarten, first, second, third, fourth) grade student. The older student of the pair serves as coach or reading mentor.
- Students read and discuss stories from age-appropriate books that might include text or situations involving comparisons.

Sustained Silent Reading (SSR)

- Students read independently and silently.
- Students read books at their instructional reading level.
- SSR provides reading practice and time for reading for pleasure.
- Students read chapter books or mature picture books.
- SSR is also known as Uninterrupted Sustained Silent Reading (USSR) or Drop Everything and Read (DEAR).

Partner reading

- Students pair up and share an agreed-upon book.
- Students take turns and assist one another.
- Designate a special place for partner reading in the room.
- You may want to pair students by reading ability: high/medium and medium/low.

Guided reading

- Teacher coaches students individually while other students read text silently or in a low voice.
- Teacher focuses on targeted "aim" or "skill."
- The teacher and students work together as they read, think about, and talk through the text.
- The teacher and student "echo read."
- Small groups at the same reading level.
- Students read the same text.

Choral reading

- Choral reading is also known as unison reading.
- It provides many opportunities for repeated readings of a selected piece.
- It provides an opportunity to practice oral reading.
- Choral reading is excellent for poetry, rhymes, and chants.

Popcorn reading

- The teacher asks a student to begin reading aloud; any willing student can start. When the student stops, he or she selects the next student (who has not already had a turn), and that student continues reading (without direction from the teacher). This process continues until all students have taken a turn reading. With larger classes, keep track of who has already read, especially if the session spans more than one day.
- A variation is to alternate boys and girls.
- Popcorn reading builds student responsibility for participation.

Timed reading

- Students work toward a designated number of words: 140 words per minute is the goal for fifth graders. However, student proficiency will vary.
- Students read as much of a passage as they can in one minute in an attempt to reach the designated words per minute.
- Students read the passage twice, attempting to read further the second time; each reading is timed.
- Timed reading builds fluency.

Reading workshop

- Teacher introduces targeted "aim" or "skill" and models it in action.
- Students read books at their level/that they choose for a sustained period of time.
- Students have individual goals they work on as well as introduced skills.
- Teacher can informally conference with individual students, asking how they are applying a goal or the aim of the day.
- Whole group shares how skills were used.

Follow-up activities after reading stories

- Students think-pair-share about their favorite parts of a story.
- Hold small group and class discussions about the author's purpose, the main idea, and so on, of a story.
- Students respond to a story by writing in their journals; they engage in predicting, summarizing, and sequencing, through simple sentences and/or illustrations.
- Students respond to a story by illustrating their favorite scene(s).
- Students retell a story on a storyboard through meaningful sentences and illustrations. Use the **Storyboard Organizer** template.
- Students describe designated parts of a story in pairs, in small groups, or as a whole class, using the pictures as a guide.
- Students identify word parts (prefixes and suffixes) while reading.
- Have a volunteer take the "hot seat." Other students ask questions, and the student in the "hot seat" answers as if he or she were a character in the story.

46
Storyboard
Organizer

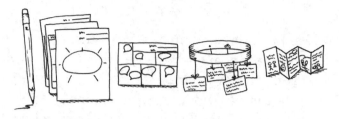

Writing activities

The following strategies and topics are ways to teach writing to fifth graders.

Writing genres

- **Research reports** Students write reports about their research that explain and inform, give information and facts with the purpose of educating the reader, and predict based on data.

- **Persuasive letters and compositions** Students convey a message and try to persuade the reader in their favor about an issue.

- **Narratives** Students write narratives that tell a story, use imagination, and give a personal account. The narratives are written in first or third person.

- **Responses to literature** Students respond to literature that they've read, using strategies such as inference, prediction, opinion, and connection through their own ideas and experiences. Responses are written by retelling, summarizing, analyzing, and/or generalizing.

- **Summaries** Students summarize a document, maintaining the integrity of the original document and using its main ideas to make a point.

- **Expository essays (informational reports)** Students explain, define, and give information, while presenting facts and statistical information, cause-and-effect relationships, and examples. Expository essays are usually written in third person.

- **Poems (rhymed and unrhymed)** Students write an arranged composition using sound and rhythm. The composition may use any one of many forms, including haiku, cinquain, limerick, closed verse, lyric, nonsense verse, narrative, jump rope, and concrete (shape) poetry.

Ways to write

38
Sandwich
Organizer

41
Stair
Organizer 1

42
Stair
Organizer 2

45
Story
Organizer

62
Web
Organizer

- **Independent writing** There are a variety of forms (journals, mini-books, and so on) that work well for fifth graders. You might have students use writing prompts to help them in brainstorming what to write, and then have them use a graphic organizer to write a short essay on a relevant topic. Use the **graphic organizer** template that is most appropriate for the assignment.

◆ **Interactive writing** With the help of the substitute teacher or classroom aide, students plan and write on a relevant topic as a group, taking turns. Students may add sentences to an existing paragraph or begin new paragraphs related to the opening.

◆ **Shared writing** The substitute teacher writes a short paragraph or sentences, and students transcribe them and add their own writing to them.

◆ **Guided writing** The substitute teacher and the students, who are grouped in pairs or small groups, write together as a community of writers. You might use one of the **graphic organizers** or provide a starter paragraph for an essay.

◆ **Writer's workshop** Writers learn through their own experience, teacher models a skill, students write independently while teacher conferences with individuals on individual skills needs or the skill for that day and students share with class and get feedback.

Additional writing activities

◆ Students create relevant word lists, using words from current topics of study.
◆ Students use spelling words to write sentences and paragraphs.
◆ Students write a friendly letter to the author of a book that the class enjoys.
◆ Students use graphic organizers to organize ideas for a writing activity.
◆ Students sequence a story or ideas on a storyboard.
◆ Students create silly poems about real-life situations.
◆ Students create a new style of poetry writing.

Math activities

The following strategies and topics are ways to teach math to fifth graders.

Number sense

- **Decimals** Give students practice multiplying and dividing decimals, converting fractions to decimals, and ordering decimals. Start the math period by writing several practice problems on the board as a warm-up. Write sets of two or three decimal problems for each type: multiplication, division, and converting fractions to decimals. Ask volunteers to come to the board and solve the problems. If the teacher has individual whiteboards available, you might make this an individual or small group game: See which student or team can come up with correct answers most quickly to given problems in which decimals are the focus.

- **Fractions (mixed numbers)** Have students practice working with mixed numbers by playing a game, where students convert improper fractions to mixed numbers. Divide the class into four groups, and have students in each group decide who will go first, second, and so on, for the game. Divide the board into four sections. (Tip: Prepare four identical sets of 5″ × 7″ index cards with problems written on them ahead of time.) Post the same improper fraction on each section of the board. Ask the first person from each group to come up to the board, and when everyone is ready, give students the "go" command. The first person who correctly converts the improper fraction to a mixed number gets a point for their group. Repeat with a new problem until all students in each group have had a turn. You may also have students turn given mixed numbers into improper fractions.

Graphing

- **Graph and plot with ordered pairs** Before students come into the classroom, create a large grid on the whiteboard. On specific sections on the grid, post pictures of places on the school campus that students will recognize, such as the office, the playground, the bathrooms, and the gymnasium. Then post copies of the same pictures next to the grid, and have students help determine the ordered pairs of numbers that coincide with

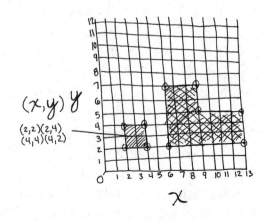

each of the drawings. Next, hand out an empty grid with 10 or more sets of ordered pairs, and have students choose a scene (for example, a circus tent, at the park, at the grocery store) to illustrate with a number of things that might be found in their scene at points that match the given ordered pairs.

Geometry/Measurement

◆ **Circumference of a circle** Review the following terms with the class: circumference, diameter, pi, and radius. Have students illustrate the meaning of these words by drawing and labeling a circle. Once you are comfortable that students understand the terms, have them review and use the formulas for finding the circumference of a circle:

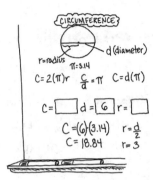

$C = 2\pi r$ OR $C/d = \pi$ OR $C = d\pi$

Next, write some problems on the board, where you provide a value for "C," "d," or "r," and have volunteers come to the board to solve the problems. Allow students to use any of the appropriate formulas.

◆ Demonstrate π with string and a small paper plate. Have students cut a piece of string the length of the diameter of the paper plate. Then have them mark a starting point on the edge of the paper plate. Students wrap the string around the perimeter (circumference) of the paper plate, marking each point where the string has to be re-placed. This demonstrates that it takes a little more than three lengths of the string to go around the paper plate, or the value of π: π = 3.14.

Probability/Statistics

◆ **Probability** Have students review probability. Hand out a paper plate and paper clip to each student. Have students divide the paper plate into 4 equal sections and either color each section a different color or number the sections 1, 2, 3, 4. Demonstrate how to hold a paper clip on the end of a pencil and then flick the paper clip onto the plate. Working independently, students flick the paper clip onto the paper plate and record where it lands each time—on which color or number. Have students do this 50 times and then tally their results. Have students express their final results in terms of fractions (for example, 14/50 times it landed on a certain color or number). As a class, have students discuss the likelihood of the paper clip landing on each of the colors or numbers, based on their results.

Social studies activities

The following strategies and topics are ways to teach social studies to fifth graders.

States

- **50 states and their capitals** Show students the classroom map of the United States. Call on students randomly to come to the board. Give them the name of a state, and ask them to point to the state and identify its capital. After reviewing all the states and capitals, hand students a blank copy of the United States map. Use the **United States Map** template. Have students work individually, in pairs, or in small groups to label as many states and capitals as they can in a given amount of time. Project a map that has been completed correctly onto the whiteboard so that all students can see it easily and will be able to correct their own maps.

60
United States
Map

History

- **Slavery character swap** Read aloud a book on slavery, such as *Nettie's Trip South* by Ann Turner. Discuss the differences of the opposing sides. Have students think about what it would be like to be each of the characters in the story. List the names of the characters on the board, and have students discuss in small groups how they would have had to act, talk, respond, and complete their work if they were each of those characters.

- **Colonial era** Have students make mini-books based on the life of a child or family of the Colonial era. They may include topics such as education, food, recreation, occupations, a typical girl's life, and a typical boy's life. Have students create a mini-book of at least six to eight pages.
  - A good resource for students is *Chronicle of America: American Revolution 1700–1800* by Joy Masoff.

Declaration of Independence and the US Constitution

♦ **Declaration of Independence** Read aloud *The Declaration of Independence* by Elaine Landau or a similar book. Have a copy of the Declaration of Independence available, and project it onto the whiteboard so that all students can easily see it. As a whole class, discuss its significance. Discuss the Fourth of July as a time when Americans celebrate the men who gathered together in July 1776 to sign our nation's Declaration of Independence. Review the key persons involved in Creating this

document, such as Thomas Jefferson (who drafted it) and John Adams. Remind students that there were many reasons for the colonial leaders' decision to leave English rule and establish their own country. Conclude by telling students that since 1776, the principles of the Declaration of Independence have served as the foundation of our country's Constitution and have inspired freedom movements across the world. Have students work in small groups to discuss the Declaration of Independence at greater length. Ask them to determine whether their group would have been comfortable signing it. They should explain why they would or wouldn't sign it, and they can use what they know today as a basis for their conclusion. If you have access to a computer lab or classroom computers, let students go online to research more about this topic to help them make their decision.

♦ **US Constitution** Read aloud *The US Constitution and You* by Syl Sobel or a similar book. Choose a book that tells students about the document itself, explaining what the Constitution does and how it affects and protects people today. Have a copy of the Preamble of the US Constitution available to hand out to each student: *We the People of the United States, in Order to form a more perfect Union, establish Justice, insure Domestic Tranquility, provide for the common defence, promote the general Welfare, and secure the Blessings of Liberty to ourselves and our Posterity, do ordain and establish this Constitution for the United States of America.* Read it aloud as the students follow along. Then have students work in small groups to analyze the Preamble and put it in their own words, as it would relate to Americans in the twenty-first century. Have each group share their understanding of what the Constitution was meant to establish with the entire class.

Science activities

The following strategies and topics are ways to teach science to fifth graders.

Life sciences

◆ **Photosynthesis**   Have students research the greenhouse effect and tree planting programs on the Internet. You may have them work independently, in pairs, or in small groups. Ask students to write down any words that are new to them as they do their research. Have them find the answers to the following questions, which will be shared later with the rest of the class.

1. What is the sun's role in photosynthesis?
2. How do plants absorb carbon dioxide?
3. What is chlorophyll, and what does it do?
4. How is glucose created?
5. Why do plants release oxygen?

Ask students if they have ever heard about programs to plant trees in cities or other areas. What do they remember about those programs? What were the purposes of those programs? What benefits can students think of for planting new trees in their community? in other parts of the world? Have students list five to ten places where planting new trees would be beneficial, along with their reasons for choosing those places.

Earth sciences

◆ **Solar system (planets, sun, moon)**   Have students choose a topic for research: one of the planets, the sun, or the moon. Once students have selected their research topic, hand out guidelines for what information they should find out. If you have access to a computer lab, schedule time for students to do their research there; otherwise, have students take turns at classroom computers or do research with print materials in the school library or the classroom. After all students have completed their research, have students meet with others who have chosen the same research topic so they can compare notes and fill in gaps. They may also continue their research as homework. Then have students who share the same research

154

topic work together to create a poster to share with the class. Each group will serve as the expert on their topic and will teach the rest of the class about their topic. (Because this lesson idea could take multiple days, it works best if you have a long-term assignment in the classroom.)

◆ **Water cycle (evaporation, condensation, precipitation)**
Demonstrate the water cycle by simulating it in a clear, airtight container. Put a small amount of water in the bottom of the container and seal it. Then put some ice in a small plastic zipper bag, and put the bag on top of the container. Leave the container in the sun, either by a window or outside. Water from the bottom of the container will evaporate, the water vapor will rise and be cooled by the ice, and condensation will form on the inside of the container and collect into drops, which will run down to the bottom of the container. This process illustrates evaporation, condensation, and precipitation. Have students journal what they observe.

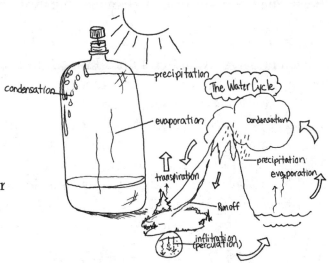

◆ **Ocean environment (physical, biological)** Have students discuss, in small groups, how human actions affect the health of the ocean environment, including ways in which the ocean environment has been polluted by industry, business, and vacationers. Then have students create posters that show the effects of throwing trash on the ground—how it gets caught in gutters and ends up in the ocean. Students' posters should show how this affects marine life. Have them share their posters with the rest of the class. Students may continue to investigate the geological features of the ocean environment and create a labeled drawing of the ocean floor.

Suggested books for fifth grade

The Blue and the Gray by Eve Bunting, illustrated by Ned Bittinger (Scholastic, 1996)

The Butter Man by Elizabeth Alalou and Ali Alalou, illustrated by Julie Klear Essakalli (Charlesbridge, 2008)

Chronicle of America: American Revolution, 1700-1800 by Joy Masoff (Scholastic Reference, 2000)

The Declaration of Independence by Elaine Landau (Children's Press, 2008)

First Day in Grapes by L. King Pérez, illustrated by Robert Casilla (Lee & Low Books, 2002)

Going Home by Nicholasa Mohr (Dial Books for Young Readers, 1986)

The Happiest Ending by Yoshiko Uchida (Margaret K. McElderry, 1985)

Indian Shoes by Cynthia Leitich Smith, illustrated by Jim Madsen (HarperCollins, 2002)

It Doesn't Have to Be This Way: A Barrio Story by Luis J. Rodríguez, illustrated by Daniel Galvez (Children's Book Press, 1999)

The Jacket by Andrew Clements, illustrated by McDavid Henderson (Simon & Schuster Books for Young Readers, 2002)

My Diary from Here to There (Mi Diario de Aquí Hasta Allá) by Amada Irma Pérez, illustrated by Maya Christina Gonzalez (Children's Book Press, 2002)

Nettie's Trip South by Ann Turner, illustrated by Ronald Himler (Aladdin, 1995)

One Green Apple by Eve Bunting, illustrated by Ted Lewin (Clarion Books, 2006)

Taking Sides by Gary Soto (Harcourt, 1992)

Suggested websites for fifth grade

http://www.arcademicskillbuilders.com/games
http://www.internet4classrooms.com

Link a picture book across the curriculum

A single picture book can be used to cover all curricular areas for fifth grade. These ideas can be tweaked and used at other grade levels as well.

The Blue and the Gray by Eve Bunting

PUBLISHER	Scholastic
PUBLICATION DATE	1996
AGE RANGE	9–12
SUMMARY	The families of two friends are building new houses on a field where a Civil War battle took place. One boy's father describes the battle to the two boys, and these scenes are shown side by side with calm scenes of the present. After hearing these stories, the boys say that they'll remember what took place in those fields.

Reading

- Read the story aloud to the class, stopping to predict, review, clarify, and summarize. After reading the story, discuss the main idea of the story, and write any new words on the board. Divide the class into groups of four students, and have a student in each group perform one of the following roles within the group: summarizer, illustrator, vocabulary finder, or responder. The responder will share the group's findings with the rest of the class.

- If multiple copies of this book are available (or even one copy for every two or three students), this is a good book to use with literacy circles. If literacy circles are possible, divide the class into groups of five students, and have them read the book aloud within their group.

- After the read-aloud, have each student perform one of the following roles in their group's literacy circle.

    1. Summarizer: This person summarizes the story.
    2. Vocabulary finder: As the story is read, this person writes down words that might be new to the group and defines the words after the story has been read.
    3. Illustrator: This person illustrates one to three scenes from the story.
    4. Travel tracer: This person describes the settings that come up in the story.
    5. Responder: This person helps with each of the other roles and then shares their findings with the entire class.

Writing

- Have students team up to do research on the Civil War. Ask students to develop a list of eight to ten key events of the Civil War, which they will place on a time line made from construction paper. Students may use printed materials from the school library for their research, or they may do their research online if you have access to a computer lab or classroom computers.

- Have students create a mini-book that compares and contrasts the present with the past, using this story as the basis for their mini-book. Tell students to present a "past" page on the left-hand side and a related "present" page on the right-hand side of each two-page spread.

Math

- Much of this book is based on measurement, such as building a house. Introduce the concepts of perimeter and area, and discuss with students the importance of knowing about perimeter and area when it comes to building a structure. Have students share reasons for this, especially as it relates to getting the appropriate amount of materials for building the space that has been measured.

Social studies

♦ Have students team up to do research on the causes and effects of the Civil War. Ask students to develop a list of eight to ten facts about the Civil War, which they list on chart paper. Have small groups of students compare the facts that they have listed, and teach one another about the causes and effects of the Civil War. Students may use printed materials from the school library for their research, or they may do their research online if you have access to a computer lab or classroom computers.

♦ Using lesson ideas from a teacher resource book such as *The Organized Teacher's Guide to Building Character* by Steve Springer and Kimberly Persiani, teach students about friendship and teamwork. Relate these character traits to the Civil War, especially how people felt about the results of the Civil War, depending on their role in it.

Science

♦ Discuss weather and the seasons. Include topics such as basic weather, appropriate clothing for certain weather conditions, and food eaten at certain times of the year. Explore details about weather in different time zones, differences in seasons around the world at the same time of year, weather patterns, how to read the weather, and crops that grow best in specific seasons.

♦ In this book, many of the illustrations are done using watercolors, and many show the blending of colors. Demonstrate art chromatography to students. This is a method of separating the components of a substance for analytical purposes and can be demonstrated by using a black nonpermanent felt pen, a coffee filter, scissors, and a small glass of water. Draw a horizontal line in the middle of a coffee filter with the felt pen. Put the filter into the water, with the felt pen line above the water level. The water rises slowly through the coffee filter, and when the water rises above the point where the felt pen line is, the water will take parts of the ink with it. The lighter parts of the ink will rise with the water, up toward the upper edge of the filter line, while the heavy parts of the ink will stay where they are. That's the principle of chromatography. Remove the coffee filter from the glass just before water reaches its top edge. Put the filter on a sheet of newspaper, and let it dry.

Art

♦ Have students use watercolors to paint their favorite scene from the book or a picture of their own that relates to the story line.

♦ Have students create an American flag, using torn construction paper.

chapter 9
Sixth grade (11–12 years old)

This chapter gives a brief overview of sixth grade students and what learning takes place at that grade level. Students vary in personality and maturity at any grade level, so keep in mind that this is a general overview—a "sneak peek" at what you might expect. Be sure to address your own state standards when doing any necessary lesson planning.

Sixth graders—Who are they?

Sixth grade students are beginning to go through physical and emotional changes that can cause mood swings. This may lead to distraction from their work. At times, their social life can take priority over their academic life, and they enjoy time away from adults. They are very conscious of what their peers think of them, despite having a stronger sense of self. Peer approval is very important to them. They are aware of societal trends and care about having the very latest material possessions. They enjoy social media, music, humor, discussing deep topics, and exploring issues and their role in the world.

What are they learning?

Reading

Sixth graders

... are working toward reading fluency of 150 words per minute

... read more in-depth text, for a purpose and to engage in rich discussions

... read chapter books (fiction and nonfiction), informational texts, and poetry

... can better interpret meaning, literary devices, relationships, and conclusions

... are able to identify inconsistencies and propaganda in what they are asked to read

... review more complex poetry

... learn more about style, tone, and meaning (structure, implied meaning, imagery)

... do online research and use a variety of reference data to develop their ideas about the world

Writing

Sixth graders

... continue to use the writing process to write multiparagraph essays (persuasive, expository, narrative), letters, reports, and responses to literature

... write with purpose, tone, and a clear point of view or voice

... consider their audience

... use, compile, and interpret research material, and decide what will be most meaningful to draw from

... focus on grammar, writing conventions, spelling, details, and voice in their essays

Math

Sixth graders

... continue with decimals, fractions, and percents

... plot decimals, fractions, mixed numbers, and integers on a number line

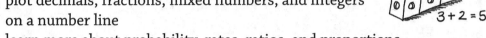

... learn more about probability, rates, ratios, and proportions

... add, subtract, multiply, and divide fractions, mixed numbers, and integers

... study mean, median, mode, range, and outliers for a data set

... organize and interpret data with a variety of graphical methods

... review prime factorization, greatest common factor (GCF), and least common multiple (LCM) of a pair of numbers

... study exponents and order of operations

... study area, perimeter, circumference, shapes, and volume of solids

... classify and measure angles

... understand congruent and noncongruent figures

... solve multistep problems

... measure, compare, and convert units of measure (US customary and metric)

Social studies

Sixth graders

... learn about world history from the late 1800s to the present, including economic, social, and religious aspects

... study the rise and fall of the ancient civilizations of Mesopotamia, Egypt, Kush, the ancient Hebrews, Greece, the Persian empire, India, China, and Rome

... study the effects of wars on the American woman's role in history

Science

Sixth graders

... study the planet Earth, including its structure, layers, and plate tectonics

... review the major events for mountain and land formations, volcanoes, earthquakes, and glaciers

... study the weather, water systems and cycles, natural resources, conservation, renewable vs. nonrenewable energy, erosion, and deposition

... explore forms of energy (potential, kinetic) and transfer (conduction, radiation, convection)

... study weather patterns and causes, convection currents in the oceans and atmosphere, and ecosystems and the role of organisms within an ecosystem

... study states of matter (solid, liquid, gas)

... study ecology, conservation, climate change, and global warming

Activities for each curricular area

Whether you are substitute teaching for one day, three days, a month, or longer, it's important to have a variety of grade level curriculum ideas and activities in your personal survival kit. You may find that no plans have been left for you; you may finish plans more quickly than expected and have extra time at the end of a period; or you may have to do lesson planning on your own, but need time to adjust to your current surroundings and the teacher's manuals you will be working with. The following lesson ideas and activities are suitable for sixth grade.

Reading activities

The following strategies and topics are ways to read to and with sixth graders.

Read aloud

◆ Read a book aloud to the class; it may be either fiction or nonfiction, a biography, an autobiography, multicultural stories, or informational text. Fiction will include setting, plot, climax, and resolution.

◆ Do not stop to summarize or ask questions.

- Students listen, and respond only when prompted to do so.
- Reading selections may include poetry and chapter books, and complex picture books with real themes are still appropriate.
- Reading selections may include a focus on the main idea, key concepts, symbolism, literary devices, cause-and-effect relationships, comparing and contrasting, and intention of the author.
- A read-aloud is usually intended to be for the pure enjoyment of hearing a story. Sixth graders still enjoy being read to.

Shared reading

- Read aloud from a textbook or other printed material.
- Model reading strategies such as predicting, summarizing, visualizing, and the use of context clues.
- Students view and follow as the teacher reads aloud.
- Students read aloud as the teacher tracks the words.

Buddy reading

- A sixth grade student pairs with a lower (kindergarten through fifth) grade student and serves as a coach or reading mentor.
- Students read and discuss stories from age-appropriate books that might include text or situations involving comparisons.

Sustained Silent Reading (SSR)

- Students read independently and silently.
- Students read books at their instructional reading level.
- SSR provides reading practice and time for reading for pleasure.
- It is recommended that students in sixth grade read chapter books, but mature picture books can also be encouraged.
- SSR is also known as Uninterrupted Sustained Silent Reading (USSR) or Drop Everything and Read (DEAR).

Partner reading

- Students pair up and share an agreed-upon book.
- Students take turns and assist one another.
- Designate a special place for partner reading in the room.
- You may want to pair students by reading ability: high/medium and medium/low.

Guided reading

- Teacher coaches students individually while other students read text silently or in a low voice.
- Teacher focuses on targeted "aim" or "skill."
- The teacher and students work together as they read, think about, and talk through the text.
- The teacher and student "echo read."
- Small groups at the same reading level.
- Students read the same text.

Choral reading

- Choral reading is also known as unison reading.
- It provides many opportunities for repeated readings of a selected piece.
- It provides an opportunity to practice oral reading.
- Choral reading is excellent for poetry, rhymes, and chants.

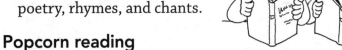

Popcorn reading

- The teacher asks a student to begin reading aloud; any willing student can start. When the student stops, he or she selects the next student (who has not already had a turn), and that student continues reading (without direction from the teacher). This process continues until all students have taken a turn reading. With larger classes, keep track of who has already read, especially if the session spans more than one day.
- A variation is to alternate boys and girls.
- Popcorn reading builds student responsibility for participation.

Timed reading

- Students work toward a designated number of words: 150 words per minute is the goal for sixth graders. However, student proficiency will vary.
- Students read as much of a passage as they can in one minute in an attempt to reach the designated words per minute.
- Students read the passage twice, attempting to read further the second time; each reading is timed.
- Timed reading builds fluency.

Reading workshop

- Teacher introduces targeted "aim" or "skill" and models it in action.
- Students read books at their level/that they choose for a sustained period of time.
- Students have individual goals they work on as well as introduced skills.
- Teacher can informally conference with individual students, asking how they are applying a goal or the aim of the day.
- Whole group shares how skills were used.

Follow-up activities after reading stories

- Students think-pair-share about their favorite parts of a story.
- Hold small group and class discussions about the author's purpose, the main idea, details, and so on, of a story.
- Students respond to a story by writing in their journals; they engage in predicting, summarizing, and sequencing, through simple sentences and/or illustrations
- Students respond to a story by illustrating their favorite scene(s).
- Students retell a story on a storyboard through meaningful sentences and illustrations. Use the **Storyboard Organizer** template.
- Students describe designated parts of a story in pairs, in small groups, or as a whole class, using the pictures as a guide.
- Students identify word parts (prefixes and suffixes) while reading.

46
Storyboard
Organizer

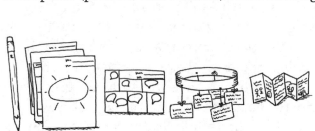

Writing activities

The following strategies and topics are ways to teach writing to sixth graders.

Writing genres

- **Research reports** Students write reports about their research that explain and inform, give information and facts with the purpose of educating the reader, and predict based on data.
- **Persuasive letters and compositions** Students convey a message and try to persuade the reader in their favor about an issue.

- **Narratives** Students write narratives that tell a story, use imagination, and give a personal account. The narratives are written in first or third person.
- **Responses to literature** Students respond to literature that they've read, using strategies such as inference, prediction, opinion, and connection through their own ideas and experiences. Responses are written by retelling, summarizing, analyzing, and/or generalizing.
- **Summaries** Students summarize a document, maintaining the integrity of the original document and using its main ideas to make a point.
- **Expository essays (informational reports)** Students explain, define, and give information, while presenting facts and statistical information, cause-and-effect relationships, and examples. Expository essays are usually written in third person.
- **Poems (rhymed and unrhymed)** Students write an arranged composition using sound and rhythm. The composition may use any one of many forms, including haiku, cinquain, limerick, closed verse, lyric, nonsense verse, narrative, jump rope, and concrete (shape) poetry.

Ways to write

- **Independent writing** There are a variety of forms (journals, mini-books, and so on) that work well for sixth graders. You might have students use writing prompts, then have them use a graphic organizer to write an essay on a given topic related to a complex issue (such as history, the environment, or politics). Use the **graphic organizer** template that is most appropriate for the assignment.

38
Sandwich
Organizer
41
Stair
Organizer 1
42
Stair
Organizer 2
45
Story
Organizer
62
Web
Organizer

- **Interactive writing** With the help of the substitute teacher or classroom aide, students plan and write on a relevant topic as a group, taking turns. Students can add sentences to an existing paragraph or begin new paragraphs related to the opening. You might begin an essay on a relevant issue on the board, and have students take turns coming up to write the next sentences until the first few paragraphs are complete; then students finish the essay on their own. Have students complete a graphic organizer together by taking turns writing words, phrases, or sentences that relate to the topic; have students complete the essay on their own.

◆ **Shared writing** The substitute teacher models a poem, a few sentences, or a short paragraph, and students transcribe them and add their own writing to them. Structure it to involve the give-and-take of oral discussion about the topic or issue being written about. This offers a model for students to refer to and gives them an opportunity to participate, contributing ideas as the teacher writes them down.

◆ **Guided writing** The substitute teacher and the students, who are grouped in pairs or small groups, write together as a community of writers. This helps motivate students who are struggling with putting ideas into writing. You might use one of the graphic organizers or provide a starter paragraph for an essay.

◆ **Writer's workshop** Writers learn through their own experience, teacher models a skill, students write independently while teacher conferences with individuals on individual skills needs or the skill for that day and students share with class and get feedback.

Additional writing activities

◆ Students create relevant word lists, using words from current topics of study.
◆ Students use spelling words to write sentences and paragraphs.
◆ Students write a letter to the author of a book that the class enjoys.
◆ Students use graphic organizers to organize ideas for a writing activity.
◆ Students sequence a story or ideas on a storyboard.
◆ Students create silly poems about real-life situations.

Math activities

The following strategies and topics are ways to teach math to sixth graders.

Geometry/Measurement

◆ **Measure, compare, and convert units of measurement (US customary and metric)**
Read aloud *Millions to Measure* by David Schwartz or a similar book to the class. Then have students convert US customary measurements to the metric system. Begin with easy conversions and move to the more difficult ones. Use basic measurements of length, weight, and volume. You may do this activity as a game by dividing the class into small groups and having a student from each group come to the board to complete the conversion. Give points to each group for every correct answer, and the group with the most points at the end wins.

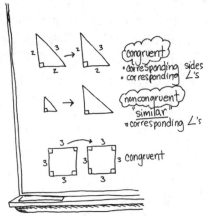

◆ **Congruent and noncongruent figures** Review with students the vocabulary related to congruent and noncongruent figures: Two figures are congruent if they have the same shape and size and if one could fit exactly on top of the other; and figures that have similar shapes are not necessarily congruent. Draw several different triangles (obtuse, acute, equilateral, right) on the board. Show examples where equal lengths of sides appear in different types of triangles, as well as triangles that look to be the same shape but have sides of different lengths. Ask students to identify which triangles are congruent and which are not, explaining the reasons for their answer. Then have students create several examples of congruent and noncongruent figures (not just triangles) on their own.

 ◆ Have students draw several triangles, cut them out, and use them to create a picture on a separate sheet of paper. Students may then exchange papers and try to find the congruent triangles in their partner's picture.

♦ **Classify angles** Demonstrate different types of angles, using colored paper plates. If possible, have a set of two different colored paper plates for each student. If you have only one set, demonstrate and have the students respond to questions. Hold the plates together, and cut a radius through both plates. Slide one plate on top of the other at the cut to create a two-color plate. Model the three different types of angles (acute, right, obtuse) by sliding the plates to reveal different angles where the colors meet. Ask students to identify each angle as you display it for them. You may also have students draw each angle on their own paper and label it.

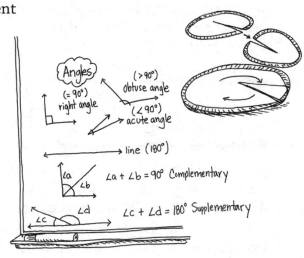

Probability/Statistics

♦ **Mean, median, and mode** Use coins to teach students about finding the mean, median, and mode. Graphing and sorting activities can also be easily incorporated. Give each student (or group of students) a small bag of mixed coins (pennies, nickels, dimes, quarters), but tell them not to open the bags. First, ask students to predict how many of each type of coin is in the bag. Next, have students open the bag, separate the coins by type, and count the coins of each type. Have the students, working in small groups, compare their results. Then have them find the mean, median, and mode for each type of coin in their bag.
  ♦ Variation: Have the students add the values of all their coins; then have them count out the coins needed for given amounts from the possible coin combinations.

Rates/Proportions

♦ **Proportions** Teach proportions through recipes, using word problems. Present one word problem as an example, and then have students create and solve word problems of their own in pairs or small groups. Begin by modeling the following word problem that uses a recipe for Fettuccini Chicken Alfredo.
  ♦ Fettuccini Chicken Alfredo calls for 1 pound of fettuccini, 4 chicken breasts, and 8 cups of pre-made Alfredo sauce. The recipe serves 4, but 10 people are having dinner with you. How can you adjust the recipe so everyone gets a serving?

SOLUTION For the fettuccini, use the proportion of 1 pound/4 servings = *x* pounds/10 servings. Cross-multiplying reveals that 2.5 pounds of fettuccini will feed 10 people. For the chicken, use the proportion of 4 chicken breasts/4 servings = *x* chicken breasts/10 servings. Cross-multiplying reveals that you will need 10 chicken breasts for the recipe. For the Alfredo sauce, cross-multiply 8 cups/ 4 servings = *x* cups/10 servings to find that 20 cups of Alfredo sauce will be needed

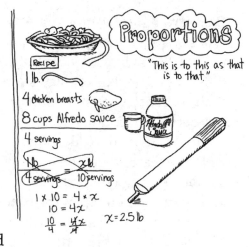

for 10 servings. Work through this process with the students, then have them work together to create their own word problem based on a recipe. As a variation, bring in recipes and have students double or triple them.

♦ **Rates** Have students practice calculating rates by working with problems where they calculate distance over time. If possible, have the students run around the perimeter of the playground. (You should be able to find out the distance by asking the playground personnel or office staff.) Record how much time it took students to run four laps. Once students are back in the classroom, give them their personal times for the four laps and have them calculate their distance over time. They can compare their times with one another.

  ♦ Variations: If the distance is unknown, assign an arbitrary number for the distance; for example, if you say that a lap equals 100 yards, 4 laps would be 400 yards. If it isn't possible for the students to do the physical activity, give them random distances and times to use for word problems; for example, "It took 3 hours to travel 60 miles. What is the rate?" or "At a rate of 60 miles per hour, how long would it take to travel 115 miles?"

Social studies activities

The following strategies and topics are ways to teach social studies to sixth graders. Many of these are research-oriented and work best if you have a long-term assignment in the classroom.

Research projects: Mesopotamia, Egypt, China, Rome

◆ **Research projects** Students may use printed materials from the school library for their research, or they may do their research online if you have access to a computer lab or classroom computers.

◆ **Time line** Have students show events from history over time by creating a time line from construction paper. Students take a sheet of construction paper (11″ × 14″), fold it in half lengthwise, cut along the fold, then tape the two pieces together to create one sheet of paper approximately 28″ long. This enables students to fit at least eight events from the history of the country they 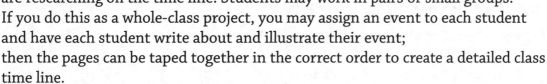 are researching on the time line. Students may work in pairs or small groups. If you do this as a whole-class project, you may assign an event to each student and have each student write about and illustrate their event; then the pages can be taped together in the correct order to create a detailed class time line.

◆ **Travel brochure** Have students create a travel brochure for the country they are currently studying. You may choose to have them create their brochure for today's time or for a specific time in the past. Have students fold an 8½″ × 11″ sheet of white paper as a trifold brochure. The front cover will show the country's location on the world map (either an illustration or a picture from the Internet). On the inside of the brochure, have students include information about neighboring countries, the country's geography (including on which continent it is located), sources of income, cultures, languages, religion, education system, and the like. Require that students include at least six important aspects of life in this country, with a corresponding illustration or picture for each one. Students should be as creative as possible, using a lot of color to appeal to the traveler they are trying to persuade to visit the country.

◆ **Travel poster (past or present)** Have students create a travel poster for the country they are currently studying. You may choose to have them create their poster for today's time or for a specific time in the past. Have students use a sheet of 11″ × 14″ construction paper (white or manila) to create a poster that features illustrations and pictures, with minimal text, as a way to persuade people to visit their country.

- **Mobile** Have students create a mobile that features five important aspects of the country they are currently studying. You may choose to have them create their mobile for today's time or for a specific time in the past. Have students use five index cards (3″ × 5″) on which they write about a chosen aspect of the country on one side and illustrate it on the other. The index cards can be hung with string on a hanger, a sentence strip joined into a circle, or a heavy drinking straw. (Tip: Coffee shops that have extra-long straws for their drinks would likely donate them for you to use in the classroom; these work very well for mobiles.)

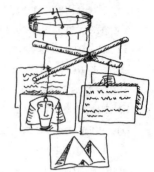

American women's role in history

- **Time line** Have students study American women's role in the history of our country. Ask students to research the topic and select six to ten important events that show women's role in US history, especially during times of war, when women went to work, played baseball, and served as nurses for the wounded. They should also include events related to the women's suffrage movement. If students fold the time line in half, they can cut flaps for the top layer, so that students can create an illustration on the outside with an explanation underneath.

Science activities

The following strategies and topics are ways to teach science to sixth graders.

Physical sciences

- **Forms of energy (potential, kinetic)** Discuss the different forms of energy with students: Energy that is stored is potential energy; energy in motion is kinetic energy. Demonstrate the difference between potential energy and kinetic energy with a ramp (a long piece of cardboard supported on one end) and a toy car. Hold the toy car at the top of the ramp, and ask students if this shows potential or kinetic energy. Then release the car, and ask students the same question as the car rolls down the ramp. Project a series of pictures onto the whiteboard that show potential or kinetic

energy, and let the students identify which type of energy is being shown. Suggestions are pictures of an apple hanging from a tree, an apple falling from a tree, a person sitting in a car, a person driving a car, and so on. Then have students develop a list of ten pairs of examples of kinetic and potential energy.

Earth sciences

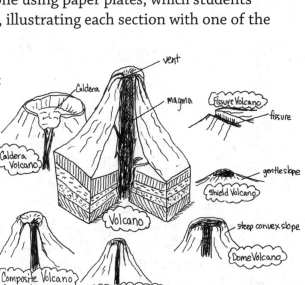

♦ **Earth's structure** As a whole class, review the key elements of the Earth's structure. Include the upper mantle, the mantle, the crust, the outer core, the inner core, the mesosphere, the stratosphere, and the troposphere. Show students a visual of Earth's layers. Once they have an understanding of the role each element plays for the planet, hand out 8½" × 11" sheets of white paper so students can create eight-page mini-books plus a cover. Students will illustrate and define each of the eight elements on a separate page of their mini-book. The project can also be done using paper plates, which students divide into eight pie-shaped sections, illustrating each section with one of the eight elements of Earth's structure.

♦ **Volcanoes** Discuss the six different types of volcanoes with the students: fissure, shield, dome, ash-cinder, composite, and caldera. Then review the main components of the volcano: lava, fissure, magma, cinder, vent, branch pipe, and cone. Have students illustrate and label one of the six types of volcanoes, showing the seven main components in their drawing.

♦ **Water cycle** Have students close their eyes while you tell them a story about a water droplet and its journey through the different stages of the water cycle. After you have finished the story, write the first sentence on the board as a story starter for students, and let them create their own story about the journey of a water droplet. Encourage students to be creative: They may set their story in a different time and/or place, include people and/or animals on the journey, and so on. If time permits, students may re-create their story as a mini-book or a flip book.

173

◆ **Global warming** Conduct a whole-class discussion about global warming. Students may hold different opinions about it; respect each student's opinion. (Global warming is part of most sixth grade curriculums and may be in their science textbook.) Share pictures, slogans, and ideas with students (from books, magazines, or the Internet). Then, if possible, have students visit the computer lab or use classroom computers and/or nonfiction books to research global warming and the implications of it for our planet. Have students identify one of the factors that contributes to global warming, and suggest a solution to that aspect of the problem to the class. Their solution can be real or it can be a fictitious machine or plan, as long as it makes sense. Have students work in small groups to brainstorm ideas and then share their ideas with the rest of the students. Students may create posters showing ways to "Reduce, Reuse, and Recycle" in order to help save our planet.

Suggested books for sixth grade

Baseball Fever by Johanna Hurwitz, illustrated by Ray Cruz
  (Avon Books, 2000)
The Breadwinner by Deborah Ellis (Groundwood Books, 2001)
The Day of Ahmed's Secret by Florence Parry Heide and Judith
  Heide Gilliland, illustrated by Ted Lewin (HarperCollins, 1995)
Eagle Song by Joseph Bruchac, illustrated by Dan Andreasen
  (Puffin Books, 1997)
Hello, My Name is Scrambled Eggs by Jamie Gilson, illustrated by
  John Wallner (Pocket Books, 1985)
A Jar of Dreams by Yoshiko Uchida (Aladdin Paperbacks, 1981)
Millions to Measure by David M. Schwartz, illustrated by Steven Kellogg
  (HarperCollins, 2003)
Music for Alice by Allen Say (Houghton Mifflin, 2004)
Music from a Place Called Half Moon by Jerrie Oughton (Laurel Leaf, 1997)
Samir and Yonatan by Daniella Carmi, translated by Yael Lotan (Scholastic, 2002)
Walk Two Moons by Sharon Creech (HarperCollins, 1996)

Suggested websites for sixth grade

http://kids.yahoo.com/games
http://www.funbrain.com/kidscenter.html
http://www.playkidsgames.com

Link a picture book across the curriculum

A single picture book can be used to cover all curricular areas for sixth grade. These ideas can be tweaked and used at other grade levels as well.

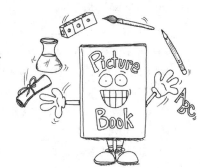

The Lorax by Dr. Seuss

PUBLISHER	Random House
PUBLICATION DATE	1971
AGE RANGE	6–12
SUMMARY	In this story, students meet the Once-ler, and they see how his greedy actions destroyed a beautiful and thriving environment. Students will enjoy the characters and the rhyming verse, but they will also understand the subtle messages about the negative effects of deforestation, habitat destruction, and air and water pollution.

Reading

- Read the story aloud to the class, focusing on the cadence and rhyme. Take time to clarify the subtle messages that some of the children might otherwise miss. This book lends itself to summary and visualization. As you are reading, you will find logical places in the story to stop and have students participate in discussion.

Writing

- Model writing poetry with the students, using the verse and rhyme in the story as inspiration.
- Have students write to a public official about an aspect of the story that is related to conservation in the community (recycling at school, conserving natural resources, using less water, and the like).
- Have students write a proposal to the Lorax with suggestions about how to solve his problem with the greedy Once-ler.
- Have students write a persuasive letter to try to persuade the Once-ler to stop the deforestation.

Math

◆ Based on the scene in the story where the Once-ler discusses his product and how much he'll make for each one, have students work in small groups to develop their own product, determine what materials would be needed to make it, and decide how much it would cost to produce. Then have groups share information about their products with the rest of the class.

◆ Have students vote on the product that uses the least amount of natural resources to produce.

Social studies

◆ Present to the class a scenario where nearby fields or forests are to be cut down or destroyed in order to build a mall or housing development. Have students share how they would feel if the nearby orange trees, strawberry fields, or forest were going to be cut down or taken out in order to build a mall or housing development.

◆ Divide the class into small groups, and assign "for" and "against" positions to the groups. Give the groups time to discuss the issue and develop their arguments in favor of or opposed to the new project. Hold a class debate on the issue. Assign roles to students within each group to make sure that every student has a chance to participate.

Science

◆ Teach students about the environment and the direct impact of using our natural resources without replenishing them in some way. Have students work in groups to devise a plan of action for helping the Lorax save the forest.

◆ Have students discuss habitat destruction, with the point of departure being what happened to the wildlife in the story as a result of all the trees being cut down.

◆ Have students discuss air and water pollution, with the point of departure being what happened to the wildlife, plants, and water in the story as a result of all the trees being cut down.

Art

◆ Have students, working in small groups, create a recycling poster that they will share with the rest of the class.

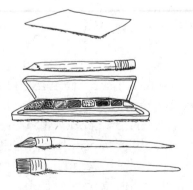

chapter 10

Secondary Grades (13–18 years old)

This chapter gives a brief overview of students in secondary school grades 7 through 12 and learning strategies that can be applied to more specific subject coursework across these five grades. You will find strategies and lesson ideas that can be applied to higher-level coursework. The idea is to bring nontraditional, out-of-the-box activities that review what is being learned. You may not be an expert in chemistry or algebra, but you can facilitate an engaging, hands-on activity that is student driven.

Student personalities and maturity will vary within a grade level and across these grade levels, so keep in mind that these are general activities that lend themselves to a variety of coursework. As always, consider district and school policies when taking on potentially controversial activities.

Secondary students (seventh through twelfth graders)—Who are they?

Secondary students are very conscious of what their peers think of them. They are coming to terms with their identity and are developing a stronger sense of self. Peer approval is very important to them, and their social life often takes priority over their academic life. They are aware of societal trends and care about having the very latest material possessions, especially in terms of technology. They are developing a social, cultural, and conscious voice and are willing to discuss deep topics as well as explore issues and their role in the world.

What are they learning?

Reading

Secondary students

... are reading fluently

... read in-depth texts, for a purpose and to engage in rich discussions

... read chapter books (fiction and nonfiction), informational texts, and poetry

... interpret meaning, literary devices, relationships, and conclusions

... are able to identify inconsistencies and propaganda in what they are asked to read

... review complex poetry

... learn more about style, tone, and meaning (structure, implied meaning, imagery)

... do online research and use a variety of reference data to develop their ideas about the world

Writing

Secondary students

... continue to use the writing process to write multiparagraph essays (argumentative, persuasive, expository, narrative) and responses to literature

... write position papers, speeches, public service announcements, research reports, and social media pieces

... write with purpose, tone, and a clear point of view or voice

... consider their audience

... use, compile, and interpret research material, and decide what will be most meaningful to draw from

... focus on grammar, writing conventions, spelling, details, and voice in their essays

Math

Fundamental skills (seventh graders)
Students will:

- continue with decimals, fractions, and percentages; plot decimals, fractions, mixed numbers, and integers on a number line
- learn more about probability, rates, ratios, and proportions
- add, subtract, multiply, and divide fractions, mixed numbers, and integers
- study mean, median, mode, range, and outliers for data sets
- organize and interpret data with a variety of graphical methods
- review prime factorization, greatest common factor (GCF), and least common multiple (LCM) of pairs of numbers
- study exponents and order of operations
- study area, perimeter, circumference, shapes, and volume of solids
- classify and measure angles
- understand congruent and noncongruent figures
- solve multistep problems
- measure, compare, and convert units of measure (US customary and metric)
- use a coordinate plane to plot points on an X and Y axis in the four quadrants

Starting in seventh or eighth grades, students move into higher-level math courses:

- Algebra
- Geometry
- Algebra 2
- Trigonometry
- Calculus

Social studies

Secondary students are adhering to the following social studies content:

Seventh graders The focus is on medieval and early modern world history. They study empires and their rise and fall, as well as the spreading of religions, languages, ideas, products, and people. The focus is on questions that get at those larger geographical, historical, economic, and civic patterns. Grade seven topics include The Roman Empire, Quanzhou, Site of Encounter, the Spanish Conquest of Mexico, and more.

Eighth graders The focus is on US history, from the founding of the American Republic through the end of the nineteenth century. Students study the themes of freedom, equality, and liberty and their changing definitions over time. They also explore the geography of place, movement, and region, starting with the Atlantic Seaboard and then exploring American westward expansion and economic development, the Civil War, the Reconstruction, and industrialization.

Ninth graders The focus is on world and regional geography, survey of world religions, women in US history, ethnic studies, and financial literacy.

Tenth graders The focus is on world history and geography from the late eighteenth century to the present. They study the world, including diverse topics such as industrialization, colonialism, the causes and effects of the world wars, revolutions, and globalization and how it affected people, nations, and capitals, of the modern period. Students examine how national identity is constructed. In contrast, students study other countries like Japan, Germany, Italy, and the Soviet Union that implement totalitarianism in various ways. Students examine economic growth and collapse and global independence and connections across the globe.

Eleventh graders The focus is on American history with an emphasis on the contributions of many diverse groups of people to the story of America, including ethnic, cultural, and religious minorities; lesbian, gay, bisexual, and transgender individuals; and the disabled. They address working children, the Harlem Renaissance, Communism, and the Vietnam War.

Twelfth graders The focus is on the principles of American democracy and how government works, with an emphasis on the United States and how its system contrasts with other kinds of government. Also, they address the principles of economics, such as classic micro- and macroeconomic concepts, as well as the impact that the government has on the economy, the effects of globalization, and the importance of national literacy.

Science

Secondary students are becoming more focused in their science studies. Specific courses could include:

- Biology
- Biochemistry
- Biotechnology
- Earth science
- Physics
- Chemistry
- Anatomy/Physiology
- Genetics
- Environmental science

These courses can be taught in isolation or in a more collective theme-based manner as outlined in the Next Generation Science Standards (NGSS). Regardless, secondary students are adhering to the following science content.

Grade focus

The following topics are addressed throughout the various secondary grade levels.

Seventh–eighth grades Matter and Its Interactions; Motion and Stability: Forces and Interactions, Energy, and Waves; Structure and Properties of Matter and Its Interactions; Molecules to Organisms; Ecosystems; Life science, anatomy, physiology Heredity/Inheritance; Natural Selection and Adaptations; Biological Evolution; Earth's Place in the Universe; Earth's Systems; Earth and Human Activity; Engineering Design; History of Earth; Human Impacts; Gas Laws; Weather and Climate; Space Systems; Oxidation/Reduction; Decomposition/Synthesis; Chemical Reactions; Acids/Bases

Ninth–twelfth grades Gas Laws; Chemical Formula; Acids/Bases; Bonding, Power; Valence Electrons; Chemical Equation; and Stoichiometry; Decomposition/Synthesis; Matter and its Interactions; Oxidation/Reduction; Motion and Stability; Energy, Waves, and their Applications in Technology for Information Transfer; From Molecules to Organisms: Structure and Processes; Ecosystems: Interactions, Energy and Dynamics; Heredity: Inheritance and Variation of Traits; Biological Evolution: Unity and Diversity; Mendelian Genetics; Natural Selection; Earth's Place in the Universe; Earth Systems; Earth and Human Activity; Engineering Design; Interdependent Relationships in Ecosystems; Weather and Climate; Human Sustainability

Activities for each curricular area

Whether you are substitute teaching for one day, three days, a month, or longer, it's important to have a variety of grade-level curriculum ideas and activities in your personal survival kit. You may find that no plans have been left for you; you may finish plans more quickly than expected and have extra time at the end of a period; or you may have to do lesson planning on your own, but need time to adjust to your current surroundings and the teacher's manuals you will be working with. The following lesson ideas and activities are suitable for secondary students.

Reading activities

The following strategies and topics are ways to encourage reading with secondary students.

Shared reading

- Regardless of the subject area you are teaching, you can read aloud from a primary resource, textbook, or other printed material.

- Model reading strategies such as predicting, summarizing, visualizing, and the use of context clues and vocabulary to comprehend text.

- Students view and follow as the teacher or other student volunteers read aloud.

- Students read aloud as the teacher and other students track the words.

Sustained Silent Reading (SSR)

- Students read chapter books/novels independently and silently.
- Students read books related to theme or genre.
- SSR provides reading practice and time for reading for pleasure.
- SSR is also known as Uninterrupted Sustained Silent Reading (USSR) or Drop Everything and Read (DEAR).

Partner reading

◆ Students pair up and share an assigned article or book.

◆ Students take turns and discuss the text and elements of the text as well as meaning.

◆ The teacher can give the students specific talking points: plot, antagonist/protagonist, narrative arch, supporting details, and so on.

Guided reading

◆ The teacher coaches students individually while other students read text silently or in a low voice.

◆ The teacher focuses on a targeted "aim" or "skill" (making connections to text, visualizing, inferring, determining importance, synthesizing information, finding evidence, etc.).

◆ The teacher and students work together as they read, analyze, and discuss the text.

◆ Students read the same text.

Popcorn reading

◆ The teacher asks a student to begin reading aloud; any willing student can start. When the student stops, he or she selects the next student (who has not already had a turn), and that student continues reading (without direction from the teacher). This process continues until all students have taken a turn reading. With larger classes, keep track of who has already read, especially if the session spans more than one day.

Reading workshop

◆ The teacher introduces the targeted "aim" or "skill" and models it in action (making connections to text, visualizing, inferring, determining importance, synthesizing information, finding evidence, etc.).

◆ Students read books at their level or that they choose for a sustained time period.

◆ Students have individual goals they work on as well as introduced skills.

◆ The teacher can informally conference with individual students, asking how they are applying a goal or the aim of the day.

◆ The whole group shares how skills were used.

Follow-up activities after reading stories

- Students share about their favorite parts of a story, and explain why by using evidence from the text.

- Hold small group and class discussions about the author's purpose, the main idea, details, and so on, of a story.

- Students respond to a story by writing in their journals; they engage in predicting, summarizing, sequencing, drawing conclusions, comparing and contrasting to other texts, inferring, and so on.

- Students respond to a story by creating a comic strip with illustrations and text. It could be a specific part or a sequel to what they are studying.

47
Storyboard
Organizer

- Students retell a story on a storyboard through meaningful text and dialogues with illustrations. Use the **Storyboard Organizer** template.

- Students describe designated parts of a story in pairs, in small groups, or as a whole class, and create posters of the part. Posters are then sequenced and displayed to tell highlights of the story.

- Students script out a commercial or trailer for their text. Students can then act it out or film it.

- Students create stop motion animation of a scene from their novel.

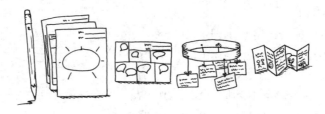

Writing activities

The following strategies and topics are ways to teach writing to secondary students.

Writing genres

- **Research reports** Students write reports about their research that explain and inform, give information and facts with the purpose of educating the reader, and predict based on data.

- **Persuasive letters and compositions** Students convey a message and try to persuade the reader in their favor about an issue/current event.

- **Narratives** Students write narratives that tell a story, use imagination, and give a personal account. The narratives are written in first or third person.

- **Responses to literature** Students respond to literature that they've read, using strategies such as inference, prediction, opinion, and connection through their own ideas and experiences. Responses are written by retelling, summarizing, analyzing, and/or generalizing.

◆ **Summaries** Students summarize a document, maintaining the integrity of the original document and using its main ideas to make a point.

◆ **Expository essays (informational reports)** Students explain, define, and give information, while presenting facts and statistical information, cause-and-effect relationships, and examples. Expository essays are usually written in third person.

◆ **Poems (rhymed and unrhymed)** Students write an arranged composition using sound and rhythm. The composition may use any one of many forms, including haiku, cinquain, limericks, closed verse, lyric, nonsense verse, narrative, jump rope, and concrete (shape) poetry.

Ways to write

◆ **Independent writing** There are a variety of forms (journals, mini-books, and so on) that can be used to hook students (even older students) and help them think outside the box and creatively. You might have students use writing prompts, then have them use a graphic organizer to write an essay on a given topic related to a complex issue (such as history, the environment, or politics). Use the graphic organizer template that is most appropriate for the assignment.

38
Sandwich
Organizer

41
Stair
Organizer 1

42
Stair
Organizer 2

45
Story
Organizer

62
Web
Organizer

◆ **Interactive writing** Students plan and write on a relevant topic as a group, taking turns. Students can add sentences to an existing paragraph or begin new paragraphs related to the opening. You might begin an essay on a relevant issue on the board and have students take turns coming up to write the next sentences until the first few paragraphs are complete; then students finish the essay on their own. Have students complete a graphic organizer together by taking turns writing words, phrases, or sentences that relate to the topic; have students complete the essay on their own.

◆ **Shared writing** The substitute teacher models a poem, a few sentences, or a short paragraph, and students transcribe it and add their own writing to it. They structure the session to involve the give-and-take of oral discussion about the topic or issue being written about. This offers a model for students to refer to and gives them an opportunity to participate, contributing ideas as the teacher writes them down.

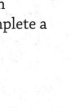

◆ **Guided writing** The substitute teacher and the students, who are grouped in pairs or small groups, write together as a community of writers. This helps motivate students who are struggling with putting ideas into writing. You might use one of the graphic organizers or provide a starter paragraph for an essay.

- **Writer's workshop** Writers learn through their own experience, the teacher models a skill, students write independently while the teacher conferences with individuals on individual skills needs or the skill for that day, and students share with the class and get feedback.

Additional writing activities

- Students create relevant word lists, using words from current topics of study.

- Students write a letter to the author of a book that the class enjoys.

- Students use graphic organizers to organize ideas for a writing activity.

- Students sequence a story or ideas on a storyboard.

- Students create silly poems/raps about real-life situations.

- Students write new endings with detail and description. Small groups select the ending they feel is best. Groups share their best selected endings and the class chooses the best new ending.

Math activities

The following strategies and topics are ways to review some basic skills in relevant math classes when you don't have any substitute plans available. Choose the one that best fits the content of the course that you are subbing for:

- **Math poster** Students can be placed in small groups or work individually. Assign a chapter/concept that has been previously studied to each group or student. Students have a designated time to create a poster that explains the assigned skill with examples and vocabulary. Students then present to the class.

- **Math quiz** Students or small groups of students create a 10-question quiz and exchange the quizzes with other students or groups. Once the quiz is completed, it is graded by the original group/student.

- **Mini-math book** Students create a mini-book focused on lessons and concepts from the chapter. This would summarize the chapter and the most important concepts taught.

- **Vocabulary cards** Students create 10 vocabulary cards (index cards) with the word, definition, and an example on the front and two problems on the back. Students can switch cards with other students and attempt to solve the problems.

- **Student as teacher** Students design a lesson related to a current concept they are learning and are randomly selected to teach their lesson. They can close out their lesson with a quiz.

- **Real-world math** Students think of real-world scenarios that can be related to what they have studied this year or in previous years and write about it with examples. Students can then share with the class.

- **Math brain games** Have Sudoku or any other challenging math or logic puzzle on hand. These math activities not only challenge students in their mathematical thinking but offer a productive break from their current line of study. Students can also have the opportunity to create their own puzzles or Sudokus.

Social studies activities

The following strategies/activities are ways to incorporate several social studies topics that are relevant in the history classes you are subbing for, especially when you don't have any substitute plans available. Choose the one that best fits the content of the course that you are substituting for:

- **Research projects** Students may use printed materials from the school library for their research, or they may do their research online if they have access to a computer lab or classroom computers. Web quests are an excellent way to set up a unit of study. Posting predetermined websites that students can research with outcome expectations can assure that students are only researching on sites you have approved. http://zunal.com/ is a great website that can assist with developing web quest and has teacher made web quests across the curriculum that are available for use.

- **Historical figure time line** Have students study specific people's roles in the history of our country. Ask students to research the topic and select six to ten important events that show the role in US history of the person they chose to study. They should also include events related to the time period of the person they are studying.

If students fold the time line in half, they can cut flaps for the top layer, so that students can create an illustration on the outside with an explanation underneath. See pp. 216-218 for mini-book ideas.

◆ **Travel brochure** Have students create a travel brochure for the geographic area related to the event in history for which they are currently studying. You may choose to have them create their brochure for today's time or for a specific time in the past. Have students fold an 8½″ × 11″ sheet of white paper as a trifold brochure. The front cover will show the country's location on the world map (either an illustration or a picture from the Internet). On the inside of the brochure, have students include information about neighboring countries, the country's geography (including on which continent it is located), sources of income, cultures, languages, religion, education system, and the like. Require that students include at least six important aspects of life in this region, with a corresponding illustration or picture for each one. Students should be as creative as possible, using a lot of color to appeal to the traveler they are trying to persuade to visit that geographic area.

◆ **Propaganda/Informational poster (past or present)** Have students create a propaganda for an event in history for which they are currently studying or just give information about a topic. You may choose to have them create their poster for today's time or for a specific time in the past. Have students use a sheet of 11″ × 14″ construction paper (white or manila) to create a poster that features illustrations and pictures, with minimal text, as a way to persuade/provoke the viewer related to the event in history for which they are currently studying.

◆ **Time line** Have students show events from history over time by creating a time line from printer paper or construction paper. Students take a sheet of construction paper (11″ × 14″), fold it in half lengthwise, cut along the fold, then tape the two pieces together to create one sheet of paper approximately 28″ long. This enables students to fit at least eight events from the history they are researching on the time line. Students may work in pairs or small groups. If you do this as a whole-class project, you may assign an event to each student and have each student write about and illustrate their event; then the pages can be taped together in the correct order to create a detailed class time line. See pp. 216-218 for mini-book ideas.

◆ **Mobile** Have students create a mobile that features five important aspects of the related event to the event in history for which they are currently studying. You may choose to have them create their mobile for today's time or for a specific time in the past. Have students use five index cards (3″ × 5″) on which they write about a chosen aspect of the event in history for which they are currently studying on one side and illustrate it on the other. The index cards can be hung with string on a hanger, a sentence strip joined into a circle, or a heavy drinking straw. (Tip: Coffee shops that have extra-long straws for their drinks would likely donate them for you to use in the classroom; these work very well for mobiles.)

◆ **Historical figure/event poster** Have students create a poster that has illustrations and facts about a historical figure or an event or series of events they are studying. You can also assign different chapters to each student or a group of students. The idea here is to be creative and add as much information and as many illustrations as possible.

◆ **Historical figure/event mini-book** Have students select an event or an important historical figure and create a mini-book that tells about the event or the significant impact that the person had on history. They would include text and illustrations. See pp. 216–218 for mini-book ideas.

Science activities

The following suggested activities are ways to address several relevant science topics, especially if you have no substitute plans available to you.

◆ **Science poster** on a topic or chapter they have studied. Assign the same chapter or topic or several. Posters need to be drawn accurately and labeled. Small write-ups need to be added to explain any process or system in detail.

◆ **Science brochure** on a topic or chapter. This would be the same as the poster activity, but completed on a single page that has two folds that create three sections. Be specific about what is expected. For example:

   ◆ Cover, or title/illustration

   ◆ P. 1 Detailed description overview

   ◆ P. 2 Breakdown of steps, and so on

- **Persuasive letter** in support of an aspect of science that is or has been studied in the course. It could be something as relevant as a letter to a local, state, or federal politician about climate change.

- **Accordion book** use a page that you cut into two strips, tape together, and fold using a fanfold. This is a good method for steps or a process. Students can illustrate and add descriptions and labels. See pp. 216–218 for ideas.

- **Minilessons** Assign previous topics/chapters to students to review and then present to the whole class.

- **Mini-book** Create a mini-book about a scientist in the field and write about the scientist's discoveries, why these are significant, and how the scientist made those discoveries. The scientist can be fictitious, but the content of the science should be reflective of what is being studied. See pp. 216–218 for ideas.

- **Flash cards** Create a set of cards with vocabulary from the chapter. On the front, list the word and illustration, and on the back the formal definition. Students can share and quiz each other.

- **Lesson/Quiz** Students select a topic to present to the class and create a five-question quiz to give.

- **Rap/Poem** Students create a rap or poem about an area of study to share with the class.

Discussion activities

The following strategies are ways to address discussion in any of the subject areas.

Whip-around

Just like it sounds, the whip-around is a quick pass that allows all students to give a quick response to a question ultimately yielding a general sense of what the class is thinking about that question. This can be a great way to start a discussion on a topic, encourage student involvement, and get a pulse on what the class is thinking.

Steps:

1. Pose or post a question, idea, or quote that can elicit a quick response from students. What do you think about...,? Immigration is..., How do you feel about...? What words describe..., and so on.

2. Each student shares his or her quick response until all have shared. Keep in mind that these are short responses. Remind students to listen for reoccurring thoughts and ideas.

3. The teacher or a student shares with the class any ideas, thoughts, or Ah-ha's that were reoccurring as the class shared. You may want to record and post these to refer back to as you dive deeper into your discussion or unit of study.

Circle talk

Circle talks are just what the name says, a gathering of students in a large circle to discuss and share on designated topics. These discussions can be used from kindergarten through twelfth grade, and all students can benefit regardless of their age. Often students have no other means of sharing. A circle talk is a purposeful model to use in the classroom for encouraging dialogue, respect, and sharing ideas. It's an opportunity to develop a sense of community and a way of  communicating in the classroom. When everyone has their turn to be heard in a respectful and attentive way, the learning environment becomes more inclusive, accessible, and enjoyable.

Talking circles date back to First Nations leaders and their tribal councils. It was a process they developed to provide everyone with an opportunity to speak and be heard in a respectful manner.
(http://www.firstnationspedagogy.ca/circletalks.html#)

Why circle talks?
Circle talks provide a safe platform for all students to share and be heard.

What does it look like?
Students sit in a large circle or pull their desks/seats into a circle so everyone can be seen.

A topic is shared or a question asked. A designated object or talking stick is passed from one student to the next. When a student possesses the object, they have the floor to respectfully comment on what has been said or share their perspective.

What do you need?

Historically a "talking stick" was used, but a variety of objects could be used, keeping in mind not to use something that could be potentially distracting. A small stuffed animal, a stone, a ball, a pine cone, or a shell are just a few examples of objects to consider.

What else?

- The discussion is passed along the circle in a designated direction from person to person.
- Only the person who has the object speaks.
- A student doesn't have to respond and can take a pass.
- Students are encouraged to speak from the heart, openly and honestly.
- Everything discussed stays in the circle.
- If time permits, a second round around the circle can take place.

Circle talk steps

1. **Remind.** Remind students that they listen when others are speaking, they are respectful, they speak from the heart, and what is discussed in the circle stays in the circle.

2. **Introduce.** A student or the teacher can introduce the topic or question that will be shared to the whole group before responding. How would you describe..., How do you feel about..., What is your idea of..., I feel sad when..., and so on. Be mindful that sometimes students can become emotional as they share.

3. **Begin.** The talking object is passed to the next person for them to share, comment, or pass. Remind students to share, but be mindful of the time so everyone gets a chance.

4. **Share.** Each student with the object responds to the prompt with a comment or can share their perspective on what has been shared.

5. **Close.** Once everyone has had a turn, everyone is thanked and reminded that this was a safe space and what was shared stays in the circle.

Socratic method

Based on the approach of Socrates, the Socratic method is purposeful dialogue based on a text through thoughtful open-ended questions. Questions are used to answer yet other questions as students discuss ideas, determine misconceptions, and construct knowledge. It is not a debate but a civil, polite discussion for deeper understanding that is student driven.

Role of the teacher

Select a text (paragraph, page, chapter, etc.) for students to discuss.

Value student thinking and thought because this includes providing wait time for thought to occur.

Initially help drive discussion with probing, open-ended questions, but eventually limit participation as students lead discussion and redirect discussion back to topic if needed. Additionally, tying the discussion to real-world connections can be a way to better engage students.

Call for periodic summaries of what is being discussed.

Role of the student

Read and annotate text and prepare ideas.

Develop questions that are open-ended and thoughtful.

Lead discussion.

Actively participate, share with the group, and listen to others, encouraging all to participate and not to interrupt.

Discuss, not debate. It's not about being right, but about gaining a more in-depth understanding.

Use evidence from the text to support ideas.

Questions

Use open-ended questions to discuss, expand upon, or dive deeper into the selected text. Questions may ask one to describe, list, compare, and so on, all in an open-ended and thoughtful way. Students can generate these questions to drive the discussion. At times questions can help drive the conversation as well. Questions can clarify (What is your main point? Can you give me an example?) or dive deeper (What are you assuming? What connection can you make? What effect would this have?).

Some use a fishbowl set-up for the discussion. There is an inner and outer circle. The inner circle discusses, and the outer circle poses the questions. Sometimes a "hot seat" can be available in the inner circle for students from the outer circle to join in when they have something to contribute. They would share and return back to the outer circle.

Reflect

After the discussion, it is a good idea to reflect and discuss how it went. Having students be able to have civil, polite discussions is a huge takeaway from this seminar. Upon reflection, students can look at what worked well and what didn't. They can self-reflect on their participation, interesting points raised, and so on. This helps them develop the art of discussion.

Technology for secondary grades

Technology continues to be an ever growing part of our modern-day classroom experience. Depending on the school where you are subbing, you may or may not have access to technology. Most students do, however, have access to cell phones and thus hold a powerful educational tool in their hands. (Always check the school policy for cell phone usage in the classroom.) With thousands of educational apps available to us, we can speak the language of our twenty-first-century students. Technology can be a powerful part of a successful classroom. Technology can engage and empower students. If you have even just a couple of devices, you can add them into your curriculum, creating another powerful layer to your instructional delivery. Students can manage this aspect of their learning, often showing teachers how to navigate the latest technologies. **Monitoring your students is critical not only to keep them on task but to ensure that the lesson objective is accomplished.**

As part of STEAM (Science, Technology, Engineering, Art, Math), the technology piece has several objectives. It serves as a tool that can be used to research, design, and model solutions to the problems students are exploring. It also serves as an excellent tool for the dissemination of information on multiple platforms. Additionally, technology itself requires an in-depth understanding and design. Coding, some argue, is as important as reading. Our students need not only to be able to use technology responsibly but also to know how to program technology to meet their needs.

This is perhaps one of the easiest components of STEAM because it is so engaging for students from all backgrounds and ability levels. There are numerous ways to use technology in conjunction with traditional instructional methodologies. With that said, the T (technology) can support all the other areas in the STEAM acronym.

Listed are a few:

Technology as a support

Consider using technology in the following ways as a substitute teacher:

Research—General research. Check out online resources from libraries, museums, universities, educational sites, and so on.

Skill reinforcement—using apps and websites. There are numerous sites that support learning in creative ways. Engaging students in games that reinforce specific skills can really support what you are doing in the classroom.

Frontloading/Flipping the classroom—using videos and apps. Using these resources—such as Show Me, which allows you to film your lessons—can prepare students for the next day's lesson. Students can arrive with an idea of what will be covered and any questions they may have regarding it.

Building Technology

Coding—the language of the twenty-first century

Students need to understand not only how to use technology but also how to build technology. There are numerous apps and websites dedicated to coding. Coding involves programing the computer to complete tasks. Students learn this best through play. Apps allow them to create simple projects and games that they "code" what to do. This can lay the foundation for more intensive coding as they become more skilled and crosses them over into actual coding. Exposure to this is a twenty-first-century skill should be provided to all students.

Students with this skill will have an advantage as they move forward in their education and then on toward their career. Therefore, numerous apps and websites are focused and committed to ensuring that students will be ready to meet the challenges of the twenty-first century. BOTH girls and boys can benefit from a deeper understanding of coding. Starting as young as kindergarten, students can learn coding just as they learn reading and counting. Listed here are a few of the websites that can be used to introduce and inspire young coders to help ensure that they have the foundation for this important twenty-first-century skill.

Websites

Here are a few suggested websites to get started. Search for more and have students try them out. Find what works for you and them.

    https://code.org/
    https://studio.code.org/
    https://www.allcancode.com/
    https://world.kano.me/
    https://www.thinkfun.com/
    https://scratch.mit.edu/
    https://hourofcode.com/
    https://www.tynker.com/hour-of-code/
    https://code.org/minecraft
    https://www.kodable.com/hour-of-code

Apps

Here are a few apps to get started. Search for more and have students try them out.

    LightBot
    SpriteBox: Code Hour
    Hopscotch: Coding for kids
    Daisy the Dinosaur
    Cargo Bot
    codeSpark Academy
    Mozilla Thimble

Suggested books for secondary grades

Bruchac, Joseph. *Our Stories Remember: American Indian History, Culture, and Values through Storytelling.* Age 16 and older

Cofer, Judith Ortiz. *An Island Like You: Stories of the Barrio.* Age 12–16

Dimaline, Cherie. *The Marrow Thieves.* Age 12 and older

Engle, Margarita. *The Surrender Tree: Poems of Cuba's Struggle for Freedom.* Age 12 and older

Flake, Sharon. *Money Hungry.* Age 12–16

Gansworth, Eric. *If I Ever Get Out of Here.* Age 11 and older

Hamilton, Virginia. *Sweet Whispers, Brother Rush.* Age 11 and older

Jaramillo, Ann. *La Línea.* Age 13 and older

Jiang, Ji-Li. *Red Scarf Girl: A Memoir of the Cultural Revolution.* Age 12 and older

Jiménez, Francisco. *The Circuit: Stories from the Life of a Migrant Child.* Age 12 and older

Johnson, Angela. *The First Part Last.* Age 13–18

Kadohata, Cynthia. *Kira-Kira.* Age 10–14

Magoon, Kekla. *How It Went Down.* Age 14 and older

Myers, Walter Dean. *Monster.* Age 13 and older

Na, An. *A Step From Heaven.* Age 13 and older

Nelson, Marilyn. *A Wreath for Emmett Till.* Age 14 and older

Nelson, Vaunda Micheaux. *No Crystal Stair.* Age 12 and older

Nelson, Kadir. *Heart and Soul: The Story of America and African Americans.* Age 8–14

Park, Linda Sue. *When My Name Was Keoko: A Novel of Korea in World War II.* Age 11–14

Quintero, Isabel. *Gabi: A Girl in Pieces.* Age 14 and older

Reynolds, Jason. *When I Was the Greatest.* Age 13 and older

Reynolds, Jason and Brendan Kiely. *All American Boys.* Age 13 and older

Sáenz, Benjamin Alire. *Aristotle and Dante Discover the Secrets of the Universe.* Age 14 and older

Say, Allen. *Drawing from Memory.* Age 10 and older

Sheth, Kashmira. *Koyal Dark, Mango Sweet.* Age 12 and older

Stork, Francisco X. *The Last Summer of the Death Warriors.* Age 14 and older

Tingle, Tim. *House of Purple Cedar.* Age 14 and older

Woodson, Jacqueline. *Brown Girl Dreaming.* Age 10 and older

Yang, Gene Luen. *American Born Chinese.* Age 13 and older

chapter 11
Professionalism

Substitute teachers have often been treated as glorified babysitters. In fact, most substitute teachers are credentialed, and many of them have quite a bit of experience as displaced, full-time classroom teachers, as retired teachers, or as long-term teaching assistants. Many substitute teachers are hired full-time at a school where they have been subbing.

Each day that you substitute teach is, in essence, an interview, and you must be professional in every particular—from introducing yourself to the office staff, administrators, colleagues, students, and parents, to cleaning the classroom at the end of the day.

Being professional

Following are recommendations for maintaining a professional attitude and demeanor.

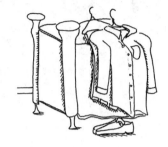

◆ **Be organized** To avoid rushing around in the morning, arrange your clothes the night before. You may even want to keep an extra set of clothes and shoes in your car—in the event of a field trip to the zoo or a cold classroom. Be sure to dress in layers.

◆ **Arrive early** Arrive early in order to orient yourself to the classroom and to the lesson plans, as well as to give yourself preparation time in case lesson plans haven't been left for you. This is especially important if you've never been in a particular school or classroom.

◆ **Be personable** Get to know the office staff and treat them respectfully. Don't be afraid to ask them for help; they are your lifeline at school. Helpful staff members include secretaries; support staff; plant managers and custodial staff; classroom aides; school nurses, physiologists, and counselors; yard supervision staff; and cafeteria staff.

◆ **Be a good neighbor** Introduce yourself to neighboring classroom teachers. They are excellent resources and are generally very helpful, and if you make a good impression on them, they may recommend that you be called to substitute teach in the future.

◆ **Meet the principal** Introduce yourself to the principal, who usually appreciates knowing who is on campus and who is teaching the students.

◆ **Know the schedule** Know the bell schedule. It's important to be on time for recess, lunch, and assemblies.

DAILY SCH
8:00 Morning Assembly
8:05 Role
8:10 Morning Warm-Up
8:30 Language Arts
9:30 Computer Lab
10:15 Recess
10:35 Writing

- **Be available** Be prepared to work on Mondays and Fridays. Since teachers occasionally take three-day weekends, you will undoubtedly get a wake-up call on these days.

Dos and Don'ts

Common sense is at the core of many of the following suggestions.

Dos

- Prepare for substitute teaching the night before; include the following items in your preparation.

  - Information about the school, including the telephone number
  - Directions to the school
  - Clothes
  - Substitute teacher's survival kit
  - Grade-appropriate picture books
  - Snack and bottled water or other drink
  - Cards or flyers containing your contact information

  The **Daily Checklist** template is a useful preparation tool.

12
Daily Checklist

- Become familiar with the rules of the school and classroom before the day begins. Most schools have the same basic rules and management systems. Familiarize yourself with a specific school by asking a neighboring teacher about school-specific policies and programs (for example, lockdown codes/policies and procedures for students who are ill).

- Write your name and the day's agenda on the board, so that students know who you are and what will be expected of them.

- Follow the lesson plans that have been left for you. If no plans have been left or if there is extra time in the schedule, you must be resourceful.

- Have a "Must Do" activity posted for students as soon as they enter the classroom in the morning, after recess, and after lunch. The list may include the following.

  - Silent reading
  - Finishing an assignment
  - Solving a word problem
  - Brainstorming a topic
  - Journaling
  - Reading assigned pages of text
  - Writing a letter, for example, to the teacher or a friend
  - Summarizing what was learned earlier

- Speak in a quiet voice to get students' attention; they must quiet down in order to hear you. Speaking quietly demonstrates control and has a calming effect.

- Reinforce appropriate behavior throughout the day. Focus on what is right with a lesson or student, not on what is wrong.

06
Classroom
Log
32
Out-of-My-
Seat Log

- Use a sign-out system for restroom and water breaks during class; the **Classroom Log** and **Out-of-My-Seat Log** templates serve this purpose well. While some students have medical issues that warrant leaving the classroom at unscheduled times, others may try to abuse the system. If you suspect the latter, check with a neighboring teacher.

- Call the office or a neighboring teacher if an emergency occurs. Ask the office staff about emergency procedures, and familiarize yourself with the exit strategy in the event of a fire, earthquake, or other emergency.

- Eat your lunch in the staff lounge in order to network with and obtain assistance from other teachers. Don't become involved in negative gossip or in school dynamics unless it directly affects you; stay neutral and polite.

- Grade assignments that you give, if possible. This reduces stress on the regular classroom teacher when he or she returns. If time doesn't permit you to grade assignments, clip them together and attach the answer key.

- Clean up the classroom, preferably with students' help, and leave a note for the classroom teacher about how the school day went. A clean room may be the teacher's first impression of your worth as a substitute teacher; this may lead to your being called to sub in the future. Your note should be positive and upbeat and should focus on what worked. You may use the **Student Behavior Tracker** template and the **Substitute Teacher Feedback Note** templates for this purpose.

Don'ts

47
Student
Behavior
Tracker
50
Substitute
Teacher
Feedback
Note 1
51
Substitute
Teacher
Feedback
Note 2

- Don't arrive late, and don't leave school immediately after students are dismissed. Tidy the classroom, grade assignments, leave a note for the regular teacher, and, if time allows, visit with other teachers.

- Don't forget to introduce yourself and explain what the class will be working on. Present yourself as a professional teacher.

- Don't waste time at the beginning of the school day—be ready to go. In the first five minutes, set the tone for the day and let students know what to expect.

- Don't disregard lesson plans that are left for you. It is important to conform to the regular classroom teacher's instructional goals and to give students continuity.

- Don't expect students to accurately explain school and classroom rules to you. As a substitute teacher unfamiliar with rules, you are vulnerable to their attempts to mislead.

- Don't focus only on incorrect responses and inappropriate behavior. Maintain a positive outlook as much as possible, and be sure to give compliments for work well done.

- Don't yell at students or talk over them to get their attention. Doing so may backfire and lead to a loss of control, and it may give students and others a bad impression.

- Don't allow students to abuse restroom and water privileges. Establish a policy and be consistent.

- Don't leave students unattended under any circumstances. You are legally responsible for them.

- *Never* be alone with a student behind closed doors.

- Don't use student restrooms. Enter only if you are managing a behavior situation and there are several students present. If possible, ask a yard supervisor or classroom aide to accompany you.

- Don't isolate yourself from the rest of the faculty. If they are acquainted with you and your abilities, they are more likely to request you as a substitute teacher in the future.

- Don't assign homework that the regular classroom teacher hasn't seen and approved. Homework should be a quick review of what was covered in class. Assigning too much homework could cause a backlash in calls to the office and teacher. A safe guide to the amount of homework to be assigned is 10 minutes per grade level.
  - Kindergarten   10 minutes
  - First grade   20 minutes
  - Second grade   30 minutes
  - Third grade   40 minutes
  - Fourth grade   50 minutes
  - Fifth grade   60 minutes
  - Sixth grade   70 minutes

- Don't leave the classroom in a mess. The classroom is a snapshot of you as a teacher; a clean classroom is a simple way to impress the classroom teacher.

The day's agenda, step-by-step

Once you have obtained the classroom keys from the office and have located the regular classroom teacher's lesson plans, seating chart, and notes to you, it is helpful to follow a set procedure in preparing for the school day and delivering instruction.

1. Walk around the classroom, noting whether there are name tags on the desks. Their presence will help you take attendance and call on students individually. Learn a few names right away, especially if the regular classroom teacher has provided a list of helpers. If there is no seating chart, sketch the desk layout, which can be completed during attendance and used throughout the day. Students can create their own name tags by using the **Desk Name Tag** template.

13
Desk
Name Tag

2. Review the teacher's lesson plans. If you have questions or need clarification, ask another teacher in the same grade/subject area for help. Write the day's agenda on the board, with an empty box in front of each item and the item's allotted time. Incorporate the agenda in a reward system by calling on a student to check off each item as it is completed. You may use the **Agenda Checklist** template for this purpose.

01
Agenda
Checklist

3. Organize required materials for the entire day, and place them on a table for easy access.

4. Post a "Must Do" activity on the board. Once students have hung up their backpacks, they will know exactly what to do. The activity, which should be related to material you'll be teaching after students have settled in, will keep them busy while you take attendance.

5. Walk to the student lines and locate your class before the opening bell. Welcome the students while they are in line, even though you will introduce yourself formally in the classroom.

6. Once in the classroom, tell students that they have three minutes to put their personal items away and get started on the "Must Do" activity.

7. Introduce yourself. Discuss rules and consequences, the daily agenda, and what you expect of them throughout the day.

8. While students are working on the "Must Do" activity, take attendance and lunch count, and complete other administrative tasks.

9. Review the results of the "Must Do" activity with the students. Have two to four volunteers share with the rest of the class.

10. Begin the morning's instruction according to the teacher's lesson plans.

11. At recess or break, give yourself a break too. After walking students to the playground or nutrition area, have a snack, use the restroom, and proceed to the teachers' lounge. A few minutes of downtime allows you to regroup and prepare for the next part of your day. Return to the classroom five minutes before the bell rings and post the next "Must Do" activity. If math is taught immediately after recess, the activity should be related to what students learned the day before or a preview of what you'll be teaching shortly.

12. Bring the students into the classroom and get them involved in the "Must Do" activity right away. Start the next lesson after the "Must Do" responses have been shared.

13. Take or send students to the nutrition area for lunch. Prepare for the afternoon's agenda by making sure all required materials are at hand.

14. Bring the students into the classroom and complete the afternoon's lessons. Allow time at the end of the day for students to complete notes to the teacher, fill out evaluation forms, and collect their backpacks. Hand out notes for students to take home.

15. Dismiss students in an orderly fashion. To incorporate interest and fun in dismissal, students may leave the classroom as they

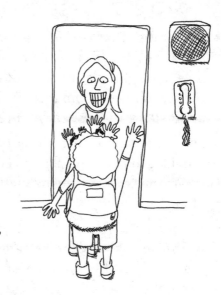

- Answer a content-related question correctly
- Identify a current technology app
- Identify current video game titles
- Play I Spy
- Play Twenty Questions

You may also dismiss students by birth month, colors they are wearing, and so on.

Getting called to substitute teach

A substitute teacher may teach every day of every week, one or two days a week, or in long-term assignments of more than one week. To be called, you must make yourself known to administrators and to other teachers.

- Always pack a lunch and eat in the teacher's lounge, if permitted. Networking is essential.

- Order or create business cards that include your name, photograph, substitute number, and contact information. Consider creating flyers to be placed in teacher mailboxes.

- Order pencils or pens with your name and phone number.

- Be available on hard-to-fill days like Mondays and Fridays, as well as for multiple-day assignments.

Tips for a successful day

- **Be resourceful** As a substitute teacher, you will have to improvise and make decisions on the spur of the moment. Teachers are not perfect, and not all lesson plans make sense or are complete. The regular classroom teacher may give an assignment, but fail to provide the materials to complete it. In this case, you must be resourceful. Since students know the classroom and the teacher, they can often help find the missing materials.

- **Remember that you're the boss** Even though students can be helpful, it's important not to allow them to tell you how to run the classroom. You may not run it exactly as the regular classroom teacher does, but students should understand and respect your teaching style and methods.

- **Set expectations** If the classroom teacher hasn't provided a discipline plan, make sure that students know what you expect of them; tell them the consequences of misbehavior.

- **Be aware** As you start the day, observe the students; you will quickly recognize potential troublemakers. Once they are identified, you can ask them to help, pay them a compliment, or use proximity to ward off misbehavior. Establish your presence and indicate that you are aware and ready to handle potential problems.

- **Know names** Pay attention while you take attendance. Look at students' faces as they raise their hands. Students respect a teacher who attempts to learn their names, and you have more authority with misbehaving students when you can call them by name rather than saying, "You in the blue shirt, pay attention." It is helpful to use name tags or to create a seating chart as you take attendance.

- **Be organized** Students know when you are not prepared. Have materials ready for each lesson, and have backup activities to fill extra time.

- **Be professional** Conduct yourself with respect and others will respect you as well. If you have long hair, consider pulling it back. Cover tattoos and remove nose and lip jewelry, if possible. Maintain a professional appearance, and wear appropriate, functional clothing. Arrive on time and conduct yourself as a professional: You are representing the school for the day.

School and office culture

You may work for a school district that has 20 elementary schools, five middle schools, and four high schools—you could sub for a full year and still not teach at every school. Or you could have a long-term substitute teaching assignment at a rural elementary school. Certain details are the same from one school to the next, no matter what their location or size.

Parking

Some schools provide parking spaces for teachers; if yours doesn't, you may have to park on the street. (Be sure to check for restricted parking areas.) If possible, call the school office in advance for advice on parking.

Logistics

Most schools are very welcoming: The principal wants to meet you, and someone will walk you to your classroom. At other schools, you walk into the office, are handed the classroom keys, and are pointed in the right direction. Don't take this personally: Many schools are hectic, busy places and don't have the time or personnel for a proper orientation. If this happens, seek out another teacher or a staff member to help you get your bearings. It is important to know the location of the following important offices in a school (in addition to your classroom).

- The principal's office
- The copy room
- The mailroom
- The adult restroom
- The teacher's lounge
- The nutrition area

Some schools give you a map of the campus and highlight the easiest route to the classroom, as well as important facilities. Keep these maps in a folder for schools where you teach, along with information like phone numbers and directions to each school (see "School log" below).

Scheduling

Confirm schedule changes caused by assemblies, emergency drills, school maintenance, inclement weather, or special events like parent conferences and staff development meetings.

Restroom use

Most schools require you to use adult restrooms instead of student restrooms. Even if a school doesn't have such a rule, you should *never* use a student restroom.

Lunch

Some schools require that you eat lunch with your students; at others, you may be asked to eat lunch in the classroom or teacher's lounge. Contact the office for the school's lunch policy.

Growth and sharing

Beginning substitute teachers often believe that they have to take every job offered—in order to pay the bills and continue to be asked. However, once you have established yourself at a few schools and teachers have gotten to know you, you will have more freedom to choose where and for whom you sub. In fact, once you establish yourself as a trustworthy substitute teacher, you will start getting requests.

Choice of assignment

Don't accept a substitute teaching job at a school or for a regular classroom teacher if it will involve a difficult situation that you aren't prepared to handle. Accepting such a job would be unfair to the teacher, unfair to the students, and stressful for you.

School log

39
School Information Card
49
Substitute Teacher Assignment Log
52
Substitute Teacher Job Log
53
Substitute Teacher Travel Log

Keep a file with information about the schools and teachers that you enjoy working for. Create a folder for each school, and use the **School Information Card**, the **Substitute Teacher Assignment Log**, the **Substitute Teacher Job Log**, and the **Substitute Teacher Travel Log** templates to note important information about each school. This will help you remember if you enjoyed the job or not. Add the following information to each folder.

- School name
- Principal's name
- Names of office manager/staff
- Date
- Beginning time
- Dismissal time
- School address and directions
- Teacher's name
- Room number
- Grade level/subject area
- Names of helpful students
- Lesson plan notes
- Additional notes

Self-evaluation

As a substitute teacher, you may find it easy to teach assigned classes, follow the lesson plans provided for you, keep students as organized and calm as possible, clean the classroom, and leave with no other thought but where you will sub the next day. However, this attitude won't help you get asked again by the classroom teacher you subbed for or by other teachers at the school, and it won't ensure that school principals will remember you.

In order to improve your substitute teaching, it is important that you reflect on each day you teach. Consider the following.

- ◆ Your actual teaching practice
- ◆ Your communication with students
- ◆ Your attention to the agenda and lesson plans
- ◆ How well you maintained classroom control and discipline

You may want to respond to the following questions in an electronic journal, in a written journal, or on the **Teacher Self-Evaluation Form** template.

59
Teacher
Self-
Evaluation
Form

Classroom environment

- ◆ Did I leave the classroom as neat and clean as it was when I arrived?
- ◆ Was all the furniture in its proper location?
- ◆ Were student and teacher materials returned to the point of access?
- ◆ Did I leave all student work organized and clearly labeled? Did I grade as much student work as I could?

Curriculum

- ◆ Did I review each of the lesson activities and teacher's manuals before teaching the concepts?
- ◆ Did I model hands-on experiences in a way that all students could understand?
- ◆ Did students have access to required materials?
- ◆ Did I use assigned manipulatives correctly?
- ◆ Did I meet the needs of all learners (for example, English Language Development (E.L.D) students, gifted students, and students with multiple modalities)?
- ◆ Did I encourage student participation throughout the day?
- ◆ Did I motivate students to be part of the learning process?
- ◆ Did I provide opportunities for student interactions, pair work, and small groups?

- Did I deliver instruction with ease and conviction?
- Did I make my expectations clear?
- Did I achieve the learning goals?

Daily schedule

- Did I post and review the daily agenda with the students?
- Did I answer students' questions?
- Did I stick to the agenda?
- Did I adjust the schedule based on students' response to my teaching?
- Were my pacing and timing effective for maximum comprehension?
- Did I manage my time efficiently?

Interactions with students

- Did I speak with each student and small group?
- Did I review rules and consequences with students? Did I adhere to the rules and consequences throughout the day?
- Did I encourage students and give them positive feedback throughout the day?
- Did I manage the discipline plan effectively?
- Did I listen to students' needs?
- Did I circulate in the classroom and interact well with students?

You are a professional teacher undertaking one of the most difficult challenges in the field of education: substitute teaching. Maintaining your professionalism is the key to your success—with faculty, staff, students, and parents. A good substitute teacher provides uninterrupted, well-delivered instruction in the regular classroom teacher's absence.

chapter 12

Extra activities and fillers

In this chapter, you will find extra activities and fillers that involve several curricular areas—writing, geography, art, physical education, and health. Many of these will help you fill 10 to 15 minutes of unstructured time in the classroom with an activity that's fun for the students, but still challenges them academically. And most of the activities included in this chapter can be tweaked to fit multiple grade levels.

Sponge activities

Sponge activities are an excellent and productive way to make use of downtime. What do you do in those 10- to 15-minute gaps in the school day before a transition (such as before lunch or recess) or at the end of the day before dismissal? They can easily be filled with a quick academic activity—if you're ready with one. Sponge activities challenge students to think in a fresh, "out of the box" way that is fun and purposeful. You can use sponge activities with individual students, or with pairs, small groups, by row, or as a whole class. Challenge students by setting a time limit, or have students compete in a friendly way by setting up teams. Following are suggestions for sponge activities that can be used for lower grades and others that are more appropriate for upper grades. Just make sure you choose an activity that's appropriate for the grade level you're subbing for, and you'll be fine.

Lower grades

- Students tell two playground rules.
- Students put spelling words in alphabetical order.
- Students draw something that is only drawn with circles (or squares, triangles, or some other shape).
- Students name animals that live in the jungle, on a farm, in the mountains, in water, and so on.

- Students give names of fruits, vegetables, meats, or other foods.
- Students list things you can touch, things you can smell, big things, small things, and so on.
- Students think of a number and write it down—and then draw a face from it.
- Say a number, day of the week, or month, and ask a student to say what comes next.
- Have the name of a color on the board and have students draw something that color.
- Write a long word on the board and have students make a list of words using letters from that word.

Upper grades

- Students make up three names for rock groups.
- Students name as many kinds of natural disasters as they can.

- Students name as many gems or precious stones as they can.
- Students list as many states as they can.
- Students write as many abbreviations as possible for
  - Roman numerals
  - Trademarks
  - Proper names of people
  - Proper names of places

- Students name as many countries and capitals as they can.
- Students name as many current technology apps as they can.
- Students list five current video games.
- Students list one manufactured item for each letter of the alphabet.
- Students list the mountain ranges in the United States.
- Students list one proper noun for each letter of the alphabet.
- Students list as many presidents of the United States as they can.
- Students name as many countries in the world as they can.
- Students write as many homonyms as they can. (EXAMPLE: past/passed)
- Students name as many types of dogs as they can.

Writing activities

The following ideas for writing activities can be modified to work with different grade levels.

Story starters

The first thing in the morning, you need to be tending to administrative duties such as taking attendance, collecting homework, getting familiar with the seating chart, and the like. So what do you do when students (grades 1–6) walk into the classroom? Have a story starter written on the board, so students have something to do right away. Story starters are a simple, fun, and creative way to get the students geared up and ready to begin the day. Story starters are a perfect "Must Do" activity. They also work well when you need to get students' heads back into academic thinking after they come in from recess or lunch. Story starters engage students' creative writing aspect. After about ten or fifteen minutes (or longer, depending on their engagement), you may ask three to five students to share their stories before moving on to the curriculum routine.

The following story starters include silly, imaginative, deep-thinking, and relatively simple ways to get students excited about writing. Encourage them to have fun writing these stories, even if the stories don't make sense in the real world.

- Imagine you are a dolphin. What do you look like? What do you do all day? What interesting things do you see? What worries you? What makes you happy? Use your answers to write a story.

- The rain fell from the sky right after the lightning brightened the sky and the thunder blasted, and when the electricity went out, my best friend and I . . .

- I woke up this morning and realized that I was five inches tall. Why did this happen? What will I do?

- My family took a safari tour of Africa. I felt something behind me coming from the jungle. When I went to yell, out of the trees came . . .

- I dreamed I was stuck in a video game. I had a blast . . .

- I woke up this morning and heard on the news that school was canceled. I . . .

- Have you ever seen an anaconda? It . . .

- My best friend and I were playing in an empty lot. We came across two large barrels with the words DANGER on them. We . . .

- My little brothers and sisters are terrified of ghosts. When a storm knocked out the phone lines and we had to go to the haunted house up the street, they . . .

- If you could "cook up" a perfect day, what would the ingredients be, and what steps for mixing and cooking the recipe would you include? Use the terms *cups, teaspoons, tablespoons, pinch, bowl, stir, pour,* and *bake.*

- I was home alone watching a funny movie on TV when the electricity suddenly went out. That was followed by a scream, and then the telephone rang. I . . .

- I received money to develop a new gadget. I bought springs, a coil of wire, rubber stoppers, and . . .

- The new classroom snake escaped from his cage during math time. It . . .

- Last night my friends and I dug up a time capsule by mistake. We opened it and found . . .

- My dad bought my mom a huge diamond ring for her birthday. When she was in the shower one day, I tried it on. I guess I shouldn't have done that over the sink, because . . .

- Dear Mr. President, I don't understand . . . (Be specific.)

- Dear Principal _____, the school year should be one month shorter, because . . .

- I was startled by the booming sound heard throughout the neighborhood. I woke up in the middle of the night and realized we were in the middle of a . . .

- I was so scared when the biggest tree in the park started talking to me. It said . . .

- Looking at the view from the window of the castle . . .

- If I won the lottery . . .

- Yesterday was a no-good, very bad day. I . . .

- My favorite TV show sucked me right out of the couch and into the script. I . . .

- If I were the teacher for the day . . .

Mini-books

A mini-book activity can enhance a lesson plan for most curricular areas, whether it's one that has been left for you or one you are planning on your own. Adding a creative element can make a big difference. These ideas will motivate and help meet the needs of all learners.

Single sheet mini-book

Using a single sheet of paper, students can fold a simple eight-page mini-book that they can use to take notes, summarize the key points of a lesson, or write a story.

1. Start with a single sheet of 8½″ × 11″ paper, and follow the diagram.
2. Fold the sheet of paper three times, folding it in half each time.
3. Open the paper, then re-fold it crosswise as shown, and cut along the folded edge to the middle point.
4. Open it fully, then fold it lengthwise.
5. Push the ends together to form an eight-page mini-book.
6. Press hard on all the creases to help the paper hold its book shape.

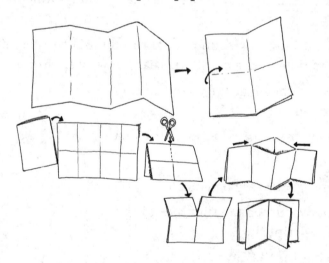

You may have students use mini-books to review a lesson; if so, you may specify that certain information from a unit should be on each page, so students have it in an easy-to-review format for later. Students can write and illustrate their own mini-books. Encourage them to be creative.

Flip book

Flip books are a good way to add creativity to a lesson. Students can use flip books to break down major components of a lesson, analyze a writing piece or a story they have read (plot, setting, characters, problem or conflict, resolution or solution), or simply take notes.

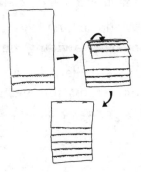

1. Start with three sheets of 8½″ × 11″ paper.
2. Stagger the sheets, with about half an inch between the edge of one sheet to the edge of the next, as shown.
3. Fold over the top, leaving about half an inch between the two edges of the paper that now overlap.
4. Staple along the top folded edge.

Accordion book

Accordion books are good to use for time lines, sequencing of events, and even stories. They can be made as long as they need to be.

1. Start with a sheet of 8½″ × 11″ paper, and cut it in half lengthwise.
2. Tape the short ends together, as shown.
3. Repeat with additional sheets of paper if a longer accordion book is needed.
4. Fold the paper back and forth like a fan, from one end to the other, as shown.

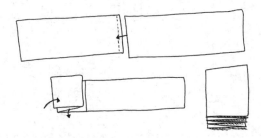

Tri-fold brochure

A tri-fold brochure is a fun and creative way to extend a lesson. Have students create a travel brochure or a sales pamphlet about a unit of study to motivate them and give them an opportunity to think outside the box.

1. Start with a single sheet of 8½″ × 11″ paper.
2. With the long edge at the top, fold both sides toward the center until they overlap, dividing the paper into thirds.
3. Have students create a cover on the first panel, and then tell them what sections or information they must include in their brochure.
4. Students may illustrate their brochure throughout.

Eight-box fold

Folding a sheet of 8½″ × 11″ paper three times will divide it into eight boxes when opened. This grid of eight boxes can be used for a variety of activities: math problems, spelling words, sequence of events, vocabulary words, and the like.

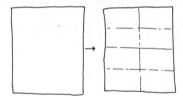

Flip-up mini-book

A flip-up mini-book is a fun way for students to study and review problems for which an answer can be hidden and then revealed. Math story problems, vocabulary, events of a story (beginning, middle, end), scientific process, life cycles, and the like are all ways students can use a flip-up mini-book. On the top, students can illustrate or write a problem; underneath, they can write an explanation or solution.

1. Start with a single sheet of 8½″ × 11″ paper.
2. Fold the paper in half lengthwise.
3. Determine how many flip-up sections are needed, and mark them for cutting.
4. Cut to the fold, as shown, to create the flip-up sections.

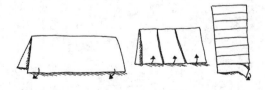

Geography activities

Geography can easily be adapted to many curricular areas, and one of the easiest ways to incorporate geography in simple and interesting ways is through mapping. Whenever you discuss space in the classroom; at the school; or within the community, the city, the state, the country, or the world, you are teaching students about geography. Because it involves different regions and cultures, geography can be exciting to study. The following ideas can be tweaked to engage students at several grade levels.

Maps

Trace maps

Have an assortment of state and world maps, tracing paper, and colored pencils. You may also want to use the blank **United States Map** and **World Map** templates. These materials can be used for a variety of activities.

- Trace and label the countries and oceans of the world map.
- Trace and label the state map, noting big cities, lakes, mountain ranges, and the like.
- Teach direction: north, south, east, and west.

60
United States Map
63
World Map

Location, location, location

Finding locations on a map adds a new perspective to lessons that students are studying throughout the curriculum. Adapt the following activities to what students are currently studying in social studies.

- Locate specific places, buildings, historic sites, and the like on a map.
- Identify where particular wars or battles took place.
- Locate historic landmarks, for example, each of the missions on a map of California.
- Locate important routes, for example, stops along the westward expansion.

- Locate important geographic sites, for example, the Wonders of the World.
- Identify where national symbols are located, for example, the Liberty Bell, the White House, and the Empire State Building.
- Locate places with a personal connection, for example, the location of the student's house, school, city, state, country, and continent. This project can be tweaked for many different contexts.

- Find popular local places such as the mall, local restaurants, and the like, using a local street map.

- Estimate distances, using the key on the map. Ask students questions like "How far is it from the school to the mall?"

- Write out directions from the school to other locations, for example, "First turn right onto Main. Travel .5 miles to Maple, and turn left onto Maple."

Map the class

Have students draw a picture of their classroom, including the north wall, south wall, east wall, and west wall. Have them include other items they can identify and place on the map. They can incorporate direction (using a compass rose) and a legend or key. Teach students that symbols are used to represent specific items on maps. For homework, students may draw and label a map of their own room or home.

Map the school

1. Take students on a walking field trip within the school campus. Note the main offices, classrooms, auditorium, gymnasium, playground, lunch room or cafeteria, bathrooms, staircases, elevators, computer lab, library, and any other significant space. Have them take sketch paper with them so that as they walk from place to place, they can sketch what they would see if they were floating above each location.

2. When back in the classroom, tape a large sheet of paper across the board and have students help you identify all the areas they noted on their sketches. Label index cards, representing buildings or areas, with the name of a building or space, and tape them to the appropriate part of the paper. After you have created a class map, have students create their own map in more detail, using their sketch and the chart paper as a reference guide. Students can use plain paper or graph paper for their own maps. They may create a key or legend to go with their map.

3. As follow-up, students may share their maps. Students may return to the yard to check their maps for accuracy.

4. Have students take turns giving directions using the large map. Ask them questions like "How do I get to the office from the classroom?"

Art activities

Hands-on art is a great way to fill time during the school day. You can connect every curricular area—from stories to history to topics in other subject areas—with art. Art projects may use coloring, painting, cutting, or gluing, or they may incorporate dance, music, or role-play. Following are several ideas for incorporating art into the school day.

Include basic art supplies in your personal survival kit to make sure that you have enough materials with you. Items such as crayons, water colors, paintbrushes, construction paper, glue, scissors, and the like are helpful additions to your survival kit. Often these supplies are found in the classroom, but don't overstep by using a teacher's supplies. Always leave things the way you found them.

Many teachers think that if they can't draw, then they can't teach art. Don't fall into this trap. All you need are some basic art materials, motivation, and a lot of enthusiasm. Even if you can't draw a straight line, armed with the following art activities that can easily be incorporated into the curriculum, you can teach art!

Color wheel

One of the fundamental aspects of art is color. Students learn as early as kindergarten how to mix colors in order to create new ones. There are three primary colors, three secondary colors, and six intermediate colors. There are cool colors and warm colors.

One of the best ways to teach color is with a color wheel. Use the **Color Wheel** template for creating a color wheel, or use a paper plate divided into sections.

08
Color Wheel

- Primary colors: red, blue, yellow
- Secondary colors: violet, orange, green
- Intermediate colors: red-orange, red-violet, blue-violet, blue-green, yellow-green, yellow-orange
- Cool colors: blue, violet, green
- Warm colors: red, orange, yellow
- Complementary colors (opposite sides of the color wheel): red and green, blue and orange, yellow and violet

Collage

A collage can be created in many different ways, using a variety of materials. When making a collage, there are no rules other than sticking to your theme. Many different materials can be used for a collage, such as pictures, magazines, newspapers, and decorative papers like wallpaper and wrapping paper. If you have access to tempera paint, magazines, scissors, pens, pencils, sponges, paper, brushes, and glue, you can have students of any age create a topic-related collage to express what they have learned or are learning.

1. **Prepare collage paper.** Have students prepare the paper that will be used for the collage. If you have access to paint, have students cover a heavy quality paper with several colors of paint. Let the paint dry completely before going to the next step. If you do not have access to paint, have students use colored construction paper. This paper will be the background for the collage.

2. **Cut shapes and pictures.** Students should know what their theme is and have a plan for what their collage will look like when finished. Have them lightly sketch out shapes that fit with the theme for their collage. Then have students cut or tear out the shapes that they are planning to use. If students are not creating a collage out of cut or torn paper, they can use pictures from magazines, newspapers, and the like, as long as the pictures are related to the topic or theme they are studying.

3. **Arrange.** After cutting the shapes or pictures for the collage, have students glue them to the background paper to create their collage.

4. **Reflect and share.** Let the collage dry completely. When the work is dry, students can share their work with the class, write stories about their collage, and so on.

Mobiles

Making a mobile is a multistep project that can be accomplished in one day or over several days. The mobile project can be related to a story, a theme, or a content standard. Mobiles can take many different forms. They are appropriate for a wide range of ages and grade levels. For the mobile shown here, you will need access to materials such as sentence strips, yarn, and index cards.

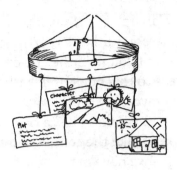

1. **Plan the mobile.** Have students plan the theme or story to be told by their mobile. They then sketch out ideas and make a list of the items to be hung from the mobile.

2. **Write, draw, and color.** Have students use five to eight index cards to write about their topic or theme. Each card should be a different concept or element related to what they are studying. For example, when students are going to sequence a story or a chapter, each of the index cards will begin with a word such as "first," "next," "then," "last," and "finally." After writing about their topic on one side of the index cards, students will illustrate what they've written on the other side. Other types of paper can be used instead of index cards to make the mobile more interesting, but plain 3″ × 5″ index cards are a perfect choice, because they are sturdy and the size works well.

3. **Assemble the mobile frame.** Staple one end of the sentence strip to the other to form a large circle for the mobile frame. Mark five to eight evenly spaced points on the sentence strip, and punch holes in the sentence strip at those points. This is where the index cards will be attached.

4. **Attach string or yarn.** Tie lengths of yarn to the frame of the mobile at the holes that have been punched. The index cards will hang from the yarn. Varying the lengths of yarn creates a more interesting mobile.

5. **Attach items.** Attach an index card to the free end of each length of yarn. A hole punch can be used to make a hole in the index cards, but don't make the hole too close to the edge, because it might tear. The index cards can also be attached to the yarn by using a needle to thread the yarn through the index card; this creates a smaller hole and is less likely to tear. A small piece of tape can be used at the hole for reinforcement.

6. **Attach yarn for hanging.** Attach four equal lengths of yarn, evenly spaced, at the top edge of the mobile frame. Tie their loose ends together to create a hanger for the mobile.

7. **Share.** Students can then share and explain their mobile.

All our many colors

Read aloud *The Crayon Box That Talked* by Shane Derolf as an introduction to a lesson for kindergartners about tolerance. Discuss how all the different colors in the crayon box got along. Whether or not you have access to this book, talk with the students about how all the crayons in a crayon box work together to make beautiful pictures, and how the pictures wouldn't be as rich and beautiful without the variety of brilliant colors. Make the connection for the students that this is like the mix of people we have in the world: Without the variety of many different people of all races, genders, ages, and abilities, our world wouldn't be as rich and beautiful as it is. Discuss with students the importance of accepting one another regardless of race, gender, age, or ability.

11
Crayon
Portrait

Have students draw self-portraits, using the **Crayon Portrait** template. If possible, hang their crayon portraits on a bulletin board decorated like a crayon box.

Multicultural masks

Masks connect us to new and interesting places or stories. These representations of faces may take many forms, perhaps a bird or a tortoise or a type of animal known only in other lands. Using paper, scissors, crayons, and found objects, students can make masks of all colors and kinds.

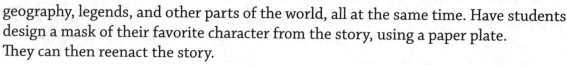

Read aloud one of Gerald McDermott's many trickster tales—*Raven, Coyote, Jabuti the Tortoise,* and *Zomo the Rabbit* are wonderful books that teach children about geography, legends, and other parts of the world, all at the same time. Have students design a mask of their favorite character from the story, using a paper plate. They can then reenact the story.

Colorful butterflies

Read aloud *The Very Hungry Caterpillar* by Eric Carle as an introduction to a lesson about the life cycle of the butterfly for lower grade students.

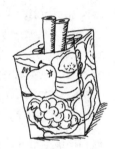

1. Discuss the stages a caterpillar goes through to become a beautiful butterfly. Include topics such as colors and symmetry.

2. Give each student a large, cone coffee filter, and have him or her fold it in half.

3. Have students color the folded coffee filters with markers. Remind them to make designs, and to watch for the colors to go through to the bottom layer of the coffee filter.

4. Have students hold up their coffee filters, and spray the filters lightly with water. Students will see that the colors spread and run together. Set the filters aside to dry.

5. Once the filter is dry, bunch it in the middle and wrap a pipe cleaner around it to create the butterfly's body and two wings. Make sure to leave small ends of the pipe cleaner unwrapped so they can serve as the two antennas.

Milk carton pen holder

Remind students to save their milk cartons from lunch and bring them back to class. Students who don't have milk at lunch should be encouraged to ask friends in another class for their milk cartons. You may want to go to the lunch tables with the students and wait for them to throw their milk cartons out so you can collect a few for this project.

1. Collect milk cartons and rinse them out.

2. Cut off the top of each carton, and leave the cartons to dry.

3. Have students decorate the milk cartons, using a variety of materials (such as pictures of healthy foods from a magazine, pictures from wrapping paper, or symbols and designs from wallpaper). Leave the milk cartons to dry.

4. To protect the pictures, brush glue over the surface and again allow the milk cartons to dry.

Physical education activities

Physical education (PE) is part of the regular routine in elementary school. Students need to stay active, and it is a natural way for them to burn off excess energy. Although PE is part of the standards-based curriculum, it is often overlooked—but PE can be an asset to a substitute teacher. Students can collectively be rewarded with PE time at the end of a productive day.

Always check with another teacher or the office for protocols that apply when teaching a PE activity. Keep games and activities controlled and organized in order to avoid injuries. Remember, safety first!

Your own PE kit

The school or classroom where you substitute teach will likely have equipment for you to use, but you may want to be proactive: Purchase a small box or crate that can easily hold PE supplies and equipment, and take it with you from school to school. Like your personal survival kit, a PE kit will include items for a number of different activities in a very compact kit—you'll have everything available whenever you need it. Consider carrying the following in your own PE kit.

- ◆ Queen-sized sheet (students hold perimeter for a variety of activities)
- ◆ Orange cones (for relay races, goals, etc.)
- ◆ Blow-up balls in several sizes
- ◆ Jump ropes
- ◆ Frisbees
- ◆ Wiffle ball and bat
- ◆ Beanbags, spoons, golf balls (for relays)
- ◆ Sidewalk chalk (for drawing stations; always clear this first with the school)
- ◆ Yardsticks
- ◆ Tennis balls, basketball, volleyball, soccer ball, Nerf football
- ◆ Paddle tennis

These items can be purchased at teacher supply stores, discount stores, and yard sales.

Physical education fillers

Motor development activities

Motor development activities help students develop throwing and catching skills, along with basic mobility skills.

1. You will need two to four playground balls (usually yellow or red rubber balls).

2. Divide the class into two teams, and select a leader for each team.

3. Place the teams on opposite half-courts. Each team has to stay on its own half-court.

4. The team leader selects two people to be catchers, who go to the opposing team's end of the court, where they stay behind the end line.

5. The players on one half-court throw to their catchers at the other end. If a catcher gets the ball, their team scores a point. The opposing team members try to block the throws to prevent the catchers from making a catch.

6. A catcher then attempts to throw the ball back to his or her teammates. The other team continues to try to block the throw from their position on their own half-court.

7. Once these two throws have been attempted, the other team gets the ball. They throw it to their catchers, who will have a chance to catch the ball for their team and then throw it back to their teammates.

8. The teams play until one team has 20 points.

Relay races

Relay races encourage all students to participate, and they foster teamwork and sportsmanship. Relays, always a favorite, can be fun and inventive.

Designate a starting point and an ending point. Team members may go to a designated location and return, or each team may split into two groups, with each member moving in only one direction.

Some examples of relay races include the following.

- Beanbag balanced on the head
- Golf ball on a spoon
- Heel to toe
- Run, skip, hop, jump, and so on.
- Partners locked arm-in-arm

227

Roll the Dice

This activity is meant to teach direction, movement, and following instructions. The goal of the game is not winning a race, but rather following the directions indicated on the dice. These dice can be stored in your PE kit so that you have them with you wherever you're teaching.

Make oversized playground dice from two large Styrofoam blocks (about 4″ on each side). Make a movement block and a number block. For the movement block, use a black permanent marker to write one way to move (such as run, walk, crab crawl, hop, jump, skip) on each side. For the number block, print the number 1, 2, or 3 on each side of the block so that you have two of each number.

1. On the playground, ask a couple of students to roll the two blocks, or "dice."

2. Have students race around a designated area as directed by the instructions that are showing on the blocks when they land. For example, if the movement block lands with "hop" on top and the number block lands with "3" on top, the students should race around the designated area three times while hopping.

Activities and numbers can also be written on strips of paper or Popsicle sticks, which are then drawn for each race.

Making Waves

An activity with an old sheet can help develop locomotor skills. The sheet can easily fold up and fit in a canvas grocery bag that can be part of your PE kit.

1. Have students spread out evenly around the sheet, and then have them grasp it with their thumbs under the sheet and their fingers on top.

2. Start by having students make waves by using only their wrists in an up-and-down motion. Then move up to using elbows, and then shoulders.

3. Have students all move in one direction while holding the sheet, using cues such as jog, walk, gallop, jump, skip.

4. Have students lift the sheet above their heads and peek across at their opposite neighbor, then gently allow the sheet to float down.

5. Have students lift the sheet to peek, and then on cue they put the sheet behind their backs and sit down inside the sheet until it floats to the floor.

Horse

1. Have students use broomsticks, yardsticks, or something similar as their "horse."

2. Set up an outside area to be used as an obstacle course for a relay race for the "horses."

3. Set up obstacles for students to go around in a zigzag pattern, weaving in and out. It works best to use orange cones, set up with some space between them. If no orange cones are available, cardboard boxes can be used.

4. Have students form two lines, one for each team.

5. Model for students how to move through the obstacle course. Zigzag through the obstacle course on your "horse" (broomstick), and then zigzag through it again as you come back to the starting line.

6. One member from each team goes through the obstacle course, and when that member returns to the starting point, the next team member starts out.

7. The first team whose members all make it through the obstacle course is the winning team.

Pass the Ball

This skill-building activity helps students develop gross motor skills and hand and foot coordination.

1. You will need several large playground balls (usually yellow or red rubber balls).

2. Begin by having students stand in a circle and hold hands. Have them back up in order to make as large a circle as possible.

3. Stand in the center of the circle and model how to kick and pass with your feet and how to pass with your hands. Be sure to model these with a student so that the group understands not only how to kick or pass the ball, but also how hard to kick or pass it.

4. When demonstrating passing, show students the chest pass, the bounce pass, and the overhead pass.

5. Remind students that kicking and passing with their feet is for sports like soccer, and passing with their hands is for sports like basketball.

6. Have students practice these skills in a circle or in two lines of students facing each other.

Red Light, Green Light

1. One student is chosen to be "it," and "it" stands 25 to 30 feet away from the rest of the students, with his or her back toward them. The rest of the students spread out side by side along the starting line.

2. "It" calls "Green light!" as a signal for the students to start running toward him or her.

3. "It" then calls "Red light!" as a signal for the students to stop running, and "it" turns around to catch any students who are still moving (who have not stopped).

4. Any student caught moving must return to the starting line.

5. The remaining students continue to play from their newly advanced position until one player makes it to the finish line where "it" is.

6. The first student to reach the finish line is then designated "it."

Boot Camp

Before class begins, set up five stations, each dedicated to a different activity. Suggested stations are for sit-ups, push-ups, jumping rope, running in place, and squats or lunges. The activities at the stations should be age-appropriate. For the most part, no equipment is necessary. If you have access to colored sidewalk chalk or orange cones, these can be used to mark the space for each station.

Once students arrive, proceed as follows.

1. Model how to perform the required activities for each station.

2. Divide the class into balanced and equal groups of boys and girls.

3. Assign each group to a station.

4. Set your watch or a timer for a given number of minutes (typically one to five minutes, depending on the grade level and complexity of the stations), and call out, "Go!"

5. When time is up, have the student groups rotate to the next station, until all students have completed the rotation one or two times.

Traditional playground games

Most schools have an outlined or designated space on their playground for traditional playground games. Students can be allowed to select a particular game, or you can organize a class tournament. Remember that this isn't free time for you, no matter what you see other teachers doing. Circulate, and monitor your students. You may join in whenever appropriate. Following are some traditional playground games.

Four Square

The game Four Square is played on a large square that has intersecting lines dividing it into four equal squares. The smaller squares are numbered 1, 2, 3, 4. A standard soft, red rubber 8½″ kickball is used.

1. Four players each take a square, with the player in the #4 square being designated the "king." The object is to advance to "king" (square #4) and stay there.

2. The "king" serves the ball with one bounce in his or her square, and then hits it (with either one or two hands) into one of the other three squares.

3. The receiving player hits the ball into any of the other squares after one bounce in his or her own square.

4. Play continues until one player is "out." A player is "out" when he or she

    ◆ has an unsuccessful serve (it doesn't bounce into another square)
    ◆ hits or is hit by the ball prior to its bouncing in his or her own square
    ◆ bounces the ball twice or not at all in his or her own square
    ◆ hits the ball with a fist
    ◆ hits the ball out of bounds (not bouncing in a square)
    ◆ momentarily holds the ball
    ◆ bounces the ball over the receiving player's head (the "hitter" is "out")

5. The "out" player proceeds to the end of the line and a new player enters the game at the #1 square, with the other players rotating up as needed to fill in the vacant square.

Hopscotch

1. Hopscotch is played on a specially drawn hopscotch grid, with numbered squares (in this example, they are numbered 1 through 9).

2. Each player has a small object that can be tossed onto the grid (such as a beanbag or a rock).

3. Players hop down the grid and back again to start the game. (Single squares are landed in with one foot, double squares are landed in with both feet— left foot in the left square, right foot in the right square.)

4. Players who successfully complete the trip take turns hopping down the grid as follows:

   ◆ They toss their objects onto one numbered square (in order, starting with #1) and then hop down the grid, always hopping over the square with their object in it.

   ◆ When they reach square #9, they turn on one foot and hop back down the grid, pausing to retrieve their object and then continuing down the rest of the grid.

5. Players must always

   ◆ toss their object into the next numbered square, without letting it touch any lines

   ◆ land their feet only in the squares, without touching a line, lowering a raised foot, or switching the raised foot

Handball

1. Two players stand between 6 feet (the service line) and 15 feet from the wall.

2. One player serves the ball by hitting it so that it bounces on the ground inside the service area and up to the wall. The ball must then bounce from the wall to the serving area to be counted (that is, it must land between 6 and 15 feet from the wall). Two attempts can be taken.

3. The second player then hits the ball on the bounce to the ground and up to the wall. It cannot bounce twice.

4. Play continues with each player taking a turn. At this point, the ball can hit anywhere in the court; it can even be hit on the fly.

5. Play continues until

   ♦ a good serve is not made in two tries
   ♦ the serve either doesn't rebound into the service area or is hit on the fly
   ♦ the ball is hit after bouncing twice
   ♦ a player interferes with (fouls) another player
   ♦ a ball bounces out of the court

6. Play continues after a new player rotates in and the remaining player serves.

Indoor Games

Inclement weather, scheduling issues, repair work, and the like mean that you may have to be inside during recess or lunch. The following activities are a great way for students to get some physical exercise when you have to stay in the classroom. These also provide a good break from the curriculum when one is needed. It is important for you to monitor any activity or game. Take care that no student feels uncomfortable or put on the spot, especially when the class is active in a smaller environment.

Hunter and Prey

This game is a safe way for students to enjoy movement and excitement in the classroom.

1. Establish a designated route around the room.
2. Two players are chosen to be "hunter" and "prey," and they take their positions at opposite ends of the route.
3. Both "hunter" and "prey" balance an object (for example, a beanbag) on their head, and they cannot touch it.
4. Both "hunter" and "prey" start to walk along the designated route. The "hunter" must tag the "prey" without the balanced object falling off.
5. If the "prey" is tagged or loses the balanced object, that student chooses a new "prey."
6. The new "prey" then chases the "hunter."
7. Whoever is tagged or loses the object chooses a replacement, and the direction of the chase is switched.

Hangman

Hangman can be played using vocabulary from a unit of study.

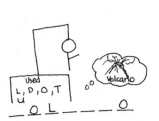

1. Horizontal lines are drawn on the board, each representing a missing letter from a word.
2. A diagram representing a gallows is drawn, which will be used for tallying the wrong guesses.
3. Students guess letters to fill in the blanks in order to spell the designated word.
4. Each letter guessed correctly is written in the appropriate blank, and this gets students closer to guessing the word.
5. Each letter guessed incorrectly is written in a separate area of the board, and a body part is drawn on the gallows.
6. Students win if they can spell the word correctly before the body is completely drawn.

Charades

Charades is a fun and easy way to review material being taught in curricular areas such as science or social studies, or to review scenes from a story or chapter book.

1. Select a student to act out a word, phrase, or concept from material currently being studied.

2. Other students guess by raising their hand and waiting their turn.

3. If the word, phrase, or concept is a title, the actor can hold up the number of fingers that represent the number of words in that title.

4. Touching the nose with one finger indicates that students have guessed a correct word.

Simon Says

Simon Says is a very popular game, especially in the primary grades. It helps with listening skills and following directions.

1. The teacher calls out a command, and students follow the command only when it is preceded by the words "Simon says."

2. For example, the teacher might say, "Simon says to raise your right hand," "Simon says to pat your head," or simply "Raise your right hand," "Pat your head."

3. A command simply stated, as in "Pat your head," should not be obeyed. Students who follow such a command are out.

4. The winner is the last student standing.

Buzz

Buzz is an excellent game for number sense, math facts, and skip counting.

1. Students stand in a circle or behind their seats. The game moves from student to student, so establish an order in which the game will proceed.

2. A designated number is selected, and the multiples of that number are called out as "buzz," as students count from 1 to 100.

3. For example, if "3" has been selected, then the students count "1, 2, buzz, 4, 5, buzz," and so on. The multiples of "3" are not stated; the word "buzz" is called out in their place.

4. If you want to make the game more challenging, add a second number and students will have to say "fizz" for that number's multiples.

Twenty Questions

Students can learn good questioning and deduction skills by playing Twenty Questions. This can be directly related to a unit of study in science or social studies.

1. Have a student think of an object on their own that pertains to the lesson or unit, or write out vocabulary pertaining to a lesson, so that the student can select from that list.

2. One student thinks of an object from one of these three categories:
   - Animal: anything alive that moves and breathes
   - Vegetable: any plant or something made from plants
   - Mineral: anything not considered a plant or an animal

3. The rest of the class asks up to 20 questions, trying to guess the object.

4. Objects should be dominantly of one material. For example, a table may be considered a vegetable because it is made mostly of wood.

5. Answers of "yes," "no," "kind of," "sort of," and the like are all acceptable, as long as the response leads students closer to guessing the object.

6. The student who guesses the object is then selected to think of the next object to be guessed.

Guess My Name

This is an excellent way to review what students know about historical figures. Students need to know details about a famous person they have studied in order to play.

1. Select a student to play the role of a specific historical figure. The student makes some statements about himself or herself, and the rest of the class asks follow-up questions to try to figure out who the historical figure is.

2. For example, assume that the historical person is Rosa Parks. The student could make statements like, "I was a major figure in the Civil Rights movement" and "I refused to give up my seat on the bus." The conversation should extend naturally from there!

3. You can also switch who does the guessing. Send one student out into the hall while you tell the class who the student "is." Then when that student returns to the classroom, he or she must guess who they are from the clues, which are given one at a time as you call on other students in the class. For example, "You were a major figure in the Civil Rights movement." "You refused to give up your seat on the bus."

Yoga

Teaching yoga to children helps them develop balance, flexibility, coordination, self-control, and awareness about their bodies. These skills can be carried beyond the class and into their daily routines. Teaching young people some basic poses will help them stretch, and it will help them relax their minds and bodies. These poses can be practiced throughout the day, at the beginning of the day, or for an actual PE activity. Today's children are under a lot of stress; yoga can help them relax. Following are four basic poses, together with the directions for doing them.

1. **Sunrise/Sunset** Stand up tall. Take three to five deep breaths. On the next inhale, lift your arms above your head. Press your legs and feet down toward the ground and stretch your spine and waist toward the sky. As you exhale, bend the upper half of your body at the waist, down toward your legs, as if diving into a pool. Bend your knees a little at first, to avoid straining your back. Bend as far as it is comfortable. Inhale again, open your arms wide, and stand up slowly, stretching your arms to the sky.

2. **Tree pose** While standing, shift your weight onto one foot, then lift your other heel up to your inner thigh. Reach your arms straight up, or press your palms together at your chest or behind your upper spine.

3. **Downward-facing dog** Start on your hands and knees, with your shoulders over your wrists, toes tucked. Make a tall V shape by lifting your hips straight up, sinking your upper chest and shoulders, and relaxing down the backs of your legs into your heels.

4. **Butterfly** Sit with your spine straight and the soles of your feet together, hands on your ankles. Sit up with a tall spine. Gently bounce your knees toward the floor 10 to 20 times.

Health activities

Health is a subject that often takes a back seat to other curricular areas, such as reading, writing, math, social studies, and science, yet it is very important in our day-to-day lives.

When there is downtime during the day, or you don't have lesson plans, or you have 15 to 30 minutes to fill, you may want to be prepared to teach a health lesson. Following are a few lessons that you can prepare in advance.

Body parts

1. Have students make life-size body outlines as a way to learn about the parts of the body.

2. Have each student (or one student out of each small group) lie down on a large sheet of butcher paper.

3. Outline the student's body, using a marker. (A parent, classroom aide, or volunteer (if available) can do this while you continue teaching the regularly scheduled curriculum for the day.)

4. After the body outlines are drawn, have the students use crayons to outline clothing on it.

5. Have students identify and label each part of the body (legs, arms, mouth, nose, eyes, etc.). Helpers can label parts of the body for students who aren't old enough to do it on their own. In upper grade classrooms, students will be able to study more in-depth anatomy (stomach, heart, lungs, liver, etc.).

6. Have students add and color the hair, eyes, mouth, ears, etc. Focus on clothing vocabulary as a good English as a Second Language (ESL) activity.

7. If you don't have access to butcher paper, scale this project down by drawing and cutting out a template for an outline that will be recognized as a child's body. Have students trace the template onto construction paper and complete the body as they would have if it were a life-size body outline of themselves.

Healthy food choices

Use the most current food pyramid to show the necessary servings for each food category required each day to be "healthy." This is an excellent way to teach children how to make healthy food choices.

1. Prepare pictures of food in advance, so that you will have them to use over and over. Cut out appropriate pictures in all food groups, glue them to construction paper or card stock, cut out the pictures again, laminate them, and store them in a plastic zipper bag. (The bags will take up very little space in your personal survival kit.)

2. Review the food pyramid with the students, using pictures of a variety of foods (such as fruits, vegetables, poultry, milk, pizza, candy bars, soda, hamburgers, tuna sandwich, etc.). If you don't have pictures prepared to use, students can create them or even cut them out of old magazines.

3. Have students help you place the pictures of these foods in one of two categories—"Healthy" or "Unhealthy" foods. Tape the pictures on the board or chart paper under the headings "Healthy" or "Unhealthy."

4. As part of a whole-class discussion about which foods are healthy and which foods are unhealthy, have students work together to create a list of other healthy and unhealthy foods. Make sure it includes a wide variety of foods.

5. Have students illustrate three healthy foods and three unhealthy foods from the list. Students may cut out their illustrations and glue them under the appropriate heading on their paper.

6. Discuss with the students what makes a healthy meal. Have students illustrate a dinner meal that includes items from the food pyramid. They will especially enjoy the activity if they can draw the meal on a paper plate.

Germs

1. Read aloud *Germs Are Not for Sharing* by Elizabeth Verdick as an introduction to a lesson about germs. After the read-aloud, engage students in a class discussion on germs. Ask them what they know about germs. Discuss covering their mouth when they cough, sneezing into the crook of their arm, why it's important to wash their hands, and so on. Transcribe their ideas onto the board or chart paper.

2. Next, put a small amount of hand lotion on each student's hands. Have them rub it in.

3. Over a bucket, sprinkle a small amount of sand into each student's hands. Have them rub their hands to spread the sand evenly, holding their hands over a large sheet of paper or outside, in order to avoid a mess.

4. Have a few students try to get the sand off with a dry napkin, and then have a few students try to get the sand off with warm water and soap. Ask students to make observations about their efforts to remove the sand. Was it easy? Did all the sand come off? How long did it take?

5. Let everyone wash their hands with warm, soapy water.

6. Bring the students back together and ask, "What does the sand represent?" (ANSWER: germs.) Follow up with questions like "What happened when you tried to get it off with just a napkin?" "What happened when you used warm, soapy water?" "Why is it important to properly wash your hands?" Transcribe their responses onto the board or chart paper.

7. Have older students (grades 2 through 6) write a paragraph about the importance of keeping clean and covering mouths and noses when sick.

Clean teeth

1. Read aloud *A Bad Day for Danny Decay* by Lisa Terry as an introduction to teaching students about the importance of brushing their teeth.

2. Label two columns on the board "Good" and "Bad."

3. Discuss what things are good for your teeth and what things are bad for them.

4. Record students' responses to questions such as "What do you think will happen to your teeth if you don't brush them?" "How can you keep your teeth in good shape?" "How do others perceive a healthy smile?"

5. Divide the class into groups of four to six students. Hand out a hard-boiled, white-shelled egg to each group. Tell them that the egg represents their teeth right now (clean and white). Remind them to handle it with care.

6. Give each group a cup of water that contains dark food coloring or dye. Tell them that the cup of water represents the bad things for their teeth.

7. Have each group drop the "tooth" into the dark water. Ask students what they think will happen to the egg overnight.

8. The next morning, look at the eggs. What happened? Why?

9. Give each group a toothbrush, and have them put toothpaste on it. Tell students to gently brush their "tooth" (the egg).

10. Have a class discussion about dental care. What happens when they use good brushing skills? (ANSWER: The egg becomes white again where they brush.)

Healthy heart

1. Discuss with students the role of physical activity and exercise in helping the body and heart stay strong and healthy. Include discussion about how exercise makes the heart beat faster and keeps it strong and healthy.

2. Give students a variety of pictures—of children sitting at a computer, watching TV, jumping rope, kicking a soccer ball, drinking water, eating French fries, and so on. Have students choose which of the pictures show situations that help keep the heart healthy and strong. (If you have no pictures, write activities on slips of paper and have students select one to illustrate.)

3. Students can share "healthy" pictures and discuss why these activities help keep the heart strong and healthy.

4. Have students illustrate three ways that they can promote a strong heart, including food and exercise.

5. Follow up with time on the playground for jumping rope, hula hooping, running on the track, or any other activity that gets their heart rate up.

6. Teach students how to test their heart rate.

Healthy choices

Help students learn how to make healthy choices from a variety of menus. Collect menus from restaurants, or print them from online restaurant sites. Students may also be assigned the task of bringing in menus over a period of a few days.

1. Read through menus.

2. Discuss what items on the menu would be considered healthy.

3. Have students write up an order for a designated number of individuals.

4. Give students a budget ($20.00 or so) and have them figure out the best meal for a specified number of individuals that allows them to stay within their budget.

5. Have students share what they have chosen as a meal "purchased" from the menu.

6. Students may then illustrate what they have purchased, and write the calculations next to their illustrations.

appendix 1
Reading

Following is an overview of the fundamentals of reading. It is especially useful for long-term substitute teaching positions (more than one week), in which you will likely be required to plan the lessons and employ a variety of reading strategies.

The alphabet

There are 26 letters in the alphabet. Kindergarten and first-grade students need to understand that the alphabet has a sequence.

A __ C __ __ F = A B C D E F
L __ N __ = L M N O

The letters of the alphabet have names and sounds. Kindergartners generally learn the uppercase, or capital, letters first (*A*, *B*, *C*, etc.). Lowercase letters (*a*, *b*, *c*, etc.) are introduced later.

Letters

The letters are divided into consonants and vowels.

CONSONANTS	b c d f g h j k l m n p q r s t v w x y z
VOWELS	a e i o u (sometimes y)
SHORT VOWELS	*apple, egg, igloo, octopus, umbrella*
LONG VOWELS	*ape, enormous, ice, oat, rule*
LONG a	*acorn, bake, pail, day*
LONG e	*feet, Pete, seat, chief, city*
LONG i	*kind, bike, high, tie, cry*
LONG o	*joke, boat, toe, show*
LONG u	*unicorn, mule*

Note that long vowels say their name and can be spelled in several ways.

The letter *y* has a long-*i* sound at the end of a one-syllable word (*cry, fly, my*). It has a long-*e* sound at the end of a word of two or more syllables (*city, pretty, realistically*).

Vowel combinations/spellings Two or more letters can form a single sound. Kindergartners learn the basic letter sounds of consonants and short vowels, and first graders build on this knowledge, adding more complex spelling patterns. The letter patterns for common vowel and consonant sounds follow.

VOWEL DIGRAPHS	Two adjacent letters combine to form a vowel sound (**ai, ay, ea, ee, ei, ey, ie, oa, oe, ow**).
VOWEL DIPHTHONGS	Two adjacent letters combine to form a gliding vowel sound (**au, aw, eu, ew, oi, oo, ou, ow, oy, ue, ui**).
r-CONTROLLED VOWEL SOUNDS	Vowels followed by *r* create a new sound (**ar, er, ir, or, ur**).

NOTE The letter *w* followed by *a* often forms the sound "wah" (*swat*, *wash*, *watch*). The letters *qu* followed by *a* often form the sound "kwah" (*quadrant*, *squat*).

Single consonants Several consonants can have more than one pronunciation.

- *C* can be pronounced soft or hard:
  - Soft *c* (*cent*, *circle*, *cytoplasm*)
  - Hard *c* (*cat*, *coat*, *cut*, *scan*)
- *G* can be pronounced soft or hard:
  - Soft *g* (*gentle*, *giraffe*, *gym*, *magic*)
  - Hard *g* (*gal*, *goat*, *gum*, *bag*)
- *S* can be pronounced with an "s" or a "z" sound:
  - "S" sound (*saw*, *see*, *sit*, *sow*, *sue*, *gas*, *pass*, *lost*)
  - "Z" sound (*bees*, *sees*, *lose*)

Note that soft *c* and *g* generally precede the vowels *e*, *i*, and *y*; hard *c* and *g* generally precede the vowels *a*, *o*, and *u*.

X has the sound of the consonant combination *ks* (*lax*, *Texas*).

Consonant combinations In some consonant combinations, the consonants are blended, so that you sound part of both consonants.

- Consonant blends with *l*: bl, cl, fl, gl, pl, sl (*blend*, *clash*, *flag*, *glue*, *play*, *slide*).
- Consonant blends with *r*: br, cr, dr, fr, gr, pr, tr (*break*, *crack*, *drum*, *friend*, *great*, *pretty*, *trap*).
- Consonant blends with *s*: sc, scr, sk, sm, sn, sp, spl, spr, st, str, sw (*scale*, *scratch*, *skip*, *smear*, *snip*, *spin*, *splash*, *spring*, *stick*, *stride*, *swim*).

Qu has the sound of the consonant combination *kw* (*quick*, *require*).

In some consonant combinations, one or more letters are silent (*autumn*, *comb*, *knit*, *night*, *rhyme*, *whip*, *write*).

Some consonant combinations form a new sound altogether (*chin*, *photo*, *ship*, *thin*, *there*, *batch*, *laugh*).

Reading

Letter sounds

Letter sounds are introduced in kindergarten and developed through first grade. Each letter has a distinct sound. When saying the letter's sound, it is important not to add a vowel: Say "b," not "bah" or "buh."

A sound can be spelled with a single letter or a combination of letters. Some sounds are represented by several letter combinations. Spelling patterns can be recognized in the following ways.

- The name of the letter: "a"
  The sound of the letter: "a," as in *apple*
  The spelling of the sound: *a*

- The name of the letter: "a"
  The sound of the letter: "a," as in *ape*
  The spelling of the sound: a, a_e (*a* with a magic *e*), ai, ay (*acorn, ape, trait, pay*)

A single sound can be spelled in several ways. In the second example above, long "a" has four possible spellings. Students can be asked about specific spellings.

TEACHER	Which spelling of long "a" is found in the word *pail*?
STUDENT	The *ai* spelling.

Sounds are blended together to create words. Beginning readers start with short vowel words. In the examples below, C = consonant and V = vowel.

CVC WORD	cat
CVCC WORD	back

The blending process begins sound by sound, then builds into sound patterns or chunks as students learn more patterns.

LETTER BY LETTER	"c" "a" "t" = "cat"
TO THE VOWEL	"c" "a" = "ca"..."t"= "cat"
THE ENTIRE WORD	"c...a...t" = cat

Sight words

Some common words are introduced and drilled as "sight" or "high-frequency" words; these words don't need to be sounded out. A list of common sight words follows.

all	for	him	on	the	was
an	from	his	one	then	we
and	go	if	out	their	went
are	got	in	said	there	were
at	had	is	saw	they	with
be	have	it	she	this	you
but	he	me	so	to	your
come	her	of	that	up	

Word families

Words that end in the same vowel/consonant spelling can be grouped into "families"; this facilitates blending and word recognition, as well as introduces rhyming patterns. Students can build word families.

-ake   bake, cake, rake, snake, etc.
-at   cat, hat, mat, rat, sat, etc.
-ock   block, clock, rock, sock, etc.

Comprehension strategies

Once fundamental reading techniques have been learned, students can read more complex text, picture books, and even chapter books. The focus shifts from reading text to understanding it.

Students use a variety of reading comprehension strategies. These strategies can be modeled for students as text is read aloud to them. The teacher should pause to make connections and to predict.

Basic comprehension

- Title
- Reading genre
- Author's name
- Illustrator's name
- Characters
  - Heroes and villains
- Setting
  - Location
  - Time period
  - Season
  - Time of day
- Main idea
- Sequence
  - Beginning
  - Middle
  - End
- Problem/resolution
- Turning point/climax of story

Advanced comprehension

- **Author's point of view** *Who is telling the story?*
  - First person: *I, me, my*
  - Third person: *he/she, him/her, his/her, they, them, their*

- **Author's purpose** *What is the author's purpose in writing this?*
  - To entertain
  - To explain
  - To inform
  - To persuade
- **Main ideas and details** *What is the primary focus of the story? What examples/ details from the text support this?*
  - Where in the text can you find examples?
  - Which page numbers can you cite to show this process?
  - What is your opinion of the story?
  - What details in the story support your opinion?
- **Compare and contrast** *What is this situation like? How is this different from others?*
  - Find similarities and differences within the text or between familiar stories. (A Venn diagram or other graphic organizer can be used.)
- **Cause and effect** *What is the cause of the situation? What is the effect?*
  - What took place (problem/dilemma)?
  - What were the outcomes (solution/resolution)?
- **Opinion and fact** *Is this story based on fact or opinion?*
  - Feeling vs. real
- **Classify/categorize** *How can you group the characters? The events?*
  - Sort story elements into groups.
- **Predict** *What do you think will happen next?*
- **Infer/interpret** *What can you infer from this? What does this mean? What conclusions can you draw?*
  - Predict, infer, make assumptions, and discover the author's meaning.
- **Make connections** *How do you relate to the story? To the characters?*
  - Relate the story to a personal experience of yours.
- **Summarize** *How can you summarize what has happened? What is the sequence of events?*
  - Clarify: Explain what you have read.
  - Visualize: Close your eyes and see the story. Which details help you see the story? Can you visualize the setting? The characters?

Reading genres

Each reading genre serves a purpose. Students need to understand the differences between genres and how to identify which genre meets the requirements of entertainment, research, information, and interest. A list of major genres follows.

- Mystery
  - Mysterious events explained in the end
  - Suspenseful
- Realistic fiction
  - Set in modern times—the here and now
  - Realistic events

- Historical fiction
  - Invented characters set in real historical events
- Nonfiction
  - Facts about any subject
  - If about a person: biography or autobiography
- Biography
  - Story of a person's life told by someone else
- Autobiography
  - Story of a person's life told by himself or herself
- Science fiction
  - Scientific fact and fiction blended
  - Futuristic technology
- Myth
  - A belief or phenomenon explained
  - Supernatural creatures involved
- Drama
  - Performed before an audience, intended for the stage
- Folktale
  - Story passed from generation to generation
  - Unknown author
- Poetry
  - Verse, often involving rhythm and/or rhyme
  - Intended to produce feelings and convey meanings beyond obvious facts

Ways to read

There are many ways for you to read with students. Some work best with small groups, and others with the whole class. Much depends on your purpose: Are you reading with students for information? For entertainment? To model comprehension? A list of reading methods follows.

- Choral ("unison") reading
  - Choral reading is an opportunity for repeated readings of a big book or text.
  - Practice in oral reading
  - Excellent for poetry and rhyming
- Shared reading
  - The teacher reads aloud from a big book or text, while students view or follow.
  - Useful as an early reading strategy
  - Useful in modeling reading strategies
  - Promotes phonemic awareness
  - Teaches that contextual clues are useful in predicting
- Independent reading
  - Students read independently.
  - Offers practice in learned reading strategies
  - Builds fluency
  - Teaches problem solving

- Sustained Silent Reading (SSR)
  - Students read independently and silently.
  - Reading at individual instructional levels
  - Practice in learned reading strategies
  - Encourages reading
  - Also known as Uninterrupted Sustained Silent Reading (USSR) and Drop Everything and Read (DEAR)
- Guided reading
  - Small groups at the same reading level.
  - Students read same text.
  - Teacher coaches students individually while other students read text silently or in a low voice.
  - Teacher focuses on targeted 'aim' or 'skill'.
- Reading workshop
  - Teacher introduces targeted 'aim' or 'skill' and models it in action.
  - Students read books at their level/that they choose for a sustained period of time.
  - Students have individual goals they work on as well as introduced skills.
  - Teacher can informally conference with individual students, asking how they are applying a goal or the aim of the day.
  - Whole group shares how skills were used.
- Read aloud
  - The teacher reads aloud to the class.
  - Includes class discussion or dialogue
  - Includes a follow-up activity (journals, art, etc.)
  - May be for pure enjoyment
  - No stopping to summarize or ask questions
- Popcorn reading
  - The teacher asks a volunteer to begin reading aloud; any willing student can start.
  - When one student stops, another student continues (without the teacher's direction).
  - Reading continues until all have read.
  - Builds responsibility to participate and promotes the choice of when to do so
  - Lower grade students can pick the next reader.
- Buddy reading
  - Students pair up to read.
  - A lower grade student can pair with an upper grade student.
  - The older student serves as a coach or reading mentor.
  - Students take turns reading aloud.
  - Students read and discuss the story.

- ◆ Timed reading
  - ◆ Measures words read within a designated number of minutes
  - ◆ Student reads twice, attempting to read further the second time.
  - ◆ Builds fluency and increases the number of words per minute
- ◆ Partner reading
  - ◆ Students in a class pair up, taking turns reading or assisting one another.
  - ◆ Showcases each student's skills
  - ◆ Allows for practice in a nonthreatening way

appendix 2
Math

Following is an overview of the fundamentals of math, beginning with basic numbers and continuing through conversions.

Numbers

Students need good number sense, including the concept of a number as a quantity. This involves counting, patterning, and comparing.

KINDERGARTEN	Numbers 1–30
FIRST GRADE	Numbers 1–100
SECOND GRADE	Numbers 1–1,000
THIRD GRADE	Numbers 1–10,000
FOURTH GRADE	Numbers 1–100,000
FIFTH GRADE	Numbers 1–1,000,000
SIXTH GRADE	Numbers 1–1,000,000,000

Greater than/less than

The alligator eats the larger number.

GREATER THAN	29 > 21	−4 > −29
LESS THAN	13 < 20	−31 < −9

Place value

Understanding a number's place value is important. An example follows.

1,657,789.489723   One million, six hundred fifty-seven thousand, seven hundred eighty-nine and four hundred eighty-nine thousand seven hundred twenty-three millionths

Millions	Hundred thousands	Ten thousands	Thousands	Hundreds	Tens	Ones	Tenths	Hundredths	Thousandths	Ten thousandths	Hundred thousandths	Millionths
1,	6	5	7,	7	8	9	.4	8	9	7	2	3

251

NOTES

- Commas are placed in front of every third number before the decimal point.
- "And" is spoken for the decimal point. "34.23" is "thirty-four and twenty-three hundreths."
- Decimals are read as fractions; the number to the right of the decimal point ends in "th(s)." (.45 is "45 hundredths," not "point 45.")
- Zeros can be added at the end of a decimal with no effect: 0.65 = 0.650000.
- Each number value can be written out in expanded notation:
  1,324 = 1,000 + 300 + 20 + 4.

Operations

Mathematical operations may be indicated in several ways.

ADD	Sum, more than, together, increased by, total
SUBTRACT	Difference, less than, decreased by, fewer than
MULTIPLY	Product, of, times
DIVIDE	Quotient, per, out of
EQUAL	Is, are, was, were, will be, same as, gives, makes, made

The following order of operations is used to solve math problems. (Use the mnemonic PEMDAS—Please Excuse My Dear Aunt Sally.)

Parentheses	( )
Exponents	x^2
Multiplication	$\times$
Division	$\div$
Addition	$+$
Subtraction	$-$

NOTE Perform all multiplication and division operations left to right (it doesn't matter which you do first). Then perform all addition and subtraction operations left to right (it doesn't matter which you do first).

EXAMPLE $5 \times (8 - 6)^2 \div (7 + 3) - 1 + 5 = ?$

1. Parentheses $\quad\quad\quad\quad\quad\quad$ $5 \times (2)^2 \div (10) - 1 + 5 =$
2. Exponents $\quad\quad\quad\quad\quad\quad$ $5 \times 4 \div 10 - 1 + 5 =$
3. Multiply or divide left to right $\quad$ $20 \div 10 - 1 + 5 =$
$\quad\quad\quad\quad\quad\quad\quad\quad\quad\quad\quad\quad$ $2 - 1 + 5 =$
4. Add or subtract left to right $\quad$ $1 + 5 = 6$

Exponents are computed as follows.

EXAMPLES $4^2 = 4 \times 4 = 16$ $\quad\quad$ (4^2 is "4 squared" or "4 to the second power.")
$\quad\quad\quad\quad\quad$ $5^3 = 5 \times 5 \times 5 = 125$ $\quad\quad$ (5^3 is "5 cubed" or "5 to the third power.")

Number lines

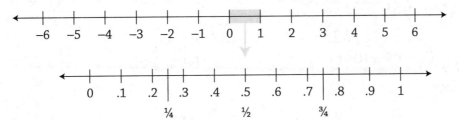

NOTE The fractions and decimals on the second line lie between 0 and 1.

Integers

An integer is a whole number.

Tallies Four lines marked through by a diagonal line represent 5.

Adding integers Integers with like signs are added and the result keeps the sign.

$$4 + 3 = 7$$
$$-5 + -7 = -12$$

Integers with unlike signs are subtracted and the result keeps the sign of the larger number.

$$-10 + 7 = -3$$
$$5 + -4 = 1$$

Subtracting integers The sign of the second number is changed and the two numbers are added. The sign of the result follows the rules for adding integers.

$$10 - 4 = 6 \qquad \rightarrow \qquad 10 + (-4) = 6$$
$$-15 - (-8) = -7 \qquad \rightarrow \qquad -15 + 8 = -7$$
$$12 - (-4) = 16 \qquad \rightarrow \qquad 12 + 4 = 16$$
$$-13 - 4 = -17 \qquad \rightarrow \qquad -13 + (-4) = -17$$

Multiplying integers The product of two numbers with like signs is positive.

$$-3 \times -3 = 9$$
$$2 \times 2 = 4$$

The product of two numbers with unlike signs is negative.

$$-2 \times 5 = -10$$
$$4 \times -5 = -20$$

Dividing integers The quotient of two numbers with like signs is positive.

$$-24 \div -3 = 8$$
$$12 \div 2 = 6$$

The quotient of two numbers with unlike signs is negative.

$$-30 \div 6 = -5$$
$$48 \div -8 = -6$$

NOTE When adding and subtracting integers, think of money: What you have is positive, and what you owe is negative.

$$-3 + 5 = 2 \qquad \text{(You owe 3 and have 5, which leaves you with 2.)}$$
$$-10 + 4 = -6 \qquad \text{(You owe 10 and have 4, so now you owe 6.)}$$

Rules of divisibility

NUMBER	RULE
2	All even numbers are divisible by 2. They end in 0, 2, 4, 6, or 8.
3	Add all digits in a number. If the sum is divisible by 3, then the number is divisible by 3. (Take 345 as an example: $3 + 4 + 5 = 12$. $12 \div 3 = 4$. Therefore, 345 is divisible by 3.)
4	If the last two digits of a number are divisible by 4, then the number is divisible by 4. (Take 1248 as an example: $48 \div 4 = 12$. Therefore, 1248 is divisible by 4.)
5	If a number ends in 0 or 5, it is divisible by 5.
6	If a number is divisible by both 2 and 3, it is divisible by 6.
7	Double the last digit of a number and subtract the result from the remaining digits. If the difference is divisible by 7, then the number is too. (Take 294 as an example: $4 \times 2 = 8$. $29 - 8 = 21$. $21 \div 7 = 3$. Therefore, 294 is divisible by 7.)
8	If the last three digits of a number are divisible by 8, then the number is divisible by 8. (Take 1392 as an example: $392 \div 8 = 49$. Therefore, 1392 is divisible by 8.)
9	Add all digits in a number. If the sum is divisible by 9, then the number is divisible by 9. (Take 4113 as an example: $4 + 1 + 1 + 3 = 9$. $9 \div 9 = 1$. Therefore, 4113 is divisible by 9.)
10	If the number ends in 0, it is divisible by 10.

Fractions

A common fraction is composed of a numerator and a denominator. The following fraction can be read as "one divided by two."

$\dfrac{1}{2}$ — Numerator
— Denominator

Equivalent fractions These fractions are equal to each other. This can be shown by multiplying both the numerator and the denominator by the same number (for example, 2 or 5 in the example below).

$$\tfrac{1}{2} = \tfrac{2}{4} = \tfrac{5}{10}$$

Common denominators The denominators of two fractions may be identical. In the fractions below, the common denominator is 5.

$$\tfrac{1}{5} \quad \tfrac{3}{5} \quad \tfrac{2}{5}$$

To find the common denominator of two fractions whose denominators are not the same, find a least common multiple for the denominators. Then multiply each fraction's numerator and denominator by the number used to derive the least common multiple. In the example below, the least common multiple for 2 and 5 is 10.

$$\tfrac{1}{2} \times \tfrac{2}{5} =$$
$$\tfrac{1}{2} \times \tfrac{5}{5} = \tfrac{5}{10} \text{ and } \tfrac{2}{5} \times \tfrac{2}{2} = \tfrac{4}{10}$$
$$\tfrac{5}{10} \times \tfrac{4}{10} = \tfrac{20}{100} = \tfrac{2}{10}$$
$$\tfrac{1}{2} \times \tfrac{2}{5} = \tfrac{2}{10}$$

Adding and subtracting fractions Find the common denominator, convert each fraction to the common denominator, add/subtract the numerators, and simplify the result, if necessary. It may be helpful to stack the fractions.

$$
\begin{array}{rl}
\tfrac{3}{5} \;\; (\times \tfrac{2}{2}) = & \tfrac{6}{10} \\
+\,\tfrac{3}{10} \;\; (\times \tfrac{1}{1}) & \tfrac{3}{10} \\
\hline
& \tfrac{9}{10}
\end{array}
$$

$$
\begin{array}{rl}
\tfrac{3}{4} \;\; (\times \tfrac{3}{3}) = & \tfrac{9}{12} \\
-\,\tfrac{2}{3} \;\; (\times \tfrac{4}{4}) & -\tfrac{8}{12} \\
\hline
& \tfrac{1}{12}
\end{array}
$$

Multiplying fractions Multiply the numerators and denominators and simplify the result, if necessary. You don't need to find the common denominator.

$$\tfrac{4}{5} \times \tfrac{2}{3} = \tfrac{8}{15}$$
$$\tfrac{6}{11} \times \tfrac{2}{3} = \tfrac{12}{33} = \tfrac{4}{11}$$

Dividing fractions Invert (flip) the second fraction, multiply the numerators and denominators, and simplify the result, if necessary.

$$\tfrac{5}{11} \div \tfrac{3}{5} = \tfrac{5}{11} \times \tfrac{5}{3} = \tfrac{25}{33}$$

Improper fractions In these fractions, the numerator is larger than the denominator; you can't leave a fraction in such a state—it will "topple over." Divide the numerator by the denominator to yield an integer (a whole number), then place the remainder over the denominator.

$$\tfrac{3}{2} = 1\tfrac{1}{2} \quad (3 \div 2 = 1 \text{ with } 1 \text{ remainder})$$
$$\tfrac{13}{4} = 3\tfrac{1}{4}$$
$$\tfrac{7}{5} = 1\tfrac{2}{5}$$

Mixed numbers These numbers consist of an integer and a fraction.

$$1\tfrac{2}{3}$$
$$4\tfrac{5}{16}$$

To convert a mixed number into an improper fraction, multiply the integer by the denominator and add the result to the numerator, then place the resulting number over the original fraction's denominator.

$$4\tfrac{1}{3} = (3 \times 4 + 1) / 3 = \tfrac{13}{3}$$

Adding and subtracting mixed numbers Treat fractions and integers separately. Find the common denominator of the two fractions, add/subtract the fractions, then add the integers.

$$
\begin{array}{cc}
1\tfrac{1}{7} & 1\tfrac{4}{28} \\
+2\tfrac{3}{4} & +2\tfrac{21}{28} \\
\hline
& 3\tfrac{25}{28}
\end{array}
$$

If the fraction is improper, convert it to a mixed number, and add the whole number to the whole number in the answer.

$$
\begin{array}{cc}
1\tfrac{3}{4} & 1\tfrac{3}{4} \\
+2\tfrac{1}{2} & +2\tfrac{2}{4} \\
\hline
& 3\tfrac{5}{4} \quad = 3 + 1\tfrac{1}{4} = 4\tfrac{1}{4}
\end{array}
$$

When subtracting, borrow if necessary.

$$
\begin{array}{cc}
6\tfrac{1}{3} & 5\tfrac{3}{3} + \tfrac{1}{3} = \ \ 5\tfrac{4}{3} \\
-4\tfrac{2}{3} & \qquad\qquad\quad -4\tfrac{2}{3} \\
\hline
& \qquad\qquad\quad 1\tfrac{2}{3}
\end{array}
$$

Multiplying and dividing mixed numbers Convert the mixed numbers to improper fractions, multiply/divide as with regular fractions, and convert the result to a mixed number.

$$
2\tfrac{1}{5} \times 1\tfrac{1}{2} = ((2 \times 5 + 1) / 5 = \tfrac{11}{5}) \times ((1 \times 2 + 1) / 2 = \tfrac{3}{2})
$$
$$
= \tfrac{11}{5} \times \tfrac{3}{2} = \tfrac{33}{10} = 3\tfrac{3}{10}
$$

Decimals, fractions, and percents

Decimals are numbers less than 1. Think of decimals in terms of $1.00: ¼ of a dollar is .25 (25¢ or 25% of a dollar).

To convert a decimal to a fraction, write the number as a fraction with a denominator of 1, then multiply the numerator and denominator by 10 for every number after the decimal point. (Tip: When reading a decimal, instead of saying "point 45," read it as "45 hundredths," which will lead students naturally to the fractional form $\tfrac{45}{100}$.)

$$
.45 = \tfrac{.45}{1} \times \tfrac{100}{100} = \tfrac{45}{100}
$$
$$
.3 = \tfrac{.3}{1} \times \tfrac{10}{10} = \tfrac{3}{10}
$$

To convert a decimal to a percent, move the decimal point two places to the right and add a percent sign.

$$
.45 = 45\%
$$
$$
.3 = 30\%
$$

To convert a fraction to a decimal, divide the numerator by the denominator.

$$
\tfrac{45}{100} = 45 \div 100 = .45
$$
$$
\tfrac{3}{4} = 3 \div 4 = .75
$$

To convert a fraction to a percent, divide the numerator by the denominator, move the decimal point two places to the right, and add a percent sign.

$$^{45}/_{100} = 45 \div 100 = .45 = 45\%$$
$$^3/_4 = 3 \div 4 = .75 = 75\%$$

To convert a percent to a decimal, move the decimal point two places to the left and remove the percent sign.

$$45\% = .45$$
$$75\% = .75$$

To convert a percent to a fraction, convert the number to a decimal, write the number as a fraction with a denominator of 1, then multiply the numerator and denominator by 10 for every number after the decimal point. (Remember: Percent is out of 100, so place the percent value over 100.)

$$45\% = .45 = ^{.45}/_1 = ^{45}/_{100}$$
$$75\% = .75 = ^{.75}/_1 = ^{75}/_{100}$$

Some common decimal, fraction, and percent equivalents follow.

DECIMAL	FRACTION	PERCENT
$^1/_5$	.2	20%
$^1/_4$	.25	25%
$^1/_3$	~.33	~ 33%
$^1/_2$	.5	50%
$^3/_4$	.75	75%

Comparing and ordering integers Integers can be ordered from greatest to least, as well as from least to greatest. To order the following integers from greatest to least, use the steps below.

1,273   126   1,209   1,300

1. Find obvious outliers: 126 and 1,300.

2. Compare numbers at the place where they differ (127 and 120) and decide which number is greater.

3. Order the numbers.

1,300   1,273   1,209   126

Comparing and ordering fractions To order the following fractions from greatest to least, use the steps below.

$^1/_2$ $^7/_{12}$ $^5/_{12}$ $^1/_3$

1. Convert all the fractions to a common denominator: 12.
   a. $^1/_2 = ^6/_{12}$ ($^1/_2 \times ^6/_6 = ^6/_{12}$)
   b. $^7/_{12}$
   c. $^5/_{12}$
   d. $^1/_3 = ^4/_{12}$ ($^1/_3 \times ^4/_4 = ^4/_{12}$)

2. Order the fractions.

$\frac{7}{12}$ $\frac{6}{12}$ $\frac{5}{12}$ $\frac{4}{12}$

3. Rewrite the fractions in their original forms.

$\frac{7}{12}$ $\frac{1}{2}$ $\frac{5}{12}$ $\frac{1}{3}$

To order the following mixed numbers from least to greatest, use the steps below.

$1\frac{1}{2}$ $3\frac{2}{3}$ $5\frac{3}{4}$ $3\frac{1}{4}$

1. Convert the mixed numbers to improper fractions.

$1\frac{1}{2} = \frac{3}{2}$ $3\frac{2}{3} = \frac{11}{3}$ $5\frac{3}{4} = \frac{23}{4}$ $3\frac{1}{4} = \frac{13}{4}$

2. Convert all the fractions to a common denominator: 12.

$\frac{3}{2} = \frac{18}{12}$ $\frac{11}{3} = \frac{44}{12}$ $\frac{23}{4} = \frac{69}{12}$ $\frac{13}{4} = \frac{39}{12}$

3. Order the fractions.

$\frac{18}{12}$ $\frac{39}{12}$ $\frac{44}{12}$ $\frac{69}{12}$

4. Rewrite the numbers in their original forms.

$1\frac{1}{2}$ $3\frac{1}{4}$ $3\frac{2}{3}$ $5\frac{3}{4}$

To order the following decimals from least to greatest, use the steps below.

.045   .9   .567   .57   .100

1. Add zeros to make all the numbers the same number of digits.

.045   .900   .567   .570   .100

2. Order the numbers as if they were whole numbers.

45   900   567   570   100   →   .045   .100   .567   .57   .9

To order the following combinations of numbers from greatest to least, use the steps below.

$1\frac{1}{2}$ .33 $\frac{5}{7}$ .5

1. Select a common equivalent for all the numbers.

1.5   .33   .714   .5

2. Order the numbers.

1.5   .714   .5   .33

3. Rewrite the numbers in their original forms.

$1\frac{1}{2}$ $\frac{5}{7}$ .5   .33

Adding and subtracting decimals Line up the decimal points and add/subtract the numbers as integers.

```
   .345
 +.521
  .866
```

```
   .859
 −.432
  .427
```

Multiplying decimals Multiply the numbers without reference to the decimal points and place the decimal point in the product by starting at the right and moving a number of places equal to the sum of the decimal places in the numbers that were multiplied. Below, .342 has 3 decimal places and .8 has 1 decimal place, so the decimal is moved 4 places to the left.

```
   .342
 ×   .8
  .2736
```

```
   1.23
 ×   .5
   .615
```

When multiplying by more than a single digit, add a zero as a placeholder in your work for each additional tens place in the multiplier.

```
    421
 ×   .31
   4 21
  126 30
  130.51
```

Dividing decimals Move the decimal point of the divisor (the outside number) all the way to the right, move the decimal point of the dividend (the inside number) the same number of places to the right, divide the dividend by the divisor, and line up the decimal point of the quotient with that of the dividend.

```
 .42)8.4
```

```
        20.0
  42.)840.0
     −84
        0
```

For some students, it is easier to turn lined paper sideways or to use graph paper when dividing.

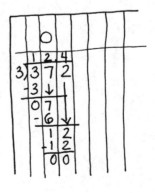

Factoring

Prime numbers A prime number is divisible only by 1 and itself; that is, its only factors are 1 and itself. Examples are 7, 11, and 13. The only even prime number is 2.

Composite numbers A composite number has factors other than 1 and itself. For example, 8 is divisible by 2 and 4, as well as by 1 and 8.

Factors A factor is a number that is multiplied to obtain a product. For example, the factors of 24 are 1, 2, 3, 4, 6, 8, 12, and 24.

To find the factors of a number, begin with 1 and the number, then work toward the center.

```
1                    24
1 2              12 24
1 2 3         8 12 24
1 2 3 4 6 8 12 24
```

Multiples A multiple is the product of a number and an integer. For example, the multiples of 9 are 9, 18, 27, 36, and so on.

To find the multiples of a number, begin by multiplying the number by 1, then by 2, then by 3, and so on.

$$12 \times 1 = 12$$
$$12 \times 2 = 24$$
$$12 \times 3 = 36$$
$$\vdots$$

Prime factorization To find the prime factors of a composite number, use a factor tree.

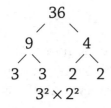

$$3^2 \times 2^2$$

Greatest common factor (GCF) The greatest common factor is the largest factor that two or more numbers have in common.

```
36   1, 2, 3, 4, 6, 9, 12, 18, 36
48   1, 2, 3, 4, 6, 8, 12, 16, 24, 48
GCF = 12
```

You may also use factor trees to determine the greatest common factor.

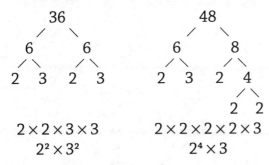

$$2 \times 2 \times 3 \times 3 \qquad\qquad 2 \times 2 \times 2 \times 2 \times 3$$
$$2^2 \times 3^2 \qquad\qquad\qquad 2^4 \times 3$$

First, circle the common factors (the apples on the branches of a tree—in the third line of the example above, circle two 2s and one 3 for each number). Then, multiply the common factors: $2 \times 2 \times 3 = 12$. For three or more numbers, find the common factors for all the numbers.

Least common multiple (LCM) The least common multiple is the smallest number that is a multiple of two or more numbers.

9   9, 18, 27, 36, 45, 54, 63, ...
6   6, 12, 18, 24, 30, 36, 42, 48, 54, 60, ...
LCM = 36

36 is the smallest number that both 6 and 9 divide into.

You may also use factor trees to determine the least common multiple.

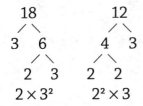

$$2 \times 3^2 \qquad 2^2 \times 3$$

For each prime factor, select its largest value, and multiply the prime numbers: $2^2 \times 3^2 = 36$. Therefore, 36 is the smallest number that is a multiple of 18 and 12.

Roman numerals

ROMAN NUMERAL	ARABIC NUMERAL
I	1
V	5
X	10
L	50
C	100
D	500
M	1,000

NOTE Generally, Roman numerals are written in order of their value, with the largest value on the left.

DCLII $500 + 100 + 50 + 2 = 652$

If a smaller number follows a larger one, the numbers are added.

VIII $5 + 3 = 8$

If a smaller number precedes a larger number, it is subtracted from the larger number.

CD $500 - 100 = 400$
MDCCXLVI   1746

Graphing

Pictures Data can be represented by a picture, which can signify one object or several. Students need to know how much each object represents in order to interpret picture graphs.

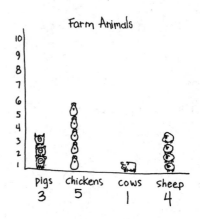

Farm Animals

pigs	chickens	cows	sheep
3	5	1	4

Pie/circle graphs Pie or circle graphs show the number of parts of a whole; each wedge, or slice, represents a percentage of the whole. Because it is easy to interpret, a pie graph is popular, but it is limited by the fact that it can only equal 100%. A key sometimes accompanies a pie graph, indicating which color or pattern stands for which category. The percentage of each slice is often given directly on the graph.

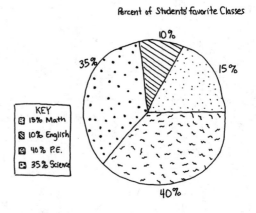

Percent of Students' favorite Classes

KEY
15% Math
10% English
40% P.E.
35% Science

262

Bar graphs Bar graphs are an excellent way to display the results of surveys and inventories—any data for which there are specific values. They are used for quick visual comparisons of categories of data. A bar graph is divided by grid lines, which mark the values on the *y*-axis.

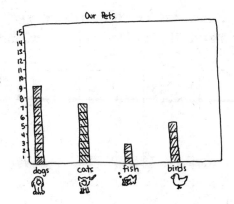

Histograms Histograms, which are similar to bar graphs, represent data groups in ranges (for example, the distribution of students' ages at a school).

Line graphs Line graphs display data (for example, variations in temperature or snowfall) as it changes over time. Data points are marked on a grid and joined by straight lines. Time is displayed on the *x*-axis.

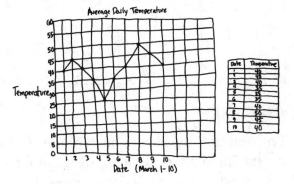

Stem-and-leaf plots Stem-and-leaf plots show the shape and distribution of data. They are often used in magazines and newspapers, since they compare different sets of data and display information efficiently. Each data value is split into a "stem" and a "leaf"; the leaf is usually the last digit of the number and the digits to the left of the leaf form the stem. For example, for the number 38, the stem is 3 and the leaf is 8. A one-digit number has a stem of 0.

Reading Quiz Scores/50	
Stem	Leaf
2	8, 9
3	5, 5, 8
4	4, 6, 6, 7, 8
5	0, 0, 0, 0

Legend: 4 | 6 means 46

Cartesian coordinates (x, y) Cartesian coordinates indicate precise location on a grid. The horizontal axis is *x*, and the vertical axis is *y*. See the accompanying grid.

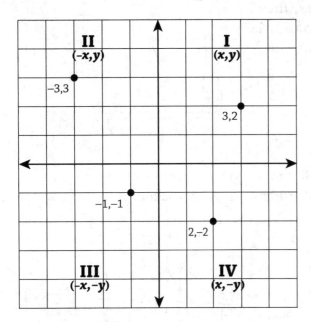

Probability

Probability is the likelihood of an event happening; for example, students can determine the probability of heads or tails when flipping a coin. Probability can be represented as a fraction (for example, ½), a decimal (.50), or a percentage (50%).

$$P = \frac{\text{Total number of successful outcomes}}{\text{Total number of possible outcomes}}$$

Example 1 For a spinner with red, blue, green, and yellow fields, the probability that the spinner will land on yellow (P_y) is ¼ (or .25 or 25%).

Example 2 For a coin flip, the probability that the coin with land heads-up (P_h) is ½ (or .50 or 50%).

Example 3 The probability of both landing on yellow and flipping a coin heads-up is determined by multiplying the numerators of the fractions and the denominators.

P_h and $P_y = P_{(h,y)}$
½ × ¼ = ⅛

Thus, there is 1 chance in 8 of both events happening.

Example 4 Consider a bag of 3 marbles, containing 1 red, 1 blue, and 1 green marble. If you select one marble, replace it, and select again, the probability of selecting a red marble the first time (P_r) and a blue marble the second time (P_b) is ⅓ × ⅓ = ⅑; this calculates the probability of independent events (where two events happen independently of each other).

If, however, you select one marble, do not replace it, and select again, the probability of selecting a red marble the first time (P_r) and a blue marble the second time (P_b) is $\frac{1}{3} \times \frac{1}{2} = \frac{1}{6}$; this calculates the probability of dependent events (where the outcome of one event affects the outcome of another).

Example 5 In the word *SHELL*, what is the probability of selecting an *L* (P_L), not replacing it, then selecting a second *L* (dependent events)?

$$\tfrac{2}{5} \times \tfrac{1}{4} = \tfrac{2}{20} = \tfrac{1}{10}$$

NOTE The total number remains the same for independent events; it decreases by one for dependent events.

Measures of central tendency

Consider the following set of nine numbers: 8 5 9 10 6 10 1 7 7.

Mean The average of a set of numbers, the mean, is determined by adding the numbers and dividing by the number in the set.

$$\frac{8 + 5 + 9 + 10 + 6 + 10 + 1 + 7 + 7}{9} = \frac{63}{9} = 7$$

Median The middle number in a set of numbers, the median, is determined by ordering the set and selecting the value of the number in the middle.

  1 5 6 7 7 8 9 10 10

The median is the number in the middle: 7.

To determine the median of two numbers, simply average the two.

Mode The number that appears most often in a set is the mode. In the set of nine numbers above, there are two modes: 7 and 10.

Range The difference between the largest and smallest numbers in a set, the range, is determined by subtracting the smallest number from the largest. In the set of nine numbers above, the range is 9 ($10 - 1$).

Outlier An outlier is a number that is distant from the rest of the numbers in a set. In the set of nine numbers above, 1 could be considered an outlier.

Ratios and proportions

Ratio A ratio is a comparison of two things. For example, if there are three girls for every boy in a class, the ratio of girls to boys is expressed as 3:1.

Proportion A proportion shows two ratios as equivalent.

   1:4 = 4:16

That is, 1 is to 4 as 4 is to 16.

To test for proportion, multiply each numerator with the opposite denominator and compare the products.

$$\frac{3}{8} = \frac{9}{24}$$

$3 \times 24 = 72$ and $8 \times 9 = 72$. Therefore, the ratios are proportionate.

Or think of it this way: 3 and 8 are proportionately increased (each is multiplied by the same number), which makes ⅜ proportionate to ⁹⁄₂₄.

$$\frac{3}{8} \times \frac{3}{3} = \frac{9}{24}$$

One can solve problems using proportions. For example, if students are divided into groups of 3 boys to 4 girls, how many boys would we need if there are 100 girls?

   $3:4 = x:100$
   $3 \times 100 = 4x$
   $300 = 4x$
   $x = 75$

We would need 75 boys if there are 100 girls.

Rate A rate is a ratio between two measurements using different units. The word *per* is often used to express rate. Two common rates are miles per hour (mph) and miles per gallon (mpg).

Example 1 If 12 apples cost $3.00, what is the unit rate? That is, what does 1 apple cost?

   $\$3.00:12\text{apples} = x \text{ dollars}:1 \text{ apple}$
   $3 = 12x$
   $x = 25¢$

Example 2 If we drove at 50 miles per hour for two hours, what is the distance we traveled?

   Distance = Rate × Time
   Rate = Distance ÷ Time
   Time = Distance ÷ Rate
   D = 50 miles per hour × 2 hours = 100 miles

Percent   Percent is expressed as follows: ____% of ____ is ____. For example, 35% of 24 is 8.4. (Tip: Read "of" as "times" and "is" as "equals.")

$$.35 \times 24 = 8.4$$

Percents can be added to or subtracted from bills.

♦ Sales tax is added to a bill.
♦ A discount is subtracted from a bill.
♦ A tip is added to a bill.

Interest is a charge for money borrowed. The interest rate is expressed as a percent of the amount borrowed, and the interest owed is calculated by the following formula.

$$I = P \times r \times t$$

I = Interest
P = Principal
r = interest rate
t = time

Example   If we borrow $200.00 at a 2% interest rate for 5 years, how much interest will we pay?

$$I = P \times r \times t = 200.00 \times .02 \times 5 = 20.00$$

NOTE: When multiplying by a percent, always convert the percent to its decimal equivalent.

Variables

A variable is a missing number in an equation; it is expressed as a lowercase letter.

$$x + 5 = 9$$
$$x = 4$$

To solve an equation, it is necessary to isolate the variable. Do this by performing the same operation to both sides of the equation. In the example above, subtract 5 from each side.

Geometric forms and solids

Perimeter A perimeter is the path around an area. The perimeter of common shapes is calculated as follows.

Rectangle $2(l + w)$, where l = length and w = width
Triangle $a + b + c$, where a, b, and c are the sides of the triangle
Circle πd, where $\pi = 3.14$ and d is the diameter of the circle

The perimeter of a circle is called its circumference. A diameter is a straight line that passes through the center of a circle and ends at the circumference. A radius is a straight line from the center of the circle to the circumference; a radius is one half of the diameter.

Area An area is the surface of a two-dimensional shape; it is measured in units squared.

Volume Volume is the space enclosed by a container or some other three-dimensional boundary; it is measured in units cubed.

Following is a formula chart for perimeters, areas, and volumes of common shapes.

SHAPE	PERIMETER (P)	AREA (A)	VOLUME (V)
Square	$s + s + s + s$ s = side	s^2 s = side	s^3 (cube) s = side
Rectangle	$2(l + w)$ l = length w = width	$l \times w$ l = length w = width	$l \times w \times h$ (rectangular prism) l = length w = width h = height
Parallelogram	$2(l + w)$ l = length w = width	$b \times h$ b = base h = height	
Triangle	$s + s + s$ s = side	$\frac{1}{2}b \times h$ b = base h = height	$\frac{1}{2}b \times h \times l$ (triangular prism) b = base h = height l = length
Circle	πd $\pi = 3.14$ (pi) d = diameter	πr^2 $\pi = 3.14$ (pi) r = radius	$\pi r^2 \times h$ (cylinder) $\pi = 3.14$ (pi) r = radius h = height

Conversions

Setting up a proportion can help perform a conversion. For example, if you want to know how many inches there are in 20 feet, set up a proportion as follows.

$$\frac{12 \text{ inches}}{1 \text{ foot}} = \frac{x}{20 \text{ feet}}$$

$12 \times 20 = 1x$

$x = 240$ inches

Following is a chart of customary units of measure.

	US CUSTOMARY UNITS	METRIC UNITS
Length	12 inches (in) = 1 foot (ft) 3 feet = 1 yard (yd) 5280 feet = 1 mile (mi) 1760 yards = 1 mile	1 centimeter (cm) = 10 millimeter (mm) 1 decimeter (dm) = 10 centimeters 1 meter (m) = 10 decimeters 1 m = 1000 mm = 100 cm = 10 dm 1 kilometer (km) = 1000 meters 1 km = 1000 m
Volume	8 fluid ounces (fl oz) = 1 cup (c) 2 cups = 1 pint (pt) 2 pints = 1 quart (qt) 2 quarts = 1 half-gallon 4 quarts = 1 gallon (gal)	1 centiliter (cL) = 10 milliliters (mL) 1 deciliter (dL) = 10 centiliters 1 liter (L) = 1000 mL = 100 cL = 10 dL 1 kiloliter (kL) = 1000 liters
Weight/ mass	16 ounces (oz) = 1 pound (lb) 2000 pounds = 1 ton (T)	1 centigram (cg) = 10 milligrams (mg) 1 decigram (dg) = 10 centigrams 1 gram (g) = 1000 mg = 100 cg = 10 dg 1 kilogram (kg) = 1000 grams 1 metric ton (t) = 1000 kilograms

US customary/metric conversions

Length
- 1 in = 2.54 cm
- 1 yd = .91 m
- 1 m = 1.09 yd
- 1 mi = 1.61 km
- 1 ft = 30.48 cm

Weight
- 1 oz = 28.35 gm
- 1 lb = .45 kg
- 1 T = .91 t

Volume
- 1 oz = 29.57 ml
- 1 c = .24 L
- 1 gal = 3.79 L

Temperature

	FAHRENHEIT (°F)	CELSIUS (°C)
Water freezes	32°F	0°C
Water boils	212°F	100°C

Fahrenheit/Celsius conversions

°F = °C × 9/5 + 32
°C = (°F − 32) × 5/9

appendix 3
Writing

Following is an overview of basic writing skills and strategies. In kindergarten, students are introduced to print as a form of communication. This foundation is critical as students progress through grade levels 1 to 6.

Handwriting

Writing involves hand-eye coordination and dexterity. Since young students are still developing their fine motor skills, it is essential that they use correct tools and techniques.

Utensils

Pencil In kindergarten through second grade, students write with a thick, easy-to-hold pencil. Some teachers modify thin pencils with pencil grips. In grades 3 and up, students use a standard No. 2 pencil.

Paper In kindergarten through second grade, students use wide-ruled paper with a broken center line. In kindergarten, the paper has space between rows for letters that descend below the line (*g, j, p, q,* and *y*). This space is smaller for first and second graders. In grades 3 and up, ordinary lined paper is used, although paper with broken center lines may be used for handwriting lessons and assignments.

Letter formation

Printing Kindergartners start with uppercase letters, then move to lowercase letters. This is related to their developing hand-eye coordination, since it is easier to print uppercase letters. Students learning to print "script" letters are encouraged to print "top to bottom, left to right." The pencil is picked up after each letter is formed.

Cursive By third grade, students are learning cursive. They first learn letters similar to those used in printing. Cursive involves keeping the pencil on the paper. Smooth letter formation with a rightward slant is emphasized.

Writing stages

Students progress through several stages of writing as they advance to complete sentences. As a substitute teacher, you must be able to determine where a student is, but it is important for you to understand the different stages.

- Precommunicative: Pictures and first attempts at letters
- Semiphonetic: Initial and final consonants of words (*in, **dog***)
- Phonetic: Vowels and syllables (***summer, bike***)
- Transitional: Sentences with emerging spelling (*My frend palyd wit me in the park.*)
- Conventional: Standard spelling and writing

It is important to validate the student at every stage and encourage progress.

The writing process

To achieve their best writing, students must learn the writing process. The basic components follow.

- Prewrite: Putting ideas on paper, perhaps with a graphic organizer
- Draft/Write: Transforming notes to a written piece, using "no worry" writing
- Edit/Revise: Rereading, clarifying, and checking content; changing information and adding details
- Proofread: Checking for spelling and grammar mistakes; cleaning the written piece up
- Publish: Writing or typing the final draft
- Share/Reflect: Sharing the written piece (even anonymously) to receive feedback and reflection

Writing methods

How you write with students depends on their ability level.

- Supported: For students in the early stages of writing
- Dictated writing: The student dictates and the teacher writes it down, then the student illustrates the text.
- Closed sentences: The student fills in a missing word or part of a sentence— they "close" the sentence. (*The dog is _____. Today we _____.*) These are also called "cloze sentence" exercises.
- Dictate to write: The student dictates to the teacher as the teacher writes and guides, then the student copies the written piece in his or her own handwriting.
- Interactive writing: The entire class and teacher plan and write together as a group; students take turns writing. The result is a whole-class story. This tactic provides opportunities to correct, decode words, and use correct grammar.
- Shared writing: The teacher models a short selection, then the students copy what was written and add their own writing to it.
- Guided writing: The teacher works with a small group of students, who work together as a community of writers.

- Writers workshop: Writers learn through their own experience, teacher models a skill, students write independently while teacher conferences with individuals on individual skills needs or the skill for that day and students share with class and get feedback.

Graphic organizers can help students organize their thoughts before they write. Students use a Venn Diagram or Web Organizer (or any fun, interactive, and engaging graphic organizer) to jot down words, phrases, and ideas that they will use in their writing; this gets students motivated and spurs creativity. Some schools have adopted sets of organizers for routine use.

Students must be able to write a sound paragraph, whose structure includes the following components.

- Opening or topic sentence: A statement of opinion or response
- Example: A specific example of the opinion or response
- Extension: Supporting details
- Closing: A restatement of the topic sentence

Writing styles

Point of view Point of view reflects the writer's position as it relates to the story being told: first person ("I"), second person ("you"), and third person ("he," "she," "they").

Genres

- **Narrative writing** tells a story or gives an account. Written in the first or third person, it is used for imagined or personal accounts.
- **Expository writing** explains, defines, and provides information. Written in the third person, it presents facts, statistical information, examples, and cause/effect relationships.
- **Descriptive writing** describes people, things, and events. Written in the first or third person, it uses descriptive language and adjectives to show, not tell. Descriptive writing is useful in all genres.
- **Summary writing** summarizes another piece of writing. It maintains the integrity of the writing while presenting its main ideas, events, and concepts. Summary writing is in the first or third person.
- **Response to literature** reacts to a literary work, creating a personal connection to the writer's ideas and experiences. The response uses techniques like retelling, summarizing, analyzing, and generalizing.
- **Report writing** informs and explains as it provides information and facts. It is used to educate, report facts, and make predictions based on data.
- **Letter writing** is a form of interpersonal communication. Even though most students use e-mail, it is important for them to understand letter format. A friendly letter includes a date, greeting, body, closing, and signature. A business letter includes the sender's address, date, greeting, body, closing, and signature.

- **Poetry writing** uses sound and, usually, rhythm in an arranged composition. There are many types of poetry, including haiku, cinquain, limericks, closed verse, lyric, nonsense verse, narrative, jump rope, and concrete (shape) poetry.
  - An **ABC** poem is a series of lines of words or phrases that create a mood, picture, or feeling. The first word of line 1 begins with *A,* the first word of line 2 begins with *B,* and so on.
  - An **acrostic** poem uses each letter of a word as the first letter of a line. The poem relates to the word.
  - A **ballad** tells a story similar to a folktale or legend and often has a refrain that is repeated. A story in poetic form, a ballad is often about love and can be sung.
  - **Cinquain** poems have five lines:
    Line 1: One word (the title)
    Line 2: Two words that describe the title
    Line 3: Three words that relate the action
    Line 4: Four words that express the feeling
    Line 5: One word that recalls the title
  - **Free verse** is composed of rhymed or unrhymed lines that have no fixed metrical pattern.
  - A **haiku** is composed of three unrhymed lines of five, seven, and five syllables. Haiku poetry, which originated in Japan, reflects on some aspect of nature and generates images.
  - **Rhymes** repeat the same or similar sounds at the ends of words, most often at the ends of lines. This technique makes the poem easy to write and easy to remember.
  - **"Auto-Bio," "I Am,"** and **"I Come From"** poems are used to teach students how to write about themselves in an abstract and creative way.

Templates

The key to laptop templates on pages 276-280 lists the accompanying templates available as PDFs. The key includes the number of each template, as well as information and instructions for its use. The symbol ⌨ next to a template number in the key indicates that the template is also available as a PDF electronic form, which can be filled in on a computer and printed. The current version of Adobe Reader is required to open PDFs.

Thumbnails of all templates are reproduced on pages 283–290.

The key to bonus templates on pages 281-282 lists bonus templates available as PDFs online. The key includes the number of each template, as well as information and instructions for its use. The symbol ⌨ next to a template number in the key indicates that the template is also available as a PDF electronic form, which can be filled in on a computer and printed. The current version of Adobe Reader is required to open PDFs.

Thumbnails of all bonus templates are reproduced on pages 291–296.

The symbol ⌨ after a template or bonus template number on the thumbnail pages has the same meaning as in the key below.

Be sure to set Adobe Reader to highlight the form fields as follows:

Preferences >
Forms >
Highlight Color: ☑ Show border hover color for fields

Note that your filled-in forms cannot be saved on the computer.

A gray arrow at the side edge of a template (for example, ➡) indicates that the template is included with an adjoining template in a multipage PDF.

Key to Laptop templates

🖥 **01 Agenda Checklist**
Use this checklist to organize and check off lessons as you complete them.

🖥 **02 Attendance/Task Log**
Use this log to record students' attendance and/or completion of assigned tasks.

🖥 **03 Attributes Organizer**
Students use this organizer to list the characteristics (attributes) of people, places, or things.

🖥 **04 Bar Graph**
Students use this sheet to graph numbers of items, either using small items such as buttons, M&Ms®, and Cheerios®, or by coloring one block for each unit counted.

🖥 **05 Bookmarks**
Cut out each bookmark along the outer edge. Fold on the dashed line and glue the halves together, or cut in half on the dashed line in order to make two different bookmarks. Encourage students to use the bookmarks when reading.

🖥 **06 Classroom Log**
Use this log to track students' time out of the classroom.

🖥 **07 Clock**
Students use this template to create their own clock with movable hands.

🖥 **08 Color Wheel**
Students color the six sections of the color wheel in the correct order.

🖥 **09 Community Helper**
Students use this template to create a favorite community helper.

🖥 **10 Counting Coins**
Students cut out and color coins to use in math activities that involve counting money.

🖥 **11 Crayon Portrait**
Students use this template to draw a self-portrait.

🖥 **12 Daily Checklist**
Use this checklist to organize each job from the assignment call to the end of your day.

🖥 **13 Desk Name Tag**
Have students print, write, or type their names in the center panel. Students may decorate their name tags. The name tags can then be folded along the dotted lines, tucking the bottom section underneath to create a name tag that stands by itself. You may distinguish classroom groups (tables, rows) with different colors of paper for the name tags.

🖥 **14 Flash Cards**
Students use this template to create their own set of flash cards.

🖥 **15 Fraction Bars**
Students label, color, and cut out the bars, and use them to learn about fractions.

🖥 **16 Geometric Shape Organizer**

Students use this organizer to name shapes and solid forms, then illustrate them.

🖥 **17 Geometric Solids: Cone**

Students cut out the shape along the perimeter, fold to create the appropriate shape, and tape the edges where they meet.

🖥 **18 Geometric Solids: Cube**

Students cut out the shape along the perimeter, fold to create the appropriate shape, and tape the edges where they meet.

🖥 **19 Geometric Solids: Cylinder**

Students cut out the shape along the perimeter, fold to create the appropriate shape, and tape the edges where they meet.

🖥 **20 Geometric Solids: Rectangular Prism**

Students cut out the shape along the perimeter, fold to create the appropriate shape, and tape the edges where they meet.

🖥 **21 Geometric Solids: Triangular Prism**

Students cut out the shape along the perimeter, fold to create the appropriate shape, and tape the edges where they meet.

🖥 **22 Geometric Solids: Triangular Pyramid**

Students cut out the shape along the perimeter, fold to create the appropriate shape, and tape the edges where they meet.

🖥 **23 Historical Person/Event Time Line**

Students use this sheet to organize significant events leading up to a person's accomplishment(s) or a historical event.

🖥 **24 Homework Pass**

Use homework passes to reward students at the end of the day. A pass can be used in place of an assignment. Note that they should not be used for specific assignments from the teacher.

🖥 **25 Ice Cream Sundae Math Fact Families**

Students use this sheet to solve problems for a math fact family.

🖥 **26 Incentive Money**

Students can earn money for good behavior and use it to buy rewards. Assign values to desired behaviors. Students may store money in plastic zipper bags bearing their names. Students may also use paper money in math activities that involve counting money.

🖥 **27 KWL Historical Person/Event Organizer**

Students use this sheet to organize what they know, what they want to know, and what they have learned about significant events leading up to a person's accomplishment(s) or a historical event.

🖥 **28 KWL Organizer**

Students use this sheet to organize what they know, what they want to know, and what they have learned about a topic they are studying.

💻 **29** Lesson Plan: Direct Instruction (with instructions)
Use this template to develop a lesson plan.

💻 **30** Lesson Plan: Direct Instruction (without instructions)
Use this template to develop a lesson plan.

💻 **31** Open Pass
Use open passes to reward students when you choose to modify an assignment.
A pass can be used to reduce the work due for an assignment.

💻 **32** Out-of-My-Seat Log
Use this log to track when students are out of their seats within the classroom.

💻 **33** Outstanding Student Tickets
Use these tickets to reward students. They write their names on the tickets and store
them in plastic zipper bags. Tickets can be redeemed for rewards.

💻 **34** Parent Letter 1
For lower grades

💻 **35** Parent Letter 2
For upper grades

💻 **36** Reward Certificates
Certificate of recognition

💻 **37** Rule Planner
Write the rule under consideration, and describe the situation that causes you to consider
this rule. Describe the effect the rule will have.

💻 **38** Sandwich Organizer
Students use this organizer to plan their writing assignment.

💻 **39** School Information Card
Use these cards to record information about each school site. Write names of additional
people related to each site on the back of the card.

💻 **40** Sort-Order-Pattern Mat
Students use these grids for sorting, ordering, and patterning activities.

💻 **41** Stair Organizer 1
Students use this organizer to sequence a process or a story.

💻 **42** Stair Organizer 2
Students use this organizer to sequence a process or a story.

💻 **43** State Facts
Students use this template to illustrate state symbols and list specific information about
a state.

💻 **44** State Profile
Students use this template when doing research about a state.

45 Story Organizer

Students use this organizer to summarize information about a book that they have read.

46 Storyboard Organizer

Students use this organizer to sequence the events of a story.

47 Student Behavior Tracker

Use this log to track students' behavior during the day.

48 Student Self-Evaluation Form

Students use this form to reflect on their behavior during the day. Use this evaluation form as a "ticket-out-the-door" and leave it for the classroom teacher.

49 Substitute Teacher Assignment Log

Use this log to record contact information for each substitute teaching assignment.

50 Substitute Teacher Feedback Note 1

Use this form to leave feedback about your day in the classroom.

51 Substitute Teacher Feedback Note 2

Use this form to leave feedback about your day in the classroom.

52 Substitute Teacher Job Log

Use this form to record basic information about each of your substitute teaching assignments.

53 Substitute Teacher Travel Log

Use this log to track mileage traveled for substitute teaching assignments.

54 Super Star Tickets 1

Use these tickets to reward students. They write their names on the tickets and store them in plastic zipper bags. Tickets can be redeemed for rewards.

55 Super Star Tickets 2

Use these tickets to reward students. They write their names on the tickets and store them in plastic zipper bags. Tickets can be redeemed for rewards.

56 Tangram Picture Cards

Students replicate the tangram picture puzzles, using a set of tangram puzzle pieces. Solutions are provided.

57 Tangrams 1

Use this template for large tangram puzzle pieces.

58 Tangrams 2

Use this template for small tangram puzzle pieces.

59 Teacher Self-Evaluation Form

Use this form to reflect on your assignment at the end of the day. Refer to it again after you have been reassigned.

60 United States Map

Students use this map for activities about the United States or the individual states.

🖥 **61** Venn Diagram

Students use this diagram to list characteristics of two things, showing which characteristics they have in common and which are unique.

🖥 **62** Web Organizer

Students use this organizer to list the details about a subject.

🖥 **63** World Map

Students use this map for activities about the world, continents, and oceans.

Key to bonus templates

BT 01 Auto-Bio-Poem 1

Students use this organizer to create their poem.

BT 02 Auto-Bio-Poem 2

Students use this organizer to create their poem.

BT 03 Bingo 1

For lower grades. Each student fills in a card with numbers or words from the current unit. As the teacher calls out a question, the student covers the answer if it appears on his or her card. The first student to cover three answers in a row (across, down, or diagonally) wins. Ideas for fill-ins are math facts, sight words, synonyms, antonyms, definitions, numbers, and fractions.

BT 04 Bingo 2

For upper grades. Each student fills in a card with numbers or words from the current unit. As the teacher calls out a question, the student covers the answer if it appears on his or her card. The first student to cover five answers in a row (across, down, or diagonally) wins. Ideas for fill-ins are math facts, sight words, synonyms, antonyms, definitions, numbers, and fractions.

BT 05 Book Report 1

Students in the lower grades use this template for checking comprehension of chapter and picture books.

BT 06 Book Report 2

Students in the upper grades use this template for checking comprehension of chapter books.

BT 07 Conflict Resolution Slip

Students work together to discuss and resolve their conflicts, filling in the slip as they proceed. They then submit the Conflict Resolution Slip to the teacher and share their resolution.

BT 08 Cycle Organizer

Students use this organizer to illustrate the steps or phases of a cycle.

BT 09 Daily Schedule Organizer

Use this organizer to list each instructional activity, including the number of minutes mandated for daily instruction in the activity.

BT 10 Hundreds Chart

Students use this chart to color counting patterns, multiples, and odd or even numbers, as well as to count, add, subtract, and discover patterns.

BT 11 "I Am" Poem Planner

Students use this organizer to plan their poem.

BT 12 "I Come From" Poem Planner

Students use this organizer to plan their poem.

BT 13 Incident Report

Use this report to document any incident for which you may need written documentation concerning the incident itself, who was present, what was done, and follow-up.

BT 14 Scavenger Hunt Questionnaire

Have students complete the questionnaire. It's a good icebreaker and gives students an opportunity to learn about one another. Each student's name can be written down only one time on a questionnaire.

BT 15 Scientific Investigation 1

Students in the lower grades use this template to record their purpose, prediction, observations, and conclusion for a scientific investigation.

BT 16 Scientific Investigation 2

Students in the upper grades use this template to record their purpose, prediction, observations, and conclusion for a scientific investigation.

BT 17 Scientific Investigation 3

Students in the upper grades use this template to record their purpose, prediction, observations, and conclusion for a scientific investigation.

BT 18 Student Interest Survey

Students complete this survey to share personal likes and interests with the teacher.

BT 19 Tens Frame

Students use this template with counters for practice with adding and subtracting numbers to 10.

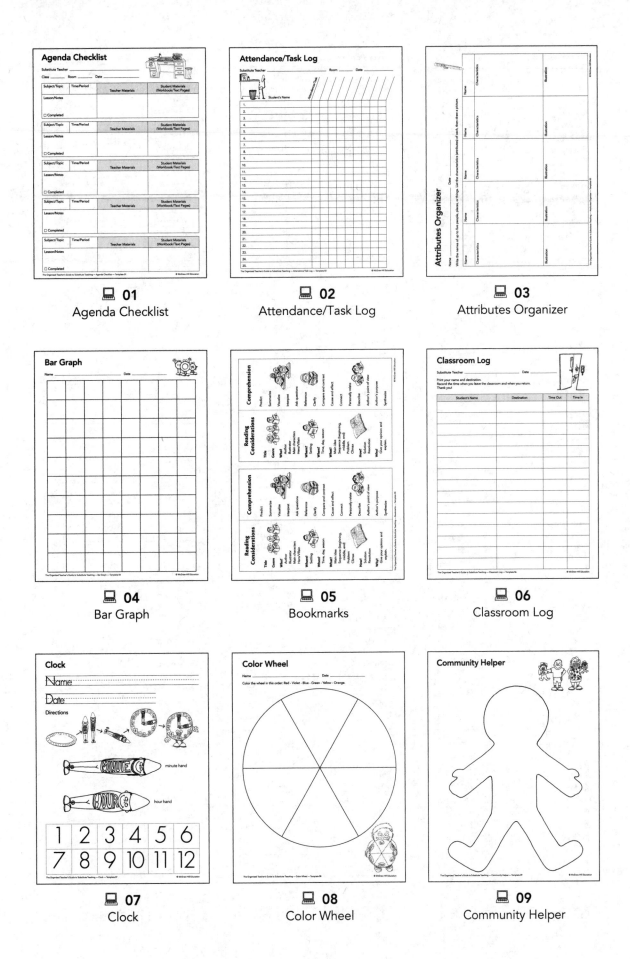

🖥 **01**
Agenda Checklist

🖥 **02**
Attendance/Task Log

🖥 **03**
Attributes Organizer

🖥 **04**
Bar Graph

🖥 **05**
Bookmarks

🖥 **06**
Classroom Log

🖥 **07**
Clock

🖥 **08**
Color Wheel

🖥 **09**
Community Helper

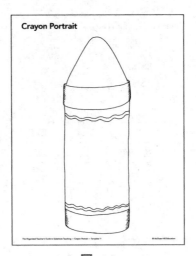

10
Counting Coins

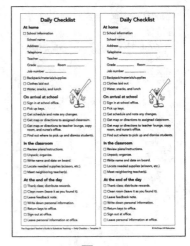

11
Crayon Portrait

12
Daily Checklist

13
Desk Name Tag

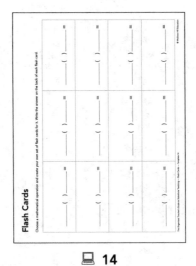

14
Flash Cards

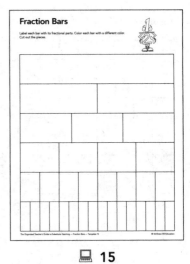

15
Fraction Bars

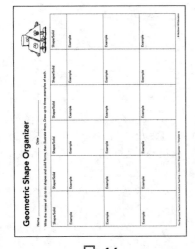

16
Geometric Shape Organizer

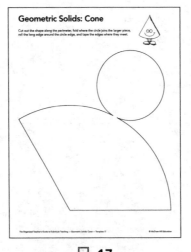

17
Geometric Solids: Cone

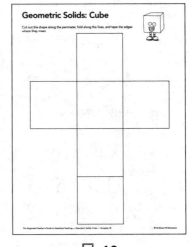

18
Geometric Solids: Cube

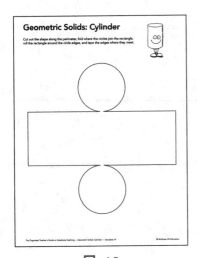

Geometric Solids: Cylinder

Cut out the shape along the perimeter, fold where the circles join the rectangle, roll the rectangle around the circle edges, and tape the edges where they meet.

🖥 **19**

Geometric Solids: Cylinder

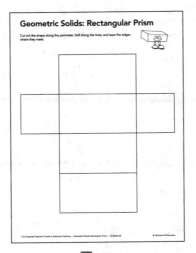

Geometric Solids: Rectangular Prism

Cut out the shape along the perimeter, fold along the lines, and tape the edges where they meet.

🖥 **20**

Geometric Solids:
Rectangular Prism

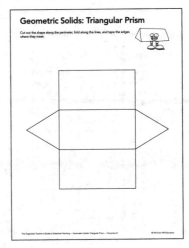

Geometric Solids: Triangular Prism

Cut out the shape along the perimeter, fold along the lines, and tape the edges where they meet.

🖥 **21**

Geometric Solids:
Triangular Prism

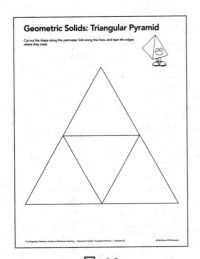

Geometric Solids: Triangular Pyramid

Cut out the shape along the perimeter, fold along the lines, and tape the edges where they meet.

🖥 **22**

Geometric Solids:
Triangular Pyramid

🖥 **23**

Historical Person/Event
Time Line

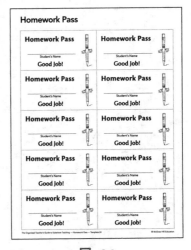

Homework Pass

🖥 **24**

Homework Pass

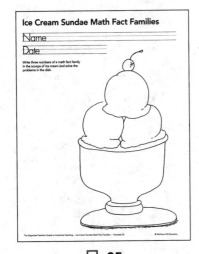

Ice Cream Sundae Math Fact Families

Name

Date

Write three numbers of a math fact family in the scoops of ice cream and solve the problems in the dish.

🖥 **25**

Ice Cream Sundae Math
Fact Families

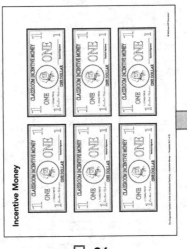

🖥 **26**

Incentive Money (1 of 3)

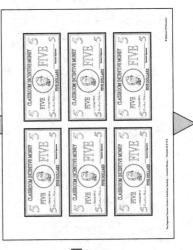

🖥 **26**

Incentive Money (2 of 3)

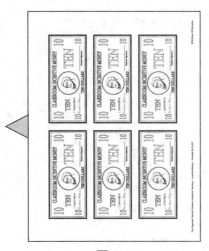

💻 **26**

Incentive Money (3 of 3)

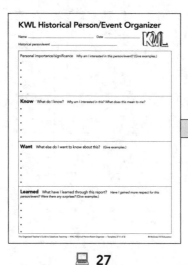

💻 **27**

KWL Historical Person/Event
Organizer (1 of 2)

💻 **27**

KWL Historical Person/Event
Organizer (2 of 2)

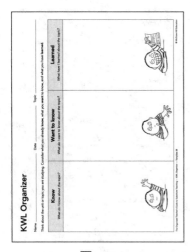

💻 **28**

KWL Organizer

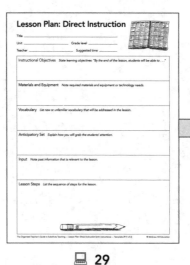

💻 **29**

Lesson Plan: Direct Instruction
(with instructions) (1 of 2)

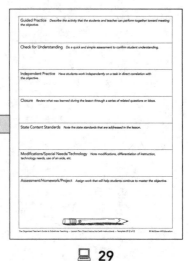

💻 **29**

Lesson Plan: Direct Instruction
(with instructions) (2 of 2)

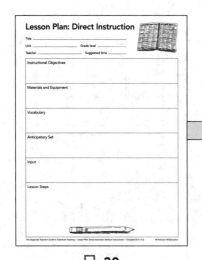

💻 **30**

Lesson Plan: Direct Instruction
(without instructions) (1 of 2)

💻 **30**

Lesson Plan: Direct Instruction
(without instructions) (2 of 2)

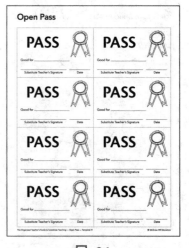

💻 **31**

Open Pass

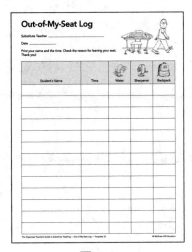

32

Out-of-My-Seat Log

33

Outstanding Student Tickets

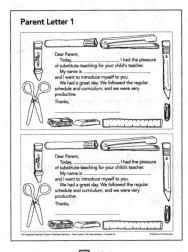

34

Parent Letter 1

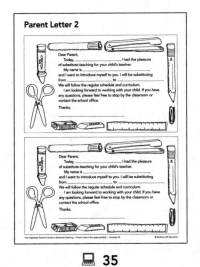

35

Parent Letter 2

36

Reward Certificates

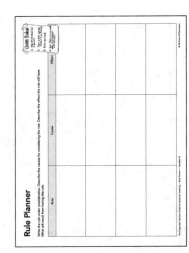

37

Rule Planner

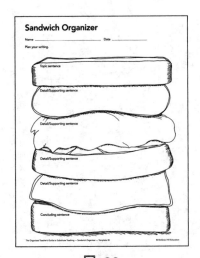

38

Sandwich Organizer

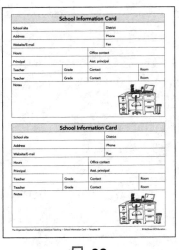

39

School Information Card

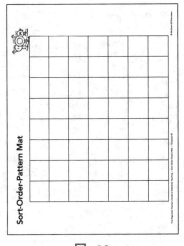

40

Sort-Order-Pattern Mat

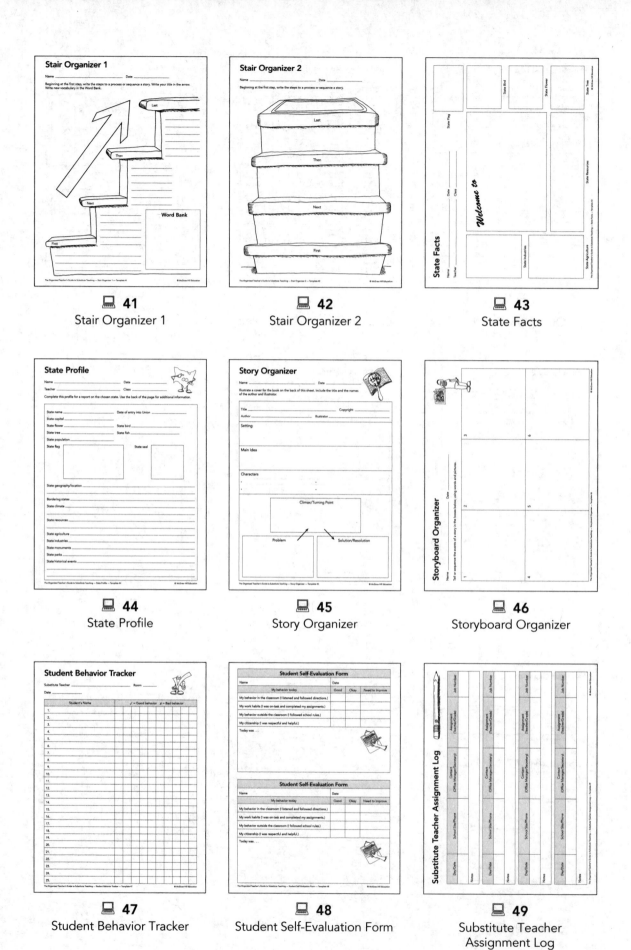

💻 **41**
Stair Organizer 1

💻 **42**
Stair Organizer 2

💻 **43**
State Facts

💻 **44**
State Profile

💻 **45**
Story Organizer

💻 **46**
Storyboard Organizer

💻 **47**
Student Behavior Tracker

💻 **48**
Student Self-Evaluation Form

💻 **49**
Substitute Teacher
Assignment Log

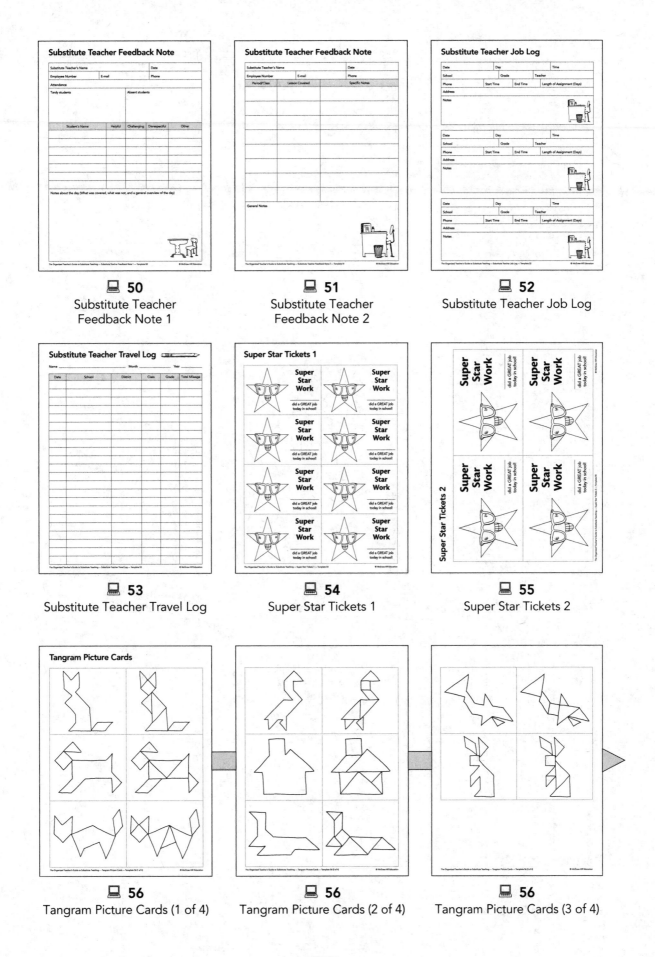

💻 **50**
Substitute Teacher
Feedback Note 1

💻 **51**
Substitute Teacher
Feedback Note 2

💻 **52**
Substitute Teacher Job Log

💻 **53**
Substitute Teacher Travel Log

💻 **54**
Super Star Tickets 1

💻 **55**
Super Star Tickets 2

💻 **56**
Tangram Picture Cards (1 of 4)

💻 **56**
Tangram Picture Cards (2 of 4)

💻 **56**
Tangram Picture Cards (3 of 4)

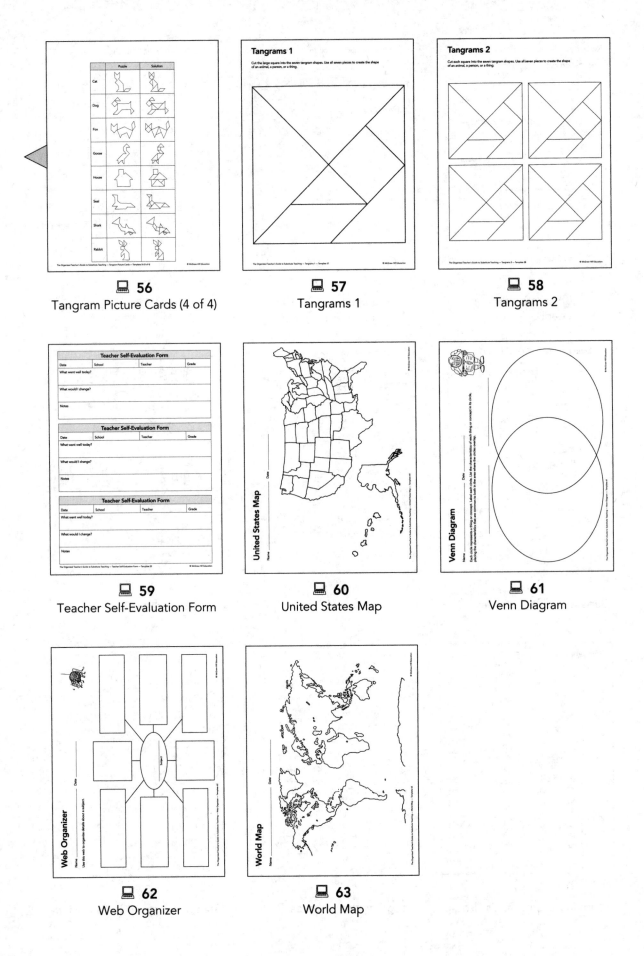

📟 **56**
Tangram Picture Cards (4 of 4)

📟 **57**
Tangrams 1

📟 **58**
Tangrams 2

📟 **59**
Teacher Self-Evaluation Form

📟 **60**
United States Map

📟 **61**
Venn Diagram

📟 **62**
Web Organizer

📟 **63**
World Map

Auto-Bio-Poem 1

Name _____ Date _____

Use the following poem to introduce yourself to your pen pal. Complete each line of the poem about yourself as a rough draft; after editing, rewrite the poem on lined paper before sending to your pen pal.

1 Your first name _____

2 Two words that describe you _____

3 Friend of (name three friends) _____
   _____

4 Who is happy when _____
   _____

5 Who is sad when _____
   _____

6 Who is afraid of _____
   _____

7 Who has fun _____
   _____

8 Who is loyal to _____
   _____

9 Your last name _____

▢ BT 01
Auto-Bio-Poem 1

Auto-Bio-Poem 2

Name _____ Date _____

Use the following poem to introduce yourself to your pen pal. Complete each line of the poem about yourself as a rough draft; after editing, rewrite the poem on lined paper before sending to your pen pal.

1 Your first name _____

2 Four adjectives that describe you _____
   _____

3 Son/daughter of _____

4 Friend of (name the three people closest to you) _____
   _____

5 Who feels best when _____

6 Who finds happiness in _____

7 Who needs _____

8 Who gives _____

9 Who fears _____

10 Who would like to see _____

11 Who enjoys _____

12 Who is loyal to (people or ideas) _____

13 Resident of (city or neighborhood) _____

14 Your last name _____

▢ BT 02
Auto-Bio-Poem 2

Bingo 1

▢ BT 03
Bingo 1

Bingo 2

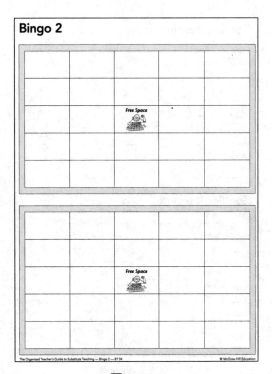

▢ BT 04
Bingo 2

Book Report

Name

Date

Title

Author

Illustrator

1. Write three sentences telling what the book is about.

_____

_____

_____

_____

_____

_____

_____

2. What was your favorite part of the book? (Write three or more sentences.)

_____

_____

_____

_____

_____

_____

_____

_____

3. Draw a picture about the story on the back of this sheet. Include characters and the setting.

💻 **BT 05**
Book Report 1

Book Report

Name _____   Date _____

Book Information

Title _____

Author _____

Illustrator _____

Copyright date _____ Number of pages _____

Genre ☐ Fiction ☐ Nonfiction ☐ Fable
        ☐ Fantasy ☐ Fairy Tale ☐ Expository
        ☐ Biography ☐ Autobiography

Book Report Outline
Use one of the following outlines for your
book report.

• 1. State the subject matter.
  2. List three facts that you learned.
  3. Describe the most interesting part.
• Describe (a) the main characters,
  (b) the setting, (c) the conflict/problem,
  (d) the resolution, and (e) your personal
  connection/opinion.

_____

_____

_____

_____

_____

_____

_____

_____

_____

_____

_____

_____

_____

Draw a picture of your favorite part of the story on the back of this sheet.

💻 **BT 06**
Book Report 2

Conflict Resolution Slip   Date _____

Student 1 _____   Student 2 _____

Statement of the conflict _____

_____

_____

Resolution checklist
☐ Discuss how the conflict makes you feel.
☐ Imagine how the other student feels.
☐ Discuss a resolution.
☐ Fill out the slip and submit it to the teacher.

Our resolution _____

_____

_____

Conflict Resolution Slip   Date _____

Student 1 _____   Student 2 _____

Statement of the conflict _____

_____

Resolution checklist
☐ Discuss how the conflict makes you feel.
☐ Imagine how the other student feels.
☐ Discuss a resolution.
☐ Fill out the slip and submit it to the teacher.

Our resolution _____

_____

💻 **BT 07**
Conflict Resolution Slip

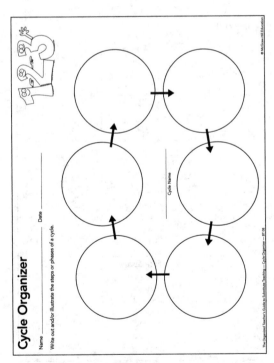

💻 **BT 08**
Cycle Organizer

Daily Schedule Organizer

Time	Activity	Minutes
7:30 AM		
7:45		
8:00		
8:15		
8:30		
8:45		
9:00		
9:15		
9:30		
9:45		
10:00		
10:15		
10:30		
10:45		
11:00		
11:15		
11:30		
11:45		
12:00 PM		
12:15		
12:30		
12:45		
1:00		
1:15		
1:30		
1:45		
2:00		
2:15		
2:30		
2:45		
3:00		
3:15		

🖥 **BT 09**
Daily Schedule Organizer

Hundreds Chart

Name _____ Date _____

Use the chart to color counting patterns, multiples, odd or even numbers, etc.

1	2	3	4	5	6	7	8	9	10
11	12	13	14	15	16	17	18	19	20
21	22	23	24	25	26	27	28	29	30
31	32	33	34	35	36	37	38	39	40
41	42	43	44	45	46	47	48	49	50
51	52	53	54	55	56	57	58	59	60
61	62	63	64	65	66	67	68	69	70
71	72	73	74	75	76	77	78	79	80
81	82	83	84	85	86	87	88	89	90
91	92	93	94	95	96	97	98	99	100

KEY ☐ _____ ☐ _____ ☐ _____
      ☐ _____ ☐ _____ ☐ _____

🖥 **BT 10**
Hundreds Chart

"I Am" Poem Planner

Name _____ Date _____
Room _____ Period _____

Line 1 I am (two special qualities about yourself) _____ and _____
Line 2 I wonder (something you are curious about) _____
Line 3 I hear (an imaginary or actual sound) _____
Line 4 I see (an imaginary or actual sight) _____
Line 5 I want (something you desire) _____
Line 6 I am (repeat the first line of the poem) _____ and _____
Line 7 I pretend (something you could pretend to do) _____
Line 8 I feel (a feeling about something imaginary) _____
Line 9 I touch (something imaginary) _____
Line 10 I worry (something that really bothers or worries you) _____
Line 11 I cry (something that makes you sad) _____
Line 12 I am (repeat the first line of the poem) _____ and _____
Line 13 I understand (something you know well) _____
Line 14 I say (something you believe in) _____
Line 15 I dream (something you dream about) _____
Line 16 I try (something you make an effort to do) _____
Line 17 I hope (something you hope for) _____
Line 18 I am (repeat the first line of the poem) _____ and _____

🖥 **BT 11**
"I Am" Poem Planner

"I Come From" Poem Planner

Name _____ Date _____
Room _____ Period _____

Describe a time in your childhood when you felt the happiest.
_____
_____

Describe a time or place in your childhood when/where you felt the safest.
_____

Describe a time with a sibling, cousin, or other family member that made you laugh really hard, and only the two of you understood why you were laughing. _____
_____

Describe the place where you grew up (the city, your street, your house, etc.).
_____
_____

Describe your favorite season in detail and tell why you love it. _____
_____

Describe your favorite food: the way it smells, when it tastes the best, and how it makes you feel.
_____
_____

Describe a time when you were sad, scared, or confused. _____
_____

Describe a day that was so perfect you couldn't possibly imagine anything better.
_____

Describe your favorite holiday/celebration spent with your family. _____
_____

🖥 **BT 12**
"I Come From" Poem Planner

Incident Report

Date _____ Time _____ Location _____

Incident (What did the student do? What happened?)

Witnesses (Who was present?)	Initial response (What did you do? What was done?)
1.	
2.	
3.	

Follow-up	Follow-up feedback/Action plan
☐ Office	
☐ Referral to _____ (nurse/counselor/specialist)	
☐ Home communication	

Incident Report

Date _____ Time _____ Location _____

Incident (What did the student do? What happened?)

Witnesses (Who was present?)	Initial response (What did you do? What was done?)
1.	
2.	
3.	

Follow-up	Follow-up feedback/Action plan
☐ Office	
☐ Referral to _____ (nurse/counselor/specialist)	
☐ Home communication	

💻 **BT 13**
Incident Report

Scavenger Hunt Questionnaire

Name _____ Date _____

I found someone who ...

1. Was born in July: _____
2. Has more than one sibling: _____
3. Likes classical music: _____
4. Has been to Disneyland or Disney World: _____
5. Speaks another language: _____ Which language? _____
6. Likes to swim: _____
7. Likes to paint: _____
8. Is from an ethnic group different from mine: _____
9. Has a pet: _____ What kind? _____
10. Owns an iPod: _____
11. Likes to dance: _____
12. Has traveled out of the state: _____ Where? _____
13. Has been on a cruise: _____ Where? _____
14. Likes Brussels sprouts: _____
15. Plays sports: _____ Which sports? _____
16. Likes Mexican food: _____
17. Dislikes pizza: _____
18. Has or has had braces: _____
19. Has met a movie star: _____ Which star? _____
20. Was born in the state where I live: _____

What do you have in common with your classmates?

I like _____, and so does _____
Sometimes I _____, and so does _____
I don't like _____, and neither does _____
I want _____, and so does _____

💻 **BT 14**
Scavenger Hunt Questionnaire

Scientific Investigation

Experiment _____

Scientist _____

Date _____

Purpose _____

Prediction: I predict _____

Observations

1. _____ ☐

2. _____ ☐

3. _____ ☐

Conclusion _____

💻 **BT 15**
Scientific Investigation 1

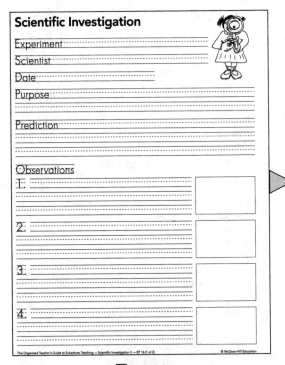

Scientific Investigation

Experiment _____

Scientist _____

Date _____

Purpose _____

Prediction _____

Observations

1. _____ ☐

2. _____ ☐

3. _____ ☐

4. _____ ☐

💻 **BT 16**
Scientific Investigation 2
(1 of 2)

Experiment ....
Scientist ....
Date ....
Observations (continued)
5: ....
....
....
6: ....
....
7: ....
....
8: ....
....
....
Conclusion ....
....
....
....
....
....

Draw a picture of your conclusion on the back.
The Organized Teacher's Guide to Substitute Teaching — Scientific Investigation 2 — BT 16 (2 of 2) © McGraw-Hill Education

💻 **BT 16**
Scientific Investigation 2
(2 of 2)

Scientific Investigation

Experiment ....
Scientist ....
Date ....
Purpose ....
....
Prediction ....
....
....
....
Observations
1: ....
....
2: ....
....
3: ....
....
The Organized Teacher's Guide to Substitute Teaching — Scientific Investigation 3 — BT 17 (1 of 3) © McGraw-Hill Education

💻 **BT 17**
Scientific Investigation 3
(1 of 3)

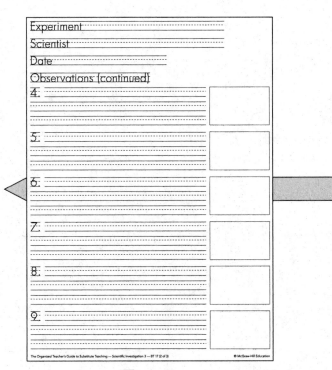

Experiment ....
Scientist ....
Date ....
Observations (continued)
4: ....
....
5: ....
....
6: ....
....
7: ....
....
8: ....
....
9: ....
....
The Organized Teacher's Guide to Substitute Teaching — Scientific Investigation 3 — BT 17 (2 of 3) © McGraw-Hill Education

💻 **BT 17**
Scientific Investigation 3
(2 of 3)

Conclusion ....
....
....
....
....
....

Illustrate and label your conclusion.

The Organized Teacher's Guide to Substitute Teaching — Scientific Investigation 3 — BT 17 (3 of 3) © McGraw-Hill Education

💻 **BT 17**
Scientific Investigation 3
(3 of 3)

Student Interest Survey

Name _____ Age _____

Three things I like to do in my spare time:

1. _____

2. _____

3. _____

My favorite things:

Favorite video game _____ Favorite sport _____

Favorite food _____ Favorite candy _____

Favorite TV show _____ Favorite movie _____

Favorite actor _____ Favorite singer _____

Favorite website _____ Favorite radio station _____

Favorite book I've read _____

Favorite subject in school _____

Best memory of school _____

When I grow up, I would like to be _____

How I describe myself:

Adjective _____

Verb _____

Noun _____

Two of my friends are _____ and _____

These things are important to me: _____

_____

🖥 **BT 18**

Student Interest Survey

Tens Frame

🖥 **BT 19**

Tens Frame

Index to templates

Template numbers are in square brackets. Bonus templates, designated [BT], are not referred to in the text.

Notes

Notes

Notes

Notes